Competition and Energy Markets

Competition and Energy Markets

What Role for Competition Policy in the Current Geopolitical Context?

Edited by

Adina Claici
Massimo Merola

Wolters Kluwer

Published by:
Kluwer Law International B.V.
PO Box 316
2400 AH Alphen aan den Rijn
The Netherlands
E-mail: lrs-sales@wolterskluwer.com
Website: www.wolterskluwer.com/en/solutions/kluwerlawinternational

Sold and distributed by:
Wolters Kluwer Legal & Regulatory U.S.
920 Links Avenue
Landisville, PA 17538
United States of America
E-mail: customer.service@wolterskluwer.com

ISBN 978-94-035-2238-8

e-Book: ISBN 978-94-035-2248-7
web-PDF: ISBN 978-94-035-2258-6

Editors

Adina Claici is director of GCLC. She is a competition economics expert whose background combines consulting experience, academia, and nearly a decade in the Chief Economist Team of DG Competition. Adina specialises in mergers, antitrust, and state aid cases. She also provides clients with insights on competition policy developments in the EU. She has been named one of the top competition economists by *Who's Who Legal*. She has been published in numerous academic journals and has authored several book chapters. In addition to her consulting work, Dr Claici is currently a Visiting Professor at the College of Europe and Barcelona School of Economics.

Massimo Merola, a professor of public competition law for over thirty years at the College of Europe, Bruges, and a lecturer on public competition procedure and litigation at Paris II Panthéon-Assas since 2018, Massimo Merola is the managing partner of the Brussels Office of BonelliErede law firm and is the scientific director of the firm's European Law group, where he oversees a broad regulatory practice specialising in EU law. He is widely recognised as one of the leading experts in State aid law and is in the forefront as regards Foreign Subsidies' control. In the broader context of EU law, his practice focuses on foreign direct investments, customs law, regulation of network industries, internal market rules, trade, EU funding, etc. He has a long and extensive experience as a litigator before the EU Courts.

Contributors

Juan José Alba Ríos joined Endesa in July 1997, where he is now in charge of regulatory affairs. Previously he was the managing director of the European trading unit of Endesa and oversaw its Joint Venture with Morgan Stanley. Between 1986 and 1997 he was a researcher at the Instituto de Investigación Tecnológica (IIT, Universidad Pontificia Comillas). He is a member of the Management Committee of aelec (the association of the Spanish electricity industry) and board member of Eurelectric. He has been a board member of EFET (European Federation of Energy Traders) and chairman of the Advisory Council of ENTSO-e. He served in the Supervisory Boards of the French and Polish power exchanges. He has a PhD in electrical engineering from Universidad Pontificia Comillas in Madrid.

Marios Andrikopoulos, Born in Athens in 1974, he holds a Maîtrise en Droit from the Université Robert Schuman of Strasbourg, an LL.M in EC Law from the College of Europe, a Master of International Economics and Management from SDA Bocconi and a Master's Degree in Public Law jointly awarded by the University of Athens and the University Montesquieu of Bordeaux. He has also obtained the Diploma of the Academy of European Law of the European University Institute. Qualified lawyer since 2002, he holds since 2013 the position of Legal Director at ELPEDISON SA, a major Greek energy company, jointly owned by HELLENiQ ENERGY Holdings SA and EDISON SpA (EDF group). He has been consecutively included within 'LEGAL500 GC Powerlist Greece and Cyprus' and within the 'Legal Leaders 25 in Energy' list, organised by the Greek magazine, 'LAWYER'. Apart from Greek, speaks fluently English, French and Italian.

Dr Lukas Cavada is the Executive Coordinator for International Affairs at the Austrian Federal Competition Authority. He studied law in Vienna and London. Lukas was seconded to the OECD Competition Division. He is a regular speaker and author of publications on various aspects of competition law.

Since 1 July 2019, **Anna Colucci** is Director for Markets and cases in Energy and Environment in DG Competition. She previously joined DG Energy in February 2016, where she was head of the Retail markets, Coal and Oil Unit. From 2007 to 2016 she held several management positions in DG Competition. In particular, she managed the State aid unit dealing with 'Post, Health and other services' and was also head of the Strategy unit. Prior to her joining DG Competition, she had thirteen years' experience in transport policy within DG Move. She was, amongst other, in charge of the European Aviation Safety Agency. Ms Colucci has a degree in Political Sciences from the Institut d'Etudes Politiques of Strasbourg, a master in European Studies from the College of Europe of Bruges and a diploma in International Relations Studies from the Johns Hopkins University Bologna.

Guillaume Duquesne is a Senior Vice President at Compass Lexecon, based in Paris and Brussels. Since joining in 2013, Guillaume has advised clients on a wide variety of competition policy issues, covering sectors as diverse as energy, financial, high technologies and digital sectors. Guillaume has advised clients in global merger or antitrust cases at the European Commission level and at the level of the French competition authorities. Some of his recent work includes advising on the competitive effects of high-profile mergers, including several recent Phase II merger cases before the European Commission: Broadcom/VMware, Arm/Nvidia, Google/Fitbit, Siemens/ Alstom, E.ON/Innogy, Deutsche Börse/LSE and EDF/Areva. It also includes advising on investigations of the European commission in the financial industry (SSA Bonds, Libor, Euribor and CDS) and advising some of the largest big tech companies in antitrust cases and litigations. Guillaume authors various papers and book chapters on revision of vertical guidelines, tech mergers, big tech banking and digital markets. Prior to joining Compass Lexecon, Guillaume worked as a quantitative analyst for Crédit Agricole – Corporate Investment Bank. Guillaume graduated from the Ecole Normale Supérieure where he specialised in economics, mathematics and finance. Guillaume holds an M.Sc. in Economics from the Paris School of Economics and an M.Sc. in Quantitative Finance from Pierre and Marie Curie University. Guillaume has held various research/teaching assistant positions.

Cani Fernandez has practiced and lectured EU and Competition Law since 1989. She was référendaire at the Court of Justice of the European Union. The first woman appointed as Co-Chair of the IBA Antitrust Committee, she also held the position of Vice-chair of the Economics Committee of the ABA Antitrust Section, Officer of the International Cartel Task Force of the ABA Antitrust Section, and member of the IBA LPD Council. She was also an NGA of the EU Commission and the CNMC before the ICN. Recognised year after year as one of the thirty best specialists in Competition/ Antitrust worldwide in the Best of the Best category of the Expert Guides. GCR recognised her as one of the '100 Women in Antitrust Worldwide'. In 2018 and 2019 Chambers named her 'Star Individual' in her specialty in Spain. She is the first woman awarded with the 'Outstanding Contribution to the Legal Profession' by Chamber.

Joaquin Garcia Gimenez works as Gas Market Team Leader in the Agency for the Cooperation of Energy Regulators (ACER) in Ljubljana. He joined ACER in 2012. Previously he had worked for four years at the Spanish Energy Regulator, and for three more years in Spanish electricity utilities. He has been mostly involved in market monitoring activities, assessing the state of the European gas wholesale markets and their trajectory towards an Internal Gas Market. He is an industrial engineer by education and has a Master's degree in Energy Business Administration.

Guillaume Gonzalez is an electricity market design expert working in the DG Competition unit in charge of State aid in the energy sector. He joined the European Commission in 2022. His career started at the French electricity Transmission System Operator, where he notably chaired an ENTSO-E expert group tasked with regulatory output (2020 ENTSO-E cross-border participation rules in capacity mechanisms). He is an engineer and economist by education, graduated from both l'Ecole Nationale des Ponts et Chaussée (engineering diploma with a specialisation in quantitative economics), and from Sciences Po Paris (economics and social science master's degree with a specialisation in European affairs).

Carsten Grave is partner at Linklaters LLP in Düsseldorf. He advises clients on competition law aspects of mergers and acquisitions, abuse of dominant positions, antitrust-related litigation, state aid as well as cartel proceedings. Carsten studied law and economics at the Universities of Bonn, Geneva, Freiburg and Hagen before passing a diploma in economics and completing a doctorate in law. He joined Linklaters Oppenhoff & Rädler in 2000. He has worked in Düsseldorf, Brussels, London, and has been on secondment with LECG in Chicago, a predecessor firm of Compass Lexecon. Since 2019, he lectures merger control at Heinrich Heine Universität Düsseldorf.

Dr Natalie Harsdorf-Borsch heads the Austrian Competition Authority since November 2023. Before that she held different roles in the agency since 2009 such as Acting Director General (Nov 2021-Oct 23), Managing Director, Head of Legal service as well as team leader and case handler. Since 2019 Natalie Harsdorf-Borsch serves as coordinator for the OECD Competition Bureau vis-à-vis UNCTAD. Harsdorf-Borsch studied Law at the Universities of Vienna and Dublin and also holds a law degree of the College of Europe in Bruges. Secondments to the European Court of Justice, the Canadian Competition Bureau and the European Commission added to her professional experience in competition law. In 2016, she was voted by Global Competition Review one of twenty-six Top Women enforcers worldwide. 2022 she was recognised as Austrian lawyer of the year as first woman in public service. Also, she is a co-founder of the women competition network Austria and author/editor of numerous publications on competition law. Harsdorf-Borsch teaches competition law in Innsbruck and Vienna.

From December 2012 to June 2023, **Dennis Hesseling** was Head of the Infrastructure, Gas & Retail Department at the EU Agency for the Cooperation of Energy Regulators (ACER). Before joining ACER, he worked as Head of Unit at the Netherland Competition Authority NMa (ACM), responsible for merger control and antitrust enforcement in the energy, telecommunications, and media sectors. Prior to that, he worked at the NMa's Energy Regulator. From 2000 he worked as a management consultant for McKinsey & Company in Brussels. Dennis Hesseling holds a PhD in Mathematics from

Utrecht University. He currently works as the IEA's Head of the Gas, Coal and Power Markets Division.

Mitja Maletin is an energy market analyst and policy officer at the European Union Agency for the Cooperation of Energy Regulators since 2016. His work focuses on monitoring gas wholesale markets, with particular emphasis on liquidity of gas trading hubs, and the effectiveness of European gas network codes in facilitating market price integration. He holds a Bachelor's degree in philosophy and economics.

Matteo Marengon is a consultant in the finance and valuation practice at Oxera. He advises clients on state aid and regulatory finance matters.

Giorgio Motta has more than twenty-five years of experience in EU, Italian and international antitrust merger control and cartel enforcement. Mr Motta advises clients on antitrust aspects of mergers, acquisitions and joint ventures. He has been involved in some of the most high-profile and complex merger control cases both in Europe and globally. He also advises clients on state aid and FSR, as well as EU and Italian competition law issues relating to vertical restraints and dominance. Mr Motta serves as a non-governmental adviser for the International Competition Network, as well as a visiting professor at the University of Lille.

Ana Palacio, a lawyer specialising in European and International law, was the first female Minister of Foreign Affairs of Spain. In the European Parliament, Ms. Palacio chaired the Legal Affairs and Internal Market Committee, as well as the Conference of Committee Chairs. She served as Senior VP and General Counsel of the World Bank Group and Secretary-General of ICSID and was a member of Spain's Council of State. Ms. Palacio was on the Executive Committee and was Senior VP for International Affairs of AREVA, and she currently sits on various corporate boards. She is a visiting professor at Georgetown University.

Nicola Pesaresi is Deputy Director for Energy at the Directorate General for Competition of the European Commission and responsible for State aid in the Energy sector. He has been previously responsible for cross-cutting policies and level playing field in the Task Force for the preparation and conduct of the negotiations with the United Kingdom under Article 50 TFEU. He has formerly been responsible for State aid policy, State aid scrutiny and State aid coordination. He joined the European Commission in 1999. His career started at the Bank of Italy where he spent nine years in the department for banking supervision. He is an economist by education, graduated from Yale University with a Master of Arts in Economics, and from Bocconi University with a degree in Economics and Social Sciences.

Albert Riera, a Vice President at Compass Lexecon, is an economist with thirteen years of expertise in the energy sector. He advises governments and major companies on regulation, market design, policy, and disputes. His background extends to antitrust and damage estimation, regularly testifying as an economic expert in court. Formerly an Advisor at the Spanish Secretary of State for Energy, he contributed to leading the EU Electricity Market Design reform negotiations. Before consultancy, he lectured microeconomics at Universidad Carlos III de Madrid. Albert holds an M.A. in Economic Analysis from Universidad Carlos III and an M.Sc. in Physics from Cambridge University.

Nicole Robins is a partner at the economics and finance consultancy, Oxera, based in Brussels where she leads Oxera's State Aid and Subsidy Control practice. She advises clients across a range of sectors, including the energy sector, on economic and financial issues in state aid cases relating to assessments of the market economy operator principle, the application of state aid rules for services of general economic interest, and the compatibility of aid.

Dr Fabien Roques is an Executive Vice President in Compass Lexecon based in Paris and Brussels. Fabien's expertise spans a range of competition, litigation and regulatory issues. He has advised clients on a variety of competition policy issues, including mergers and antitrust cases at the European Commission level and with other competition authorities. Fabien has particularly deep expertise of the energy and utilities sectors and leads Compass Lexecon's energy practice in Europe. Fabien is a recognised authority on utilities' regulation and electricity, gas and carbon market design. Over the past twenty years, Fabien has worked on numerous tailored assignments for clients including lawyers, regulators, utilities, renewables project developers and operators, and financial investors. Previously Fabien has held positions with the International Energy Agency and with the energy consultancy IHS Cambridge Energy Associates, where he led the European power, gas and renewables team. He holds a Ph.D. in Economics from the University of Cambridge and an M.Sc. in Engineering from Ecole Centrale Lyon. Fabien has authored numerous publications on the utilities industry and related regulatory issues in both practitioners and academic journals. Fabien is also an Associate Professor in economics at the University Paris Dauphine and at the Florence School of Regulation where he teaches and contributes to the research of the European Electricity Market Chair on electricity markets and utilities' regulation. He is also a research associate of the Cambridge University Energy Policy Research Group.

Francesco Maria Salerno is Managing Partner of the firm's Brussels office. Francesco Maria has extensive experience in EU law, having acted in several matters before the EU Commission and the courts in Luxembourg. Besides representing companies in antitrust matters, Francesco Maria assists on cases arising from state measures such as aids, regulation in sectors covered by EU harmonisation rules (such as digital, energy, transports, postal services, banking and finance), as well as other state measures impacting the freedoms guaranteed by the internal European market. Francesco Maria joins the firm after 18 years with a leading international law firm where he began in 1999 working in its Rome offices. In 2005 he transferred to the Brussels office of the same firm, and was appointed a Senior Attorney in 2010. After earning both Masters and Ph.D. degrees from the London School of Economics, Francesco Maria continued his academic and research interests and several of his articles and essays on State aids, independent authorities and antitrust issues have been published by prestigious,

European and American legal publishing houses. He speaks Italian, Spanish, French and English.

Ulrich Scholz has been partner at Freshfields Bruckhaus Deringer since 2002 and served several years as co-head of Freshfields global power & utilities and low carbon energy group. Besides advising on EU and national competition law, Ulrich has a particular focus on the energy sector and advises on and national energy regulation, including certification procedures, unbundling requirements, network access and network fees, implication of the EU Green deal and equivalent national law on renewable energies. Upon completion of his legal education at the universities of Bonn, Cologne, and at Tulane Law School in New Orleans, and before joining Freshfields, he worked as a research assistant at the Institute for Energy Law in Cologne.

Pascal Schönemann is associate at Freshfields Bruckhaus Deringer and specialises on competition law and energy regulation. He completed his legal education at the university of Mannheim.

Ben Smulders is currently the Deputy Director General responsible for State aid control in the European Commission's DG Competition. In addition, he is a substitute judge in the Court of Appeal of The Hague, a guest professor of international and European competition law at the Free University of Brussels and a visiting professor of the EU protection of the rule of law at the *inter alia* College of Europe in Bruges. He is the author of a series of publications on a wide range of EU policy and law related subjects.

Maximilian Weber is currently completing his legal clerkship in the district of the Higher Regional Court of Düsseldorf. At the time of writing, he was a legal assistant in the competition law and foreign investment team at Linklaters LLP in Düsseldorf. Maximilian studied law at the Universities of Passau, Düsseldorf and the Monash University Malaysia.

Peter Willis is a Partner at Bird & Bird LLP, based in London. He has been a competition and regulatory lawyer for over thirty years. He is well-known as an expert on REMIT and EU energy regulation. He has advised businesses in a number of REMIT investigations around Europe, including in two of what are thought to be the only three published decisions in which national regulatory authorities have investigated and then concluded that there was no REMIT infringement. He writes and speaks regularly on the subject of REMIT.

Table of Contents

Introduction

Massimo Merola & Adina Claici

The recent geopolitical crisis has deeply affected all socio-economic activities, raising unprecedented risks. The extraordinary restrictions that the EU implemented to address the COVID-19 pandemic were being gradually relieved when the war in Ukraine broke out on the EU's doorstep. As a result, the EU is facing unprecedented challenges, especially in the energy sector – challenges that are anything but eased by fierce economic rivalry, even between Western countries, and resurgent economic patriotism.

These repeated emergencies have radically changed the paradigm of EU policy-making. We are now confronted with a situation where we need to assess the trade-offs between various stated objectives, which can no longer be fully achieved (with the related political price to be paid).

One example is the potential conflict between the green transition on the one hand and the need to preserve European industry and its independence from third-country supplies on the other. In this context, the decoupling from Russian gas requires at least a short-term increase in the volume of gas imported into the EU from other areas of the world, even if this entails new investments that risk delaying the decarbonisation of the global economy. In the long term, it will most likely lead to the emergence of a new technological mix that strikes a balance between decarbonisation and energy security.

Against this backdrop, the 2023 Global Competition Law Center (GCLC) annual conference – in line with GCLC tradition, is oriented toward the future and aims to suggest guidelines for the development of competition policy in line with the current times. The issue has been expressed using the rhetorical device of a dilemma: namely, the dilemma of how to ensure security of energy supply – which requires a very different technological mix from the one we are used to, or the one we could have predicted, before the current geopolitical crisis – while at the same time ensuring we meet the EU's emission targets under the European Green Deal. Indeed, we must address how we can reconcile these goals in the best possible manner and what role competition policy can play in this effort.

We should perhaps first clarify that we use the word 'dilemma' not as it is commonly understood but rather in the philosophical sense: that is, a choice between two or even more options which are equally unsatisfactory as they imply the sacrifice of important achievements or values.

Other constraints beyond the security of supply and the path toward a green economy do of course exist, chief among them being affordability. However, because we see affordability as a precondition to whatever solution is found more than as a third aspect of the choice to be made. Therefore, because affordability is non-negotiable, the balance we must strike will necessarily imply a certain sacrifice on the part of the security of supply, the EU's green objectives, or both. The European Commission uses the word 'trilemma', including affordability as a third pillar to be assessed in the trade-offs, besides the security of supply and decarbonisation.

We also wanted to avoid conveying overly optimistic messages, such as that the EU will surely find a way to reconcile everything to an entirely satisfactory degree. This would be untrue, as a long-term solution will likely entail reducing or slowing down progress on some EU targets. From this perspective, the current geopolitical crisis will likely come at a cost for the EU in terms of energy and environmental welfare, and we must openly acknowledge that. Only if we put everything in the right perspective can we hope to identify the best possible method to tackle the crisis, including through the adequate use of competition policy.

When it comes to what the compromise should be, some argue that the ambitious path toward the green transition set out in the 2020 European Green Deal has been largely called into question by the Russian aggression against Ukraine. An opposing narrative is that the path to decarbonisation must be accelerated, as renewables are key to achieving a satisfactory and largely self-sufficient level of energy supply within the EU.

These competing narratives at least confirm that some balancing will be needed, and the experience from previous crises shows that competition policy can make a positive contribution to the process. However, we are just as far from reaching a consensus on competition policy's role. Competition policy is sometimes presented as an obstacle to the efficient management of energy markets, especially in crisis situations. The counterargument is that it preserves market dynamics and thereby ensures that energy markets deliver the right outcomes. This may imply that current tools are not sufficient to achieve the policy objectives and that it may be necessary to review and, possibly, amend enforcement priorities.

In this introduction, we will briefly touch upon three different challenges of the current and prospective enforcement, namely the suitability of the current architecture of incentives, Europe's openness to international investments and finally the need for legal certainty.

First, the roll-out of renewables in Europe over the last two decades has been largely associated with our architecture of incentives and EU funding to achieve climate objectives. State aid rules have allowed the Commission to influence and shape the initiatives of public authorities. The discipline imposed by the constant screening of public measures by competition enforcers has naturally contributed to achieving well-designed measures and preventing wasteful, counterproductive interventions.

However, this strength of our unique competition law tradition can easily turn into a weakness if screening and control procedures lose sight of the wider picture. In this vein, the new Temporary Crisis and Transition Framework appears to provide a balanced response to counter the introduction of the Inflation Reduction Act (IRA) in the US. Section 2.8 includes a flexibility clause for 'matching aid' that some fear, or secretly hope, will open the floodgates of subsidies in the EU. However, this is not a novel approach, as regional aid guidelines have long included the well-known 'location decision scenario'. The conditions set out in section 2.8 appear adequate to ensure a due degree of flexibility on paper, but they will need to be evaluated in practice.

A too-literal reading of the products or sectors covered by section 2.8, rather than a functional reading based on the rationale of the provision, might unduly penalise innovative projects that do not strictly correspond to the definitions provided thereunder. Conversely, a well-designed industrial policy in Europe can achieve the targeted political objectives with minimum market distortions, if the design of incentives follows economic principles used so far in State aid policy to maintain efficient outcomes.

A combination of market response (embodied in the reform of the EU electricity market design) and adequate incentives is probably the best formula. After all, even the US government adopted the IRA on top of the market response. Economic reports show that the green revolution is being fuelled by a business-friendly ecosystem and by the awareness that greener investment provides the highest returns – more than investments aided by federal handouts. So, it appears that the US has learned from the EU when it comes to the need to provide adequate incentives, and the EU – in addition to reacting to the IRA – should perhaps also learn from the US as far as the use of market responses is concerned.

Secondly, the European project's success has long been based on embracing an open-market economic system, limiting public interest considerations to strategic sectors (and with precise limits) and rejecting proposals to downgrade competition law during times of crisis. We remain sceptical of calls to create an EU fortress, as remaining open to investments from abroad is key for the EU to compete. More flexibility in State aid – together with laws that provide adequate safeguards to European industry, such as the carbon border adjustment mechanism (CBAM), the Foreign Subsidies Regulation and the foreign direct investment (FDI) screening framework – are all probably necessary, but let's not overlook the other fundamental component of a successful strategy: market mechanisms and openness to international investments. As regards investments in the green transition, there are currently many efficient and innovative options available globally and Europe should remain an attractive investment destination. The obvious need for screening foreign investments to avoid predatory deals, especially if the investor is directly or indirectly under the control or the influence of foreign governments, must not transmode into unwarranted hostility towards foreign investors, which Europe needs.

A third aspect of the enforcement in the EU intrinsically linked to the previous one is the legal certainty. One step in the right direction is certainly the Council regulation laying down a temporary framework to accelerate the deployment of renewable energy by introducing faster permitting processes for projects that have the highest potential for a quick roll-out. However, more needs to be done. It's not too late for us to make the necessary changes to avoid further eroding confidence in the EU as an attractive place for investments. To give but one example, the fact that, at the end of last year, because of State aid developments in the field of arbitration, EU Member States along with Venezuela and Russia were among the countries with the highest number of unpaid arbitration awards, is hardly a record to be proud of.

In the same vein, we cannot emphasise enough how indispensable it is to address the long-standing shortcomings in the administration of State aid rules and how short-sighted it is to reduce aid procedures to bilateral negotiations between a centralised power (the Commission) and national authorities. The current approach to the administration of State aid rules does not allow investors to obtain legal certainty from the Commission, as discussions are conducted primarily with national authorities, whose focus is to get projects done in the short term rather than safeguard long-term financial risks for private investors. This decades-old problem was already pressing in a period of strict enforcement of State aid rules; now it can no longer be ignored as the EU enters a global race to attract investments amid a fast-changing regulatory environment.

The IRA might offer an unrivalled level of financial support, but there are already doubts about the US government's poor track record of delivering similar schemes in the past and the complexity and costs of the US legal system. An overhaul that focuses on ensuring legal certainty and the protection of third parties' rights in the enforcement of EU State aid rules could give the EU a competitive advantage in attracting large investments that require stable regulatory frameworks.

To conclude, we believe in freedom and democracy, which in economic terms means an open and free market sensibly managed and corrected by public intervention only to the extent strictly necessary. Strategic autonomy is an unavoidable objective in current times, but market openness remains the paradigm, which should be derogated only in case of ascertained necessity. We hope that this edition of the GCLC conference proceedings will provide a better understanding of what is at stake in the current energy crisis. And we sincerely hope that this understanding will contribute, even if only slightly, to helping everyone (EU institutions, Member States, and stakeholders) make the right decisions to overcome the crisis while preserving the internal market and the European project as a whole.

Organising a conference on this topic has proven to be rather complex as we have been confronted with a fast-evolving legal framework and shifting market conditions. We have structured the conference's programme with the aim of providing food for thought as to the interplay between competition policy and energy crisis management in broad terms. We are extremely thankful to the speakers for their commitment to providing their thoughts in writing and also to the participants for stimulating inspiring discussions.

The structure of the book follows the themes discussed at the conference. The first part will set the scene by presenting the current challenges. The next parts will examine how the dilemma affects various EU priorities. Specifically, the second part will discuss the affordability of energy prices for households and enterprises; the third part will cover articles about the desired acceleration of the efficient roll-out of energy infrastructures and about solidarity among Member States and reciprocity in international relations.

The fourth part of the book will look more closely at the EU competition toolkit in force (as recently amended) and the Commission's practice in order to explore how competition law and policy can help address the energy dilemma and complement the reform of energy markets. The fifth part will zoom into the EU State aid tools and their appropriateness to solve the energy dilemma. The final, sixth part of this edition will present the concluding remarks of various European enforcers from competition authorities.

Part I The New EU Energy Dilemma

CHAPTER 1

Securing Gas Supplies Through an Integrated European Energy Market*

Dennis Hesseling, Joaquin Garcia Gimenez & Mitja Maletin

1 INTRODUCTION

In 2022, the European gas market faced the shock of sudden and significant reductions in Russian flows. Thanks to a well-integrated European gas market, demand reductions, new liquefied natural gas (LNG) supplies and timely policy responses, Europe came through the winter of 2022-2023 without shortages. This chapter provides insight into the dynamics at play during the 2022 gas crisis and examines which factors were crucial to getting through the winter. It not only provides lessons learned for the European gas market but also presents a highly relevant case study of how to deal with energy security of supply in a world marred by geopolitical tensions.

2 RUSSIA'S INVASION OF UKRAINE LED TO A DRAMATIC SHIFT IN GAS FLOW PATTERNS TO EUROPE

Starting in the second half of 2021 and continuing during 2022, particularly following Russia's invasion of Ukraine in February 2022, Gazprom diminished its flows to Europe in an apparent attempt to target certain routes and destinations. The reduction ended up being as high as 80% or more on particular routes, with Gazprom delivering pipeline gas to Europe mainly via Turkstream and the Ukrainian corridor (Figure 1.1).

* This chapter is based on a presentation that Dennis Hesseling gave at the 18th Annual Conference of the Global Competition Law Centre in Brussels on April 20-21, 2023. A previous version of the article, written by Dennis Hesseling and Mitja Maletin, was published under the title 'Out of the storm' in World Energy (July 2023), https://www.eni.com/static/en-IT/world-energy-magazine/the-new-routes-of-gas.html#slide17. The authors would like to thank Boyko Nitzov, Juan Lopez Vaquero and Una Shortall for their comments on an earlier draft.

Overall, Russian piped gas deliveries to the EU more than halved in 2022, dropping from almost 140 bcm in 2021 to just above 60 bcm.[1]

Figure 1.1 Natural Gas Flow Changes: April 2022–March 2023 Versus April 2021–March 2022

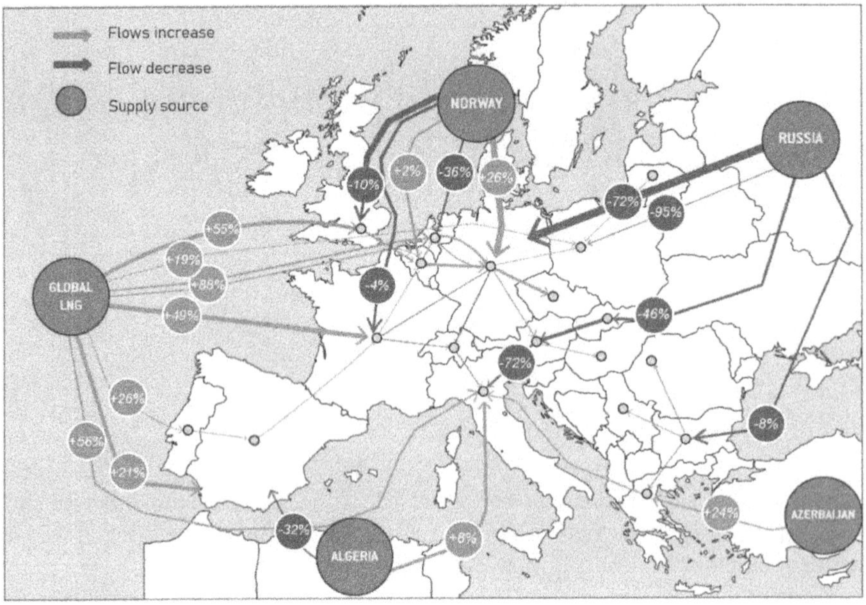

Source: ACERs re-elaboration of Bruegel policy brief: ‘A Grand Bargain to Steer Through the European Union’s Energy Crisis’, September 2022. Data from Entsog Transparency Platform (TP) & Refinitiv Eikon.

Since such flow reductions constitute prima facie a breach of Gazprom’s contractual supply obligations, Gazprom justified these cutbacks by claiming that they were carried out in the context of new regulations established by the Russian government, for instance, the requirement to pay for gas exports in rubles. Apart from such ‘contractual supply curtailments, the unexplained explosions on the Nord Stream pipelines in September 2022 rendered inoperative three of the four Nord Stream strings, thus diminishing the possibilities for physical Russian gas pipeline supplies to Europe as well.

While the European Network of Transmission System Operators for Gas (ENTSOG) had modelled Russian gas supply disruptions for years as part of its standard risk analysis, such disruption scenarios were typically limited to one major supply route at a time and for a limited duration (up to two months). What happened in 2022 was not only unprecedented but also a scenario that few foresaw. With Europe

1. IEA Medium-Term Gas Report 2023.

unprepared for it, there was much uncertainty about whether the European gas market would be able to navigate the crisis and continue to supply gas across the continent without interruption.

The fact that Europe managed to do so can be attributed to several factors, the most important of which are new LNG supplies, price-induced demand reductions, and a well-established, flexible system of gas transportation capacity allocation. Furthermore, a number of other factors played a significant role, in particular new interconnectors (such as the Gas Interconnector Poland-Lithuania, the Baltic Pipe from Norway via Denmark to Poland, and the Interconnector Greece-Bulgaria), the obligation to make all interconnection points bidirectional (already in place before the crisis), and, in reaction to the crisis, policy responses such as the Gas Storage Regulation requiring the mandatory filling of gas storages.

First, LNG: EU LNG imports rose 75% year-on-year in 2022, mainly from the US. Together with the Norwegian pipeline supply, it has become the biggest source of gas for the EU. Conversely, Russian gas declined from more than 40% of European supplies in January 2021 to less than 10% in March 2023 (Figure 1.2). This also means that the role of LNG in the European market has changed drastically. While in the past LNG cargoes supplied the marginal molecule, LNG has become a baseload supply, in a similar way as Norwegian or North African piped gas.

Figure 1.2 Monthly Evolution of Gas Deliveries into the EU by Supply Route (bcm/Month): 2021 to August 2023 (bcm/Day)

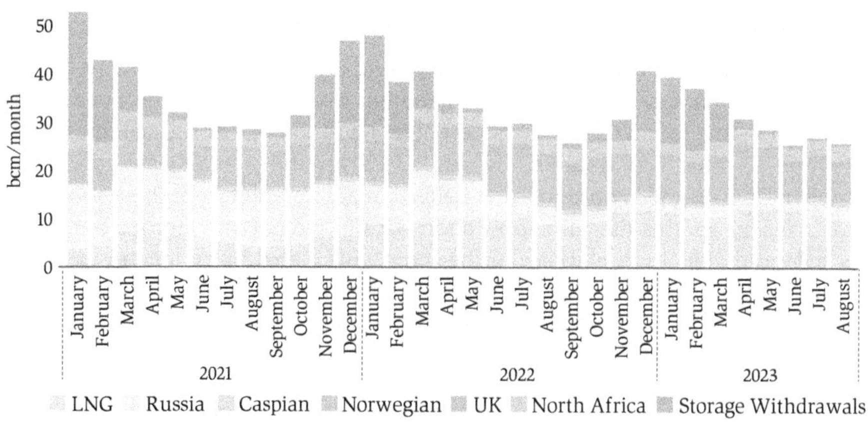

Source: ACER calculation based ENTSOG TP and GIE ALSI.

Next, significant gas demand reductions including through changed consumer behaviour played a key role in balancing supply and demand. Driven by extremely high prices, EU gas demand fell by 55 bcm in 2022, a 13% year-on-year drop. As the IEA pointed out, lower gas use in the residential and commercial sectors (down by 15% compared to 2021) accounted for almost half of the overall decline. While mild winter weather contributed to lower heating needs, it explains just over 40% of the gas demand reduction in the residential and commercial sectors. Gas-saving measures enacted in public buildings, fuel-switching in households with the option, the installation of heat pumps, efficiency gains and behavioural changes all played a critical role in reducing distribution network-related demand. In addition, rising affordability issues contributed to lower natural gas use in households. The share of households unable to keep their homes adequately warm rose from 6.9% in 2021 to 9.3% in 2022 – its highest level since 2015. Natural gas demand in the industry dropped by around 20% (or 30 bcm) in 2022, with all-time high gas prices driving fuel switching and leading to reduced production rates across most gas- and energy-intensive industries. Production curtailments accounted for around half of the decline in industrial gas use, with chemicals and fertilisers being the most affected sectors. European gas-to-power demand remained relatively resilient in 2022, declining by just 4% (or 6 bcm). The power sector contributions varied per Member State, driven by the need to *increase* gas use for power generation – despite its record-high price – in countries where nuclear or hydro faced severe limitations. On the other hand, lower electricity demand together with gas-to-coal switching and stronger wind and solar power output weighed on the overall gas burn in the power sector.[2]

Finally, thanks to a well-established and flexible system of standard transportation capacity products, it was possible to reroute gas supply flows at short notice. In this system, gas capacity products varying in duration from yearly all the way down to daily and within-day are offered through auctions on capacity booking platforms. This means that in case of shortage, the capacity will be sold to the highest bidder. The system was set up more than a decade ago and is harmonised at the EU level, thus providing a fundamental element needed for securing flexible and market-driven gas flows within the EU.

It is important to point out that Russian gas supplies that formerly reached Europe by pipeline could not easily be diverted to another route or destination. For example, while it is possible to flow Russian gas by pipeline to China, (a) the volumes pale in comparison to what was traditionally sent to Europe (Figure 1.3) and (b) the gas exported to China is mostly produced at fields that are different from those that supply Europe. This means that the gas supply shortage affected not only Europe but also the finely balanced global gas market. Furthermore, this global imbalance in gas supply and demand occurred in a situation of extremely high geopolitical uncertainty. In consequence, gas that could flow in different directions (in particular LNG) ended up flowing to the highest bidder (which in 2022 typically were European buyers). Hence, the gas shortage that Europe was facing was 'exported' to other parts of the world, affecting importing countries as far away as Japan and Korea. The situation was worse for countries like Pakistan and Bangladesh which could not afford to pay such premiums. While some of these flow changes reflect a normal global LNG market response, in other instances, they reflect a willingness of some LNG suppliers to pay the penalty to breach the contractual deliveries to Asian countries in order to divert those LNG cargoes to Europe in response to its high prices.

2. IEA Medium-Term Gas Report 2023.

Figure 1.3 Existing and Potential Russian Gas Exports to Asia Versus Russian Exports to the EU + UK

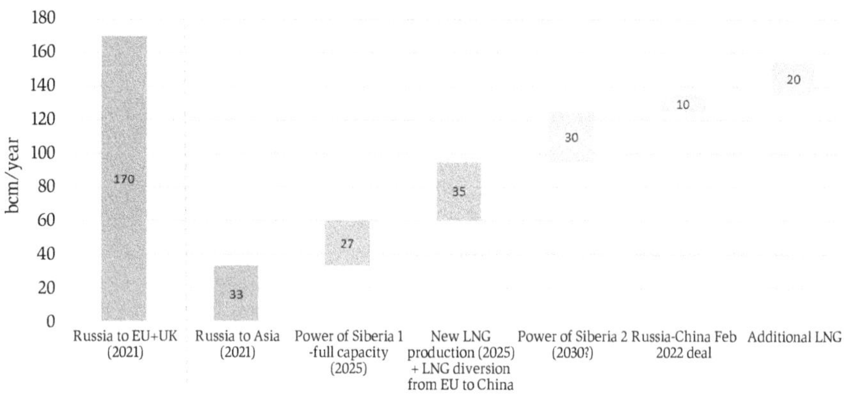

Source: Eurostat Energy database; Centre for Strategic and International Studies (May 2022); IEA: Energy Fact Sheet: Why does Russian oil and gas matter?

3 CHANGED GAS FLOWS LED TO INFRASTRUCTURE BOTTLENECKS

While it was eventually possible to flow gas across Europe accommodating the new flow patterns, this was not achieved without difficulties. The European gas pipeline system was primarily built to flow large quantities of Russian pipeline gas from East to West. The sudden and unforeseen shift in the flow patterns meant that the infrastructure now had to accommodate the opposite: large quantities of LNG landing in the West needed to be transported to consumption centres in the East. The infrastructure did not always have enough capacity to accommodate such flows, resulting in congestion at specific interconnection points.

Since capacity at interconnection points is sold through auctions, such congestion becomes visible in the form of congestion rents: the additional amount of money paid by shippers and received by Transmission System Operators (TSOs) because of auction premiums. These congestion revenues rose sharply to an unprecedented EUR 3.4 billion in 2022, compared to EUR 55 million in 2021. Furthermore, the congestion rents also showed clearly where most congestion was located, and in which direction: the most congested entry points were in Germany and the Netherlands, while the most congested exit points were in Belgium and France. In other words, shippers were trying to flow gas from Member States that were well connected to the global LNG market (like France and Belgium) to Member States with much more limited access to LNG (like Germany and the Netherlands) (Figure 1.4).

Figure 1.4 Congestion Revenues per Country in 2022 (EUR)*

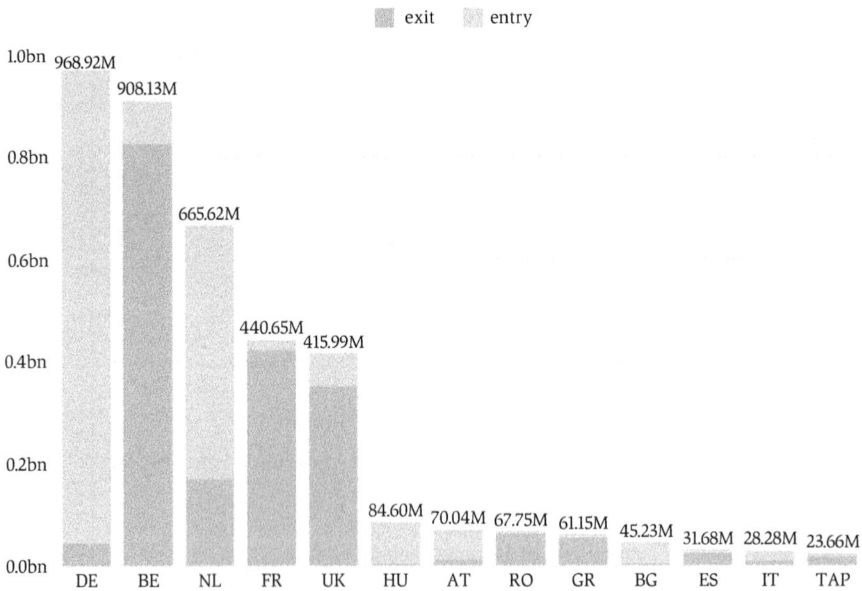

Source: ACER based on GSA, PRISMA and RBP – gas transportation congestion revenues calculation is based on auction time (in 2022), not on delivery time (i.e., includes products for delivery after 2022).

Note: *MSs & third countries with congestion revenue exceeding EUR 10 MM during auctions held in 2022. (Swiss congestion revenue for transit Wallbach-Passo Gries, estimated at EUR 245 MM, but not depicted.)

Over time, investments in new LNG receiving terminals located 'behind' the congested interconnection points not only increased security of supply but also helped address congestion. Especially Floating Storage and Regasification Units (FSRUs) were very useful for this purpose, as they were made available at short notice and were connected to the grid in record time. This particularly helped ease the situation in the Netherlands and Germany have done.

At an operational level, the congestion also revealed itself in the utilisation rates of the congested interconnection points, which were often close to 100% and sometimes even higher (Figure 1.5). This required TSOs to take operational measures to maximise the offer of transmission capacity. As ACER analysed in its Market Monitoring Report,[3] TSOs reduced capacities at underused interconnection points and reallocated them to congested routes, particularly after the termination of legacy contracts. Flows were steered towards areas of increasing demand, and compression was

3. ACER 'European gas market trends and price drivers. 2023 Market monitoring report', October 2023.

temporarily boosted above usual levels to physically push more gas through the pipelines.

National Regulatory Authorities (NRAs) also contributed to regulatory action to accommodate the new flows. The physical flow of LNG and Norwegian supplies from France to Germany became possible on a firm day-ahead basis after an agreement was reached to reconcile the different odourisation practices in both markets. After the German NRA Bundesnetzagentur issued a regulatory decision that offered financial assurances against potential damage claims from industrial users, German TSOs accepted odourised gas from the French system. The French NRA CRE adapted the internal congestion management procedures, including the use of locational price spreads, to address the internal French market area bottleneck. This enabled flowing more gas from Spain and the south of France to the north of the country, where gas was scarcer.

The gas flow changes were by no means limited to the EU but extended to the wider interconnected European gas system. As the EU Agency for the Cooperation of Energy Regulators (ACER) analysed in its special congestion report,[4] the offshore interconnectors with the UK significantly ramped up their use. Additionally, the Norwegian supplies to Europe across the North Sea reached record levels. With the opening of the Baltic Pipe at the end of 2022, with up to 10 bcm of annual capacity, Norwegian gas started flowing to Denmark and Poland, relieving some of the stress on the North-West European transmission system.

4. ACER 'Report addressing congestion in North-West European gas markets', July 2023.

Figure 1.5 Overview of the Utilisation Ratio in Selected EU Interconnection Points (Ips) in Different Time Periods (% of Firm Technical Capacity)

Direction	Interconnection Point	IP Utilisation Rate Historical Average 2019-2021 (%)	IP Utilisation Rate Phase 1 01/04/2021 - 23/02/2022 (%)	IP Utilisation Rate Phase 2 24/02/2022 - 31/05/2022 (%)	IP Utilisation Rate Phase 3 01/06/2022 - 30/09/2022 (%)	IP Utilisation Rate Phase 4 01/10/2022 - 31/08/2023 (%)
UK > NL	Bacton (BBL)	43	17	99	100	66
NL > UK	Bacton (BBL)	13	13	0	0	0
AT > SK	Baumgarten	0	0	0	0	0
SK > AT	Baumgarten	61	63	52	28	16
HU > RO	Csanadpalota	34	13	21	1	1
RO > HU	Csanadpalota	28	36	13	80	52
EL > BG	Kulata (BG) / Sidirokastron (EL)	1	1	15	26	23
BG > EL	Kulata (BG) / Sidirokastron (EL)	62	63	33	10	17
PL > DE	Mallnow	80	57	5	0	0
DE > PL	Mallnow	1	6	35	21	11
HU > AT	Mosonmagyarovar	66	31	87	56	57
LT > PL	Santaka			39	43	16
PL > LT	Santaka			0	1	11
IT > AT	Tarvisio (IT) / Arnoldstein (AT)	0	0	0	0	15
AT > IT	Tarvisio (IT) / Arnoldstein (AT)	70	65	42	22	8
DK > DE	VIP DK-THE	0	0	0	0	35
DE > DK	VIP DK-THE	90	77	80	49	25
FR > DE	VIP France Germany					47
DE > FR	VIP France - Germany	50	60	26	13	1
AT > DE	VIP Oberkappel	12	13	0	0	5
DE > AT	VIP Oberkappel	63	34	94	104	52
ES > FR	VIP PIRINEOS	3	6	61	16	41
FR > ES	VIP PIRINEOS	53	34	1	28	14
DE > BE	VIP THE-ZTP			0	0	0
BE > DE	VIP THE-ZTP			143	150	120
NL > DE	VIP TTF-THE-H			41	74	99
DE > NL	VIP TTF-THE-H			43	17	18
NL > BE	VIP-BENE	5	5	0	0	0
BE > NL	VIP-BENE	28	32	84	101	72
FR > BE	VIRTUALYS	4	59	237	336	250
BE > FR	VIRTUALYS	27	10	1	0	3
BE > UK	Zeebrugge IZT	8	7	0	0	0
UK > BE	Zeebrugge IZT	19	10	78	92	69

Source: ACER calculation based ENTSOG TP.

Note: Utilisation ratios are assessed by dividing physical flows by firm technical maximum capacity. The ratios might move above 100% in case flows are underlined by interruptible capacity. Historical utilisation ratios at some Virtual Interconnection Points (VIPs) have not been included as a result of the entry into operation of the virtual interconnection at later dates.

4 PRICES REACTED TO AND STEERED, FLOW DEVELOPMENTS

European energy prices, led by the Dutch Title Transfer Facility (TTF), surged to unprecedented levels during the summer of 2022, primarily because of the dramatically reduced Russian gas flows. The price spike was also a consequence of additional and interlinked factors, including resilient gas demand for the build-up of storage inventories ahead of winter, significant constraints on non-gas power generation capacity, congestion in accessing pipelines and LNG terminals in North-West Europe, and a tight global LNG supply market exacerbating LNG price competition. Since gas-fired power generation is often the marginal unit setting the wholesale electricity price, these elevated gas prices translated into similarly high electricity prices as well. Over time, while the market sought and found a new equilibrium, most of these tensions gradually eased, leading to a more favourable demand-supply balance that has made energy prices decrease during the last months of 2022 and across 2023 (Figure 1.6).

Figure 1.6 EU Gas and Electricity Prices and Relevant Market Fundamentals (January 2021–October 2023)

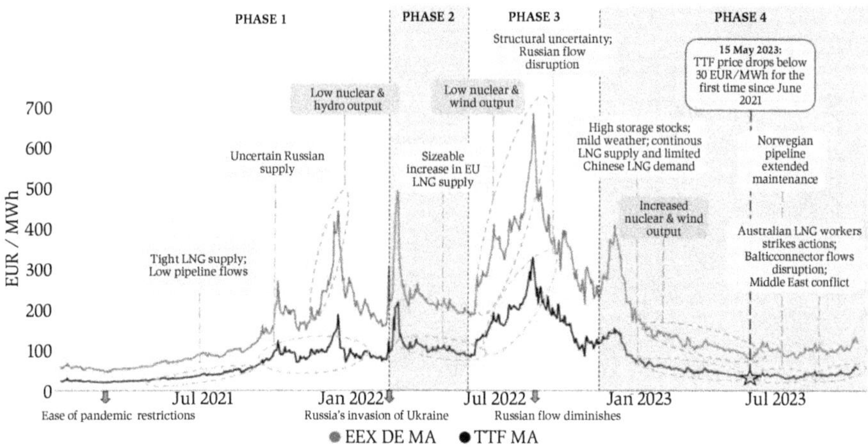

Source: ACER based on ICE and EEX data.

Within the European gas market, locational hub price spreads had often been perceived as low prior to the crisis, commonly hovering at the price levels set by tariffs for short-term transportation capacity. In fact, on many days, the spot gas price differences between interconnected EU markets were lower than this limit. This was especially the case between markets in North-West Europe, which were de facto functioning as a single price zone. While individual markets differed in aspects (such as LNG regasification capacity, level of interconnectedness, storage capacity, seasonality of consumption), the relatively high level of competition in the midstream market, the flexibility in the upstream North Sea network to redirect supply to premium markets, the availability of cross-border transportation capacity and the efficient capacity allocation system ensured that gas flows were optimised and locational price differences were arbitraged away.

However, with the Russian gas supply shock affecting some EU markets much more severely than others, the strong hub price convergence observed in previous years was upended and replaced by unprecedentedly high spreads. Some of the most noticeable differences were between TTF (based in the Netherlands), which used to set the price for the whole EU but which had more limited LNG connections, and the Spanish PVB hub, which is well supplied by LNG (Figure 1.7). These spreads in turn sent strong price signals to maximise flows to where the supply shortfall and the demand to replenish storages were highest. Since the end of 2022, price spreads between hubs have returned to pre-war levels.

Figure 1.7 Month-Ahead Convergence Between TTF and Selected EU Hubs (2021 to Q3 2023)

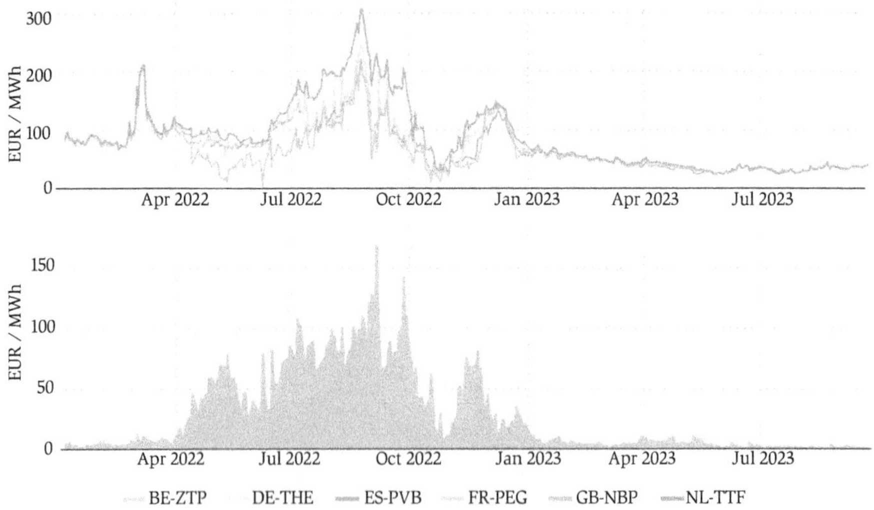

Source: ACER based on ICIS.

Note: The first graph shows the daily evolution of day-ahead prices traded at the five listed hubs, while the second graph shows the daily price spread between the Dutch TTF hub and the hub with the lowest price of the other four hubs.

5 GAS STORAGE STAYED HIGH DURING WINTER BUT CAME AT A PRICE

European gas storage reserves, or lack thereof, were one of the crucial factors in determining price outcomes throughout the energy crisis. The Russian invasion of Ukraine elicited a strong policy response at both the EU and Member State levels aimed at ensuring sufficient gas storage levels come winter. These policies proved highly effective in achieving the objective of improving security of gas supply during winter, the peak consumption season. The gas stock build over the gas summer of 2022 was one of the highest on record at the time, despite limited supply (Figure 1.8).

However, in contrast to the *effectiveness*, questions around the *efficiency* of the measures as well as their potential role in driving gas spot and futures prices remain to be fully investigated. What is beyond question is that the cost of the gas in storage build was several orders of magnitude higher than any that came before, especially when assessed on a mark-to-spot-market basis (Figure 1.9).[5]

Figure 1.8 EU Gas Storage Levels Evolution – 2017-2023 (% of Total Capacity)

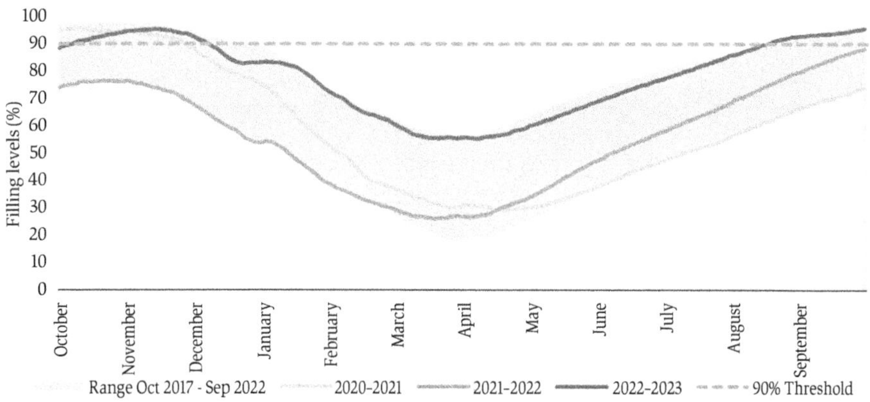

Source: ACER based on GIE data.

5. These estimates are based on the assumption that all storage injections and withdrawals during a given month were priced at the average cost of the preceding month-ahead TTF price; while the actual injection costs would have been lower in practice in 2022, as several suppliers likely hedged at least parts of the injected volumes' prices in advance, it gives a useful order-of-magnitude of the amounts involved.

Figure 1.9 Volatile Value of Gas Impacting EU Storage – 2019–2023 (bn Euros)

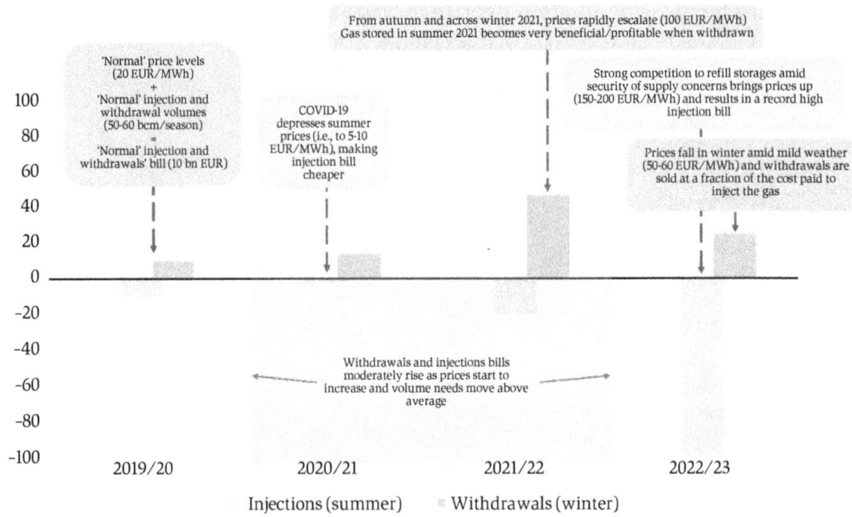

Source: ACER based on the International Energy Agency (IEA).

Note: Injections assessed as the average prompt prices across summer months and withdrawals as the average prompt prices across winter months.

6 CONCLUDING REMARKS

The European gas market found itself at the centre of a global energy crisis in 2022. Russian attempts, in the wake of its invasion of Ukraine, to use its 'gas weapon' against Europe have backfired: while 2022 was tough in terms of extremely high energy prices as the market sought a new equilibrium, Europe navigated the crisis without supply interruptions. Thanks to new LNG supplies, demand side response, policy interventions and a robust and flexible infrastructure system, it has weathered the storm. As of December 2023, wholesale gas prices have come down below 35 EUR/MWh, reaching the lowest level in two years. In the meantime, the Russian pipeline gas supply share to Europe has shrunk to less than 8 %, meaning that Russia has not only significantly less influence on Europe's energy market but also significantly lower gas export earnings. The adjusted EU gas market now places a heavier reliance on LNG supply, making it more susceptible to global competition and to potential volatility stemming from unforeseen events. However, thanks to its enhanced preparation and the foreseen evolution of demand dynamics, it is better equipped to avoid reaching extremely high price levels. A well-integrated, open and competitive European energy market goes a long way.

CHAPTER 2

State Aid Control and Energy Markets in a Time of Crisis

Ben Smulders & Anna Colucci

1 EU ENERGY POLICY OBJECTIVES: DECARBONISATION, SECURITY OF SUPPLY AND AFFORDABILITY

The core objectives of the EU energy policy - decarbonisation, security of supply, and affordability - have long guided both regulatory choices, competition and State aid policies. These objectives, integral to the Green Deal strategy,[1] remain crucial in the evolving economic and geopolitical landscape.

In the face of challenges like Russia's military aggression against Ukraine, diversification of energy sources, independence from monopolistic suppliers, and accelerated decarbonisation have become imperative for Europe's autonomy.

Competitive energy markets are essential for resilience, securing supplies, and supporting the green transition. They have helped us to manage the energy crisis without major supply issues, enabling significant energy savings and efficient electricity exchange within the European Union.

2 STATE AID RESPONSE TO THE ENERGY CRISIS: THE EVOLUTION OF THE TCTF

Competition policy has played a crucial role in mitigating the consequences of the energy price crisis. The Temporary Crisis Framework (TCF), initially designed to enable Member States to support companies and sectors in response to the aggression

1. Communication from the Commission to the European Parliament, the European Council, the Council, the European Economic and Social Committee and the Committee of the Regions, COM/2019/640 final of 11.12.2019 - The European Green Deal.

against Ukraine by Russia, has evolved into the Temporary Crisis and Transition Framework (TCTF).[2] To accompany the acceleration of the energy transition, the TCTF facilitates aid towards decarbonisation, security of supply, and resilience, allowing Member States to support renewable energy and industrial decarbonisation.

Sections 2.5 and 2.6 of the TCTF facilitate State aid, respectively, to accelerate the roll-out of renewable energy, storage and renewable heat relevant for REPowerEU[3] and to decarbonise industrial production processes. These temporary rules are more flexible than the normal rules under the General Block Exemption Regulation (GBER) and guidelines in order to enable projects to be implemented within a short timeframe to effectively accelerate the green transition, but should not result in undue negative effects on the level playing field.

Section 2.8 of the TCTF exceptionally allows Member States to grant aid to accelerate investments in key sectors for the transition towards a net-zero economy. Aid under this section is subject to strict limits and safeguards to preserve cohesion policy and to avoid any undue effects on trade and competition. In the case of aid schemes, Member States must ensure that any eligible project would not be realised in Europe without the aid and that there is no relocation of production activities between Member States. For individually notified measures, the Commission will require a number of eligibility conditions to be fulfilled. These conditions include concrete evidence of subsidies in third countries, the cohesion and cross-border effects of the project, the use of state-of-the-art environmental technologies and the absence of relocation effects. Any aid granted pursuant to such an individual notification is limited to the lower of the available third-country subsidies and the funding gap of the project to ensure that aid is kept to the minimum necessary to trigger the investment in Europe.

3 LOOKING BEYOND THE CRISIS: CEEAG, GBER AND THE GREEN TRANSITION

While temporary support during crises is essential, long-term structural actions are necessary to address the root causes of the energy crisis and to advance faster in the green transition.

State aid control, embodied in the 2022 Guidelines on State aid for Climate, Environmental Protection and Energy (CEEAG)[4] and the 2023 revised GBER,[5] plays a pivotal role in advancing EU energy policy objectives. By directing public resources

2. Communication from the Commission on the Temporary Crisis and Transition Framework for State Aid measures to support the economy following the aggression against Ukraine by Russia (OJ C 101, 17.3.2023, p. 3), as amended by Commission Communication C(2023)8045 (OJ C1188, 21.11.2023).
3. Communication from the Commission to the European Parliament, the European Council, the Council, the European Economic and Social Committee and the Committee of the Regions, COM/2022/230 final of 18.05.2022 – REPowerEU Plan.
4. Communication from the Commission C/2022/481 – Guidelines on State aid for climate, environmental protection and energy 2022 (OJ C 80, 18.2.2022, pp. 1-89).
5. Commission Regulation (EU) No 651/2014 of 17 June 2014 declaring certain categories of aid compatible with the internal market in application of Articles 107 and 108 of the Treaty (OJ L 167, 30.6.2023, p. 1).

towards faster deployment of renewables, energy efficiency, and industrial decarbonisation, it contributes significantly to the European Green Deal and the REPowerEU Plan also reducing the European dependency on energy imports and expensive fossil fuels.

In December 2019, the European Commission adopted the Communication on the Green Deal with the objective of becoming the first climate-neutral continent in the world. At the core of the Green Deal lay the three key objectives: decarbonisation, security of supply and affordability. It is with these objectives in mind that the CEEAG was developed to allow Member States to provide support for all the technologies that can contribute to the decarbonisation of the Union and to introduce security of supply measures to accompany the transition to a more flexible electricity system that is increasingly based on renewable energy sources.

In this context, the CEEAG constitute the main guidance regarding the State aid for energy and environmental protection. The CEEAG adopt a technology-neutral approach to all the technologies that can contribute to the European Green Deal, including renewable energy and energy efficiency. However, technology-specific tenders remain possible, for example, where Union law establishes sectoral or technology-based targets, e.g., for renewable energy under the Renewable Energy Directive. These rules generally allow for aid amounts up to 100% of the funding gap and introduce new aid instruments, such as Carbon Contracts for Difference (CCfDs) to help Member States respond to the greening needs of the industry. The CEEAG is not the only set of guidelines that contribute to the green transition as almost all State aid sectors have a role to play in facilitating the green transition. This is why different State aid rules have either already been revised or are also currently undergoing a revision process to ensure coherence with the objectives of the twin transition to a green and digital economy.

In 2023, the Commission approved under the CEEAG several State aid measures targeting the decarbonisation of industrial sectors such as steel and refining through the uptake of hydrogen-based technologies or through electrification of hydrogen production.[6] The challenge in these cases is the fact that the renewable and low-carbon hydrogen markets in the EU are still in a nascent state which entails substantial uncertainties and high risks to economic operators, for example, whether enough renewable hydrogen at affordable prices would be readily available in the medium term. This justifies the intervention of Member States to address such high risks and incentivise the decarbonisation of industrial processes through the shift to clean hydrogen and electrification. Also in 2023, the Commission approved other State aid measures under the CEEAG to support the development of renewable energy, covering different technologies (solar PV, onshore wind, offshore wind, hydrogen, biomass)[7] and continued assessing measures taken by Member States to support the phase-out

6. *See*, for example, decisions in cases SA.63733, SA.104904, SA.104897, SA.104903, SA.105244, SA.105337, SA.105006 (available in https://competition-cases.ec.europa.eu/search).
7. *See*, for example, decisions in cases SA.104685, SA.101998, SA.103069, SA.103648, SA.108070 (available in https://competition-cases.ec.europa.eu/search).

from coal-fired power generation[8] as well as continued providing guidance to Member States regarding measures to ensure security of energy supply.[9]

In addition, the Commission adopted revisions to the GBER on 23 June 2023 with the aim of aligning the relevant parts of the GBER with recently revised State aid guidelines to support the twin transition. However, due to the broader context of discussions on how to best combat the economic effects of the Russian military aggression against Ukraine and wider global challenges to the economic level playing field, including due to the US Inflation Reduction Act, the substantive changes to the GBER went beyond that initial scope.

The revised rules increase and streamline the possibilities for aid in the area of environmental protection and energy, among others to support the rollout of renewable energy, decarbonisation projects, green mobility and biodiversity, as well as to facilitate investments in renewable hydrogen and to increase energy efficiency. They also facilitate the implementation of certain projects involving beneficiaries in several Member States, such as Important Projects of Common European Interest (IPCEI), in the research and development field, by increasing the aid intensities as well as the notification thresholds; and block exempt aid measures set up by Member States to regulate prices for energy such as electricity, gas and heat produced from natural gas or electricity.

4 NEED FOR A STRUCTURAL RESPONSE: THE EMD REFORM

The Commission also moved towards more structural interventions to increase the resilience of the electricity market to crises, with a proposal for a reform of the Electricity Market Design (EMD)[10] on which co-legislators reached a political agreement in December 2023.

The reform reflects the experience with State aid support schemes, as well as the experience during the crisis, in particular the importance of efficient imports and exports and demand reduction driven by price signals in the internal market. This is apparent in the provisions to safeguard the efficient functioning of short-term markets, to foster the use of market-based instruments such as power purchase agreements, to use two-way contracts for difference (CfD) for the support schemes of fossil-free technologies and to support security of supply in a decarbonised electricity system by enabling additional competitive support options for non-fossil flexibility services. While it is clear that State aid and State aid control will remain important in the electricity sector, the instruments may fall outside the scope of State aid control if they are market-based and/or purchased independently from the State and without State resources.

8. *See*, for example, decision in case SA.53625 (available in https://competition-cases.ec.europa.eu/search).
9. *See*, for example, decisions in cases SA.104336, SA.103068 (available in https://competition-cases.ec.europa.eu/search).
10. Proposal for a Regulation of the European Parliament and of the Council amending Regulations (EU) 2019/943 and (EU) 2019/942 as well as Directives (EU) 2018/2001 and (EU) 2019/944 to improve the Union's electricity market design, COM(2023) 148 final of 14.3.2023.

The current market design creating the single electricity market has brought huge economic and security of supply benefits to Europe. But the recent crisis has shown the impact of high and volatile fossil fuel prices on electricity bills. The reform of the EMD addresses this exposure to fossil fuel prices through the mandatory move to two-way CfDs, which will bring the benefits of lower-cost renewables to consumers and address our affordability, decarbonisation and security of supply goals over the long term.

5 CONCLUSION: STATE AID POLICY AS A PILLAR OF STABILITY

State aid control remains a crucial pillar for maintaining a level playing field in the EU, especially in times of crisis, preventing subsidy races and preserving the single market's integrity. The Commission is committed to drawing essential lessons for the future, ensuring that State aid control continues to contribute to minimising distortions and fostering a resilient and united Europe.

The CEEAG and the revised GBER provide a flexible framework for coordinated state support, weathering the energy crisis and complemented by temporary instruments for crisis response. The synergies between this set of rules and the ongoing reform efforts, particularly in the Electricity Market Design, showcase a comprehensive approach to addressing the challenges and advancing the green transition. This strategy, anchored in competition policy and regulatory frameworks, reflects the EU's commitment to a sustainable, competitive, and secure energy future.

The Commission remains dedicated to fine-tuning these instruments to navigate the evolving challenges, preserving a level playing field in the internal market and ensuring a cost-efficient and fair green transition for Europe.

CHAPTER 3

The EU Energy Transition: Realism Confronts Dogma

Ana Palacio

1 INTRODUCTION

The European continent has been hit by energy shocks in the past years. In consequence, energy security has become the top concern of policy-makers in this field. The war in Ukraine has exposed the depth of Europe's (notably, Germany's) self-induced dependency on Russian fossil fuels, particularly gas. Pipeline bottlenecks, insufficient upstream investment, and the lack of liquified natural gas (LNG) terminals further exacerbated the crisis, compounded by the halving of France's nuclear capacity, owing to unforeseen maintenance shutdowns and hydro shortages linked to poor rainfalls. It was a significant challenge, and few expected Europe to overcome the brutal severance from Russian gas. But despite the magnitude of the obstacles and our tendency to self-flagellate, Europe has been able to "weather the storm," prevent families from freezing in the winter months and avoid the widespread closing of industries. Notwithstanding the mild temperatures last winter, which certainly alleviated the burden, the European Union's performance and agile reaction have not been properly acknowledged.

This is not to say that it will be all smooth sailing, especially as Europe braces for the 2023-2024 winter ahead. Germany, which is completing the last stages of the nuclear phase-out pledged after the Fukushima disaster in 2011, has been returning to service dismantled coal power plants and reopening coal mines. Meanwhile in Brussels, the *Fit-for-55* package, recently approved by the European Parliament, has already raised concerns about further social fragmentation.

The internal market looks equally vulnerable. The staggering amounts—close to EUR 800 billion—of state aid provided by European governments to shield companies and households from high energy costs have created imbalances favoring the continent's industrial heavyweights. To date, Berlin and Paris account for 77% of the EUR 672 billion[1] in government funds approved by Brussels after it relaxed state aid rules in March 2022. Berlin has extended an astounding EUR 356 billion in economic support to industry, green-lighted by the European Commission. In turn, roughly EUR 161 billion—24% of the total—was cleared by Paris. Such glaring imbalances have accentuated the cracks in the internal market and sown discord among the Member States.

2 OLD NARRATIVES INTO NEW REALITIES

Faced with the mounting challenges of recent months, the institutions of the European Union, particularly the European Commission, have struggled to fit the new realities that confront us into the existing Green Deal framework (widely considered to be the game-changer that will consolidate our status as Standard Bearers of the transition to Net-Zero). The Green Deal, which became the hallmark of the (first) Von der Leyen mandate, was built in 2019 when supply and affordability were not the existential concerns they are today.

But the focus on energy security has become non-negotiable for policymakers in Europe and elsewhere, making it increasingly difficult to reconcile with the Green Deal's original objectives. Since the start of the war in Ukraine, news headlines have been dominated by the legal and conceptual pirouettes of a Union that seeks to match its ambitious energy goals to a fast-moving geopolitical landscape. One such example was the Union's decision, under its 2022 "Taxonomy" rules, to include nuclear energy and gas as environmentally sustainable economic activities.

Fundamentally, a key factor contributing to the imbalances and distortions of Europe's energy policy is the very design of the Treaty on the Functioning of the European Union when it comes to energy policy: the Treaty entrusted Brussels with sustainability while it placed the responsibility for security of energy supply and the creation of the energy mix with Member States.[2]

3 NEW ACTORS, OLD TENSIONS

For decades, the European Union has been a pioneer for climate change, and a leader in promoting sustainability, with notable successes in the fight against greenhouse gas emissions. Europe's actions have made significant gains both in curbing its own emissions and in raising global awareness of climate change. But the emergence of China as a dominant player in the clean energy market has changed not only the constellation but also the game.

1. https://www.euronews.com/my-europe/2023/01/17/germany-france-account-for-most-eu-state-aid-heres-why-its-a-concern.
2. Particularly illuminating in this context is the 2022 decision of the Court of Justice of the European Union to dismiss action brought by Austria contesting Hungarian investment aid previously approved by the European Commission.

Today, Beijing has become the essential supplier of a significant proportion of clean technology—including critical minerals and rare earths, accounting for around 70%[3] of the world's extraction capability. In terms of the processing and refining of these minerals, China's control is even greater, currently performing between 60% and 90%. China's dominance of critical supply chains has effectively halted Europe's green dreams and has made an accelerated transition to clean energy even more challenging. It is a reality that Brussels has yet to confront.

The turmoil in global energy markets and the impetus to transition from fossil fuels to renewable energy sources have also caused increasing financial pressures on countries worldwide. Resolute in its fight against global emissions, Europe's dogmatism has made it increasingly oblivious to the stark realities of energy poverty—a source of tension between wealthy and poorer countries, particularly in Africa, where a generalized feeling of resentment prevails.

Consequently, the issue of the clean energy transition has become a contentious topic, especially at international climate conferences. Paradigmatic was the last Conference of the Parties to the United Nations Framework Convention on Climate Change, held in Sharm el-Sheikh, where tensions between the Global North and South were on full display.

There is a palpable frustration with wealthy nations' failure to deliver on promises for climate assistance and their direct refusal to finance hydrocarbon projects in poorer parts of the world. The Green Climate Fund, conceived during the 2009 United Nations Climate Conference in Copenhagen, aimed to raise an annual sum of USD 100 billion by 2020 to support the energy transition of developing countries. But, according to the Fund's own tracker, the participating countries' pledges have totaled a mere USD 9.31 billion to date.[4] This year's G7 Ministers Meeting on Climate, Energy, and Environment, held in Hokkaido, Japan, echoed this commitment, with participating countries reaffirming their commitment to jointly mobilize USD 100 billion annually in climate finance through 2025. It remains uncertain, however, if Western commitments still hold water.

The gap between words and deeds has thus been on full display. Developing countries rightfully chafe against the West's empty promises and lofty proselytizing given the ways in which our actions affect them, often adversely. As Russia launched its full-scale invasion of Ukraine, Europe raced to secure new energy supplies and build new infrastructure, in its haste, bidding up the price of gas. This, in turn, drove up demand for coal in Asia, resulting in record-high prices, which tightened the supply for countries such as Pakistan and Bangladesh that are struggling to afford energy in any form.

It is therefore no surprise that many countries in the Global South have opted for a pragmatic approach, which includes the use of fossil fuels, considering this more

3. https://www.heritage.org/defense/commentary/rare-earths-supply-chains-and-confrontation-china.
4. https://www.greenclimate.fund/sites/default/files/document/1706-status-pledges-website-july-31-2023.pdf.

realistic and less damaging to their economies. Furthermore, many developing countries face significant financial barriers in their transition to clean energy. One jarring example today is that only 0.6% of global investment[5] in renewable energy goes to Sub-Saharan Africa; interest rates to finance clean projects on the continent are much higher than those in the Global North. In Nigeria alone, the predominant narrative is that achieving net-zero by 2060 would require bringing nearly 100 million people out of poverty and undertaking a solid industrial transformation that would require serious investment. The financial needs of Africa—to mention our closest neighbors—are in the trillions; meanwhile, there is little notion of how funding for the Global South will materialize.

4 EUROPEAN DOGMA AND AMERICAN PRAGMATISM

After years of being a laggard on climate action, especially during the dark years of the Trump presidency, the Biden administration has put the United States at the forefront of the fight against climate change. Industrial policy is back in vogue, and the Inflation Reduction Act (IRA) is the latest action in a growing trend aimed at harnessing cutting-edge clean technology to boost domestic industry, create local jobs, and secure supply chains.

The IRA is notable for its pragmatism, which takes a technologically neutral approach to reaching net-zero emissions. Its inclusion of carbon capture, utilization, and storage (CCUS) projects marks support for a field that the Union is just beginning to explore. The IRA has also drawn the attention of European equipment suppliers due to its advantageous structure of support schemes, which directly address the off-taker price and operational expenditures; by contrast, EU capital expenditure subsidies affect the business case, which delays projects intrinsically.

Europe's travails, on the multiple regulatory fronts it has opened, have forced the bloc to face the consequences of competencies scattered across the EU directorates. The Union's attempt to ensure a secure and sustainable supply of critical raw materials or its efforts to create a feasible Carbon Adjustment Border Mechanism (CABM) are fitting examples to that end. For Brussels to break out of this siloed approach and to be able to chart an ambitious and comprehensive industrial path forward, structural changes will be required; disparate competencies will need to be focused in a way that allows the EU to effectively cover the entire cycle, from sourcing minerals to designing subsidy schemes through final sale.

5 CONCLUSION

For Europe to achieve a net-zero future, it needs a measure of pragmatism that translates into powerful industrial deployment. This will necessitate a level of regulatory predictability that transmits security to investors, and it will require the EU to

5. https://about.bnef.com/blog/scaling-up-renewable-energy-in-africa/.

project determination and realism regarding fossil fuels, critical minerals, and public and private systems that create, store, and distribute energy.

The bloc cannot be perceived as prioritizing ideologically charged tenets over effectiveness when designing climate policies. Brussels and the capitals are often caught up in endless disputes about what can be considered green, sustainable, or renewable, losing sight of the main goal: decarbonization. Instead of demonizing the fossil fuel industry, Europe needs to focus on reducing emissions from all sources—it cannot afford to discount any solutions, including technological advances for the fossil fuel sector.

Renewable energy sources face reliability and storage challenges; nuclear energy is perceived as unsafe, costly, and produces spent fuel; and fossil fuels' Achilles heel is their emissions. If we haphazardly rule out energy sources because of their disadvantages, we will be left empty-handed.

The challenges of the European energy transition converge towards the Union's competition policy, which forms the core of European construction. In the last year, it has been made clear that dogmatism is a poor weapon in times of crisis. Europe needs to take a pragmatic approach to climate action, focusing on reducing greenhouse gas emissions by all means possible while promoting a strong industrial deployment. Only then can Europe achieve a sustainable net-zero future.

PART II Affordability of Energy Prices

CHAPTER 4

From the Implementation of Emergency Interventions to the Review of Market Design: How Two Years of Energy Price Crisis Have Changed the European Electricity Market

Juan José Alba Ríos[*]

1 SUMMARY

The approval of the Clean Energy Package had been seen by many, especially in the electricity industry, as the end of the road for legislation on electricity market design. However, the gas price crisis that started in mid-2021, which led to unprecedented wholesale electricity prices that also impacted retail prices, made many politicians and part of society think that the electricity market design was not able to effectively protect consumers from this type of shocks, with prices reaching levels that some considered unjustified. This led to a flurry of national emergency market interventions, followed by actions at the EU level, which are discussed in section 2 of this chapter.

The EU debate on this topic soon moved beyond the market interventions themselves and focused on more fundamental issues of the electricity market, questioning some of the foundational principles of the market. Section 3 of this chapter summarizes some of these debates. And the obvious follow-up of this was a legislative

* Special thanks to friends and colleagues who have contributed comments and suggestions to this chapter: Eduardo Moreda, César Martinez, Marta Marañón, Elena Alonso, Andrea Villa, Teresa Luis, Simonetta Naletto, José Casas, Gabriel Tévar, Marta Castro Rafael Gómez-Elvira, Pavla Mandatova and, specially, Yvan Hachez and David Robinson, for their detailed discussions of the text.

proposal on electricity market design, whose inception and main elements are reviewed in section 4.

The rest of the chapter goes deeper into the most important and controversial elements of the proposal. Section 5 focuses on different aspects of long-term contracting. The proposal of the Commission (as well as the amendments proposed by Parliament and Council) deal with power purchase agreements (PPAs), contract for differences (CfDs), forward markets and capacity mechanisms, not only from the point of view of their impact on investment, as usual, but also considering their effect in the stability and level of the prices paid by end consumers. As the Explanatory memorandum of the legislative proposal says, it includes measures aimed at creating "a buffer between short-term markets and electricity bills paid by consumers, in particular by way of incentivizing longer term contracting."

Section 6 deals with the retail market and the network. Beyond the consideration of long-term contracts from the perspective of the consumer, the proposal includes provisions that specifically affect the retail market. The treatment of the grid in the proposal, through the introduction of the concept of "anticipatory investments," is brief, but very relevant, with the potential to have a large impact on the application of electricity to new uses and the removal of an important barrier to the energy transition.

Section 7 focuses on emergency market interventions: the market design proposal started as a response to the energy price crisis, and the new market design proposal includes some built-in crisis-response mechanisms.

Finally, section 8 presents some conclusions. The legislative process of the market design proposal will probably be over when this chapter is published. However, this discussion will still be relevant once the text has been finalized for the interpretation, implementation, development, and eventual evolution of the resulting legislation.

2 INTRODUCTION: PRICE CRISIS AND EMERGENCY INTERVENTIONS

In 2019, the so-called Clean Energy Package was approved. Finally, the European Union had a comprehensive legal framework for the electricity market, replacing several generations of rules that had always been an incomplete set of patchwork regulations. This latest legislative package covers all aspects of the electrical system: customers and retail, generation, transmission and distribution networks, wholesale market, regulatory bodies, cross-border energy exchanges, etc. For the first time, systematic legislative responses were provided for phenomena such as self-consumption, demand-side management, energy communities, the integration of renewables into the market, and more.

The market was defined as the foundation of the electrical system, and one of the objectives of the package was to define an efficient and competitive market design for the entire Union, which was supposed to allow the substantial investments needed for the energy transition.

At that time, many considered the market design to be a resolved issue. Some elements remained to be finalized (such as the deployment of new opportunities envisaged by the package for consumers), but the European Commission believed it had almost reached the end of the road.

However, controversial issues remained open, such as the need to include in the market design mechanisms that offered long-term economic signals (such as capacity markets or long-term contracts for renewable generation) to trigger investments. Much of the electricity industry was skeptical about whether the existing spot and forward markets were sufficient. Usual wholesale prices in Europe before 2021 did not allow for the recovery of the fixed and investment costs of many generation facilities, especially those capable of providing stability and flexibility to the system, such as nuclear plants, hydropower plants, hydro pumping stations, or combined cycle generation units.

By early 2020, the focus of the European Commission had shifted to the European Green Deal, a new legislative initiative that aimed to increase ambition in emissions reduction and make Europe the first climate-neutral continent by 2050, dealing with energy efficiency, mobility, fairness of the energy transition, hydrogen, "green" taxation, digitalization, and more. The electricity market design was no longer a pressing issue.

In the spring of 2020, the COVID-19 pandemic disrupted all plans and shifted attention to protecting the most vulnerable citizens and the economic recovery that would be necessary after the pandemic. In 2021, as most EU countries gradually began to return to normal life, the "fit-for-55" package was proposed by the EC to deliver the 55% emissions reduction target by 2030 as a fundamental part of the Green Deal, but turbulence in the electricity market began. In mid-2021, emission allowance prices and, above all, natural gas prices started to rise rapidly, dragging wholesale electricity prices in the spot markets to unprecedented levels. The rise in gas prices was attributed to an irregular global economic recovery that increased gas demand in Asia and raised prices for liquefied natural gas. Additionally, the reduction of Russian gas exports to the European Union started; long-term contracts were honored, but spot gas sales began to decrease.

The impact was particularly felt in Spain, where a distinctive regulated tariff, the so-called Voluntary Price for Small Consumers (PVPC by its Spanish initials), directly passed on the hourly spot market price to customers, causing millions of citizens to experience these wholesale price increases directly in their electricity bills. In the rest of Europe, where most end-customer prices were based on forward prices, consumers took months to feel the effects of the price crisis. This led the Spanish government to be the first to react: on June 1, 2021, the bill "on the Remuneration of Non-emitted CO_2" was presented, aiming to capture the revenue that hydraulic, nuclear, and older renewables generators were supposedly receiving due to the increase in spot market prices driven by higher CO_2 prices. Soon after that proposal, VAT and the Value of Production Tax paid by generators were reduced.

In September 2021, Spain adopted a new measure with Royal Decree-Law 17/2021, imposing an obligation on hydraulic, nuclear, and some renewable generators to pay an amount equivalent to the increase in spot market prices due to the rise in gas prices.[1] This regulation—which foreshadowed "windfall profit" proposals that would be adopted in other countries in 2022—was quickly adjusted to consider that much of the production during these months was sold in the futures markets or to end customers at prices that had been set many months before, much lower than those in the spot market. In other words, there were very limited "windfall" profits to tax.

From September 2021 onwards, other countries began to take measures, mostly of a fiscal nature or in support of consumers and industries, but there were some, such as Italy or Romania, which proposed similar interventions to the Spanish proposal.

In any case, even in October 2021, the crisis was perceived as temporary. Futures market prices indicated a reduction in wholesale gas and electricity prices starting in the spring of 2022. If this were to be the case, most European electricity consumers would not notice the significant rise in wholesale prices that had occurred.

In October, the European Commission published its first communication on the price crisis, the so-called Toolbox. It described the tools already available to Member States to address the crisis, with an approach aligned with the traditional positions of the Commission. It did not consider market interventions but rather short-term measures focused on protecting vulnerable customers and businesses, along with tax reductions. Additionally, it advocated accelerating the development of renewables, improving market oversight, and exploring joint gas purchasing schemes to ensure gas reserves for the upcoming winter.

In the "Toolbox" communication, the Commission asked the Agency for the Cooperation of Energy Regulators (ACER), to "assess benefits and drawbacks of the current wholesale electricity market design," and this led to "ACER's Final Assessment of the EU Wholesale Electricity Market Design," published in April 2022.[2] ACER made a generally positive assessment of the current market design and proposed several concrete measures without any disruptive change.

For several countries, this was not enough. Spain was probably the most active, but France, Italy, Greece, and Romania pushed in the same direction. The need to "decouple gas and electricity prices" began to be discussed. Others, such as Germany, the Netherlands, Austria, and the Nordic countries, opposed market intervention.

The situation deteriorated, and by the turn of the year, it was clear that prices would not normalize in the spring of 2022. Russian gas exports to Europe were decreasing; gas prices were soaring, dragging electricity spot prices with them. The pressure from Spain and other countries increased in the first months of 2022, advocating not so much for new interventionist measures but for a complete review of the electricity market design. The situation worsened after the Russian invasion of Ukraine, which jeopardized much of Europe's gas supply.

1. This measure is approximately equivalent to the "cap on market revenues" that was later established by Council Regulation 2022/1854 on emergency interventions. The difference is that, while the EU regulation sets a limit of up to 180 EUR/MWh, the Spanish measure sets a limit of 67 EUR/MWh and if market revenues are above that value the producer will pay 90% of the difference.
2. The Commission also asked ESMA for an assessment of the trading of emission allowances since speculation in this market had also been blamed as a driver of the turmoil in energy prices.

So, we arrive at Spring 2022. The Commission published a set of communications,[3,4] which marked a 180-degree turn in its approach. After traditionally defending the current market model throughout the Union, the Commission began to interpret that regulated prices could be used with much greater frequency and flexibility than previously thought[5] and opened a debate, hitherto non-existent in Europe, on "windfall profits" and the fiscal or regulatory measures to capture them. Measures to capture "windfall profits" were considered very similar to those implemented in Spain in 2021.

After this shift in the Commission's position, the debate continued about the need for further interventions, as prices continued to rise and Russian gas supply for the coming winter was threatened after Russia had already interrupted or reduced exports to several EU countries.

In June 2022, the European Council conceptually approved the principles behind interventions such as the so-called Iberian exception, and the Commission ultimately approved the specific measure:[6] it reduces the apparent cost of gas used for electricity generation, subsidizing the difference between the market gas price and the reference price set in the regulation. Finally, the regulation on emergency interventions[7] introduced a limit on the revenues of inframarginal generators, while the regulation on the Title Transfer Facility (TTF)[8] market correction mechanism[9] introduced a scheme to control the prices of the TTF natural gas market in exceptional circumstances.

The debate about short-term interventions for crisis situations was mixed with reflections on whether the electricity market design should be changed. Was the market design finally established in the Clean Energy package adequate for a market with a high proportion of renewables and subject to shocks in the supply of gas?

There were several things to consider in this discussion. First, we cannot forget that the root of the problem is the price of gas (and the fact that the international gas market has an oligopolistic structure, even more so than the oil market). It is not easy to understand how almost the entire debate of the past years (and almost all the measures adopted) focused on the electricity market. Should not we consider intervening in the gas market, controlled by an oligopoly whose principal representative has launched a war that threatens all of Europe? Second, this is a European problem that requires European solutions. We cannot break the market with exceptions: in the medium and long term, that will be worse for everyone. Third, transparency is required, along with

3. Communication on Security of supply and affordable energy prices: Options for immediate measures and preparing for next winter, Brussels, 23.3.2022.
4. Communication on Short-Term Energy Market Interventions and Long Term Improvements to the Electricity Market Design—a course for action, Brussels, 18.5.2022.
5. There are doubts about the legality of this interpretation.
6. The Spanish Royal Decree-Law 10/2022 and the Portuguese Decree-Law 33/2022 and its associated Direitiva 11/2022 of ERSE, EU's approval decision "State Aid SA. 102454 (2022/N)—Spain and SA.102569 (2022/N) - Portugal—Production cost adjustment mechanism for the reduction of the electricity wholesale price in the Iberian market," Brussels, 8.6.2022, C(2022) 3942 final.
7. Council Regulation (EU) 2022/1854 of 6 October 2022 on an emergency intervention to address high energy prices.
8. TTF is a virtual gas trading hub in the Netherlands, which is a de facto reference market for a large share of gas transactions in Europe.
9. Council Regulation (EU) 2022/2578 of 22 December 2022 establishing a market correction mechanism to protect Union citizens and the economy against excessively high prices.

dialog among all stakeholders, without demonizing anyone (governments and businesses are not to blame for the energy price crisis) and arguments based on data. We have already seen measures that did not work as expected or had to be hastily corrected or an accumulation of measures pursuing the same objectives.

3 THE DEBATE ON MARKET DESIGN

The European debate on reforming the electricity market design was unofficially launched by the intervention of President Von der Leyen in the European Parliament in May 2022:

> Electricity prices are skyrocketing, and we are doing a lot on it. We have issued a toolbox that many of our MS are using that; it is taxing the windfall profits and subsidizing vulnerable households and business. But we also acknowledge that this is a short-term relief that will not really change the structure of the market. We still have an electricity market that is designed in a way like it was necessary 20 years ago, when it was necessary to bring in the renewables. So, it is the renewables that go in first, at that time much more expensive, and then other energies like oil or gas or nuclear or coal. And the one that comes in last is the most expensive and deciding the price.
>
> Today the market is completely different. It is renewables the most cost effective and the cheapest and they come in and then, at the very end, comes gas and it is the most expensive. But it defines the whole price. This market system does not work anymore. We have to reform it; we have to adapt it to the new realities of dominant renewables.
>
> This is the task the EC has taken over now. It is not trivial it is a huge reform. It will take time and it has to be well thought through. We need to step forward to adapt our electricity market to the modern conditions.

The public debate went beyond the "usual" topic, familiar to the industry, of whether the market provides sufficient investment signals to deliver the energy transition and focused on the impact of market design on consumer prices in the context of the energy crisis. Are consumers sufficiently protected by the current market arrangements, or are they excessively exposed to short-term price volatility? Among other topics, public discussions focused on the following issues.

Is the marginal market a design choice?

Spot electricity markets are used to exchange electricity on a day-ahead horizon. Sellers and buyers present their bids for each hour of the following day, and the price for the electricity delivered in each hour is given by the intersection of the supply and demand curves, i.e., by the last supply or demand offer that is needed to ensure the supply-demand equilibrium in each hour (*see* Figure 4.1). Frequently, in most European wholesale markets, this last bid corresponds to a gas-fired power plant, and its price, in a competitive environment, corresponds to its marginal cost, i.e., to the cost of delivering one extra MWh with this power plant (therefore, the main drivers are the price of the natural gas needed for that extra production—and that price will be given by the opportunity cost of selling that gas in the spot gas market—as well as the price of the emission allowances required by this production).

Some critics of the current market design consider it unfair that the price of electricity is set by the last bid, i.e., by the most expensive generation needed to serve demand. They claim that we now have a lot of low-cost renewable generation, and it does not make sense that the price of electricity is not based on an average value that takes that reality into account.[10] These critics consider the marginal market a "design choice," a creature of the European Commission, something that can be simply changed by legislation. But the reality is that all commodity markets are marginal. Economic theory predicts that the equilibrium price in a competitive market will be given by the marginal cost of delivering an additional unit. This is the case not only for electricity but also for oil, natural gas, wheat, copper, etc. This reality cannot be changed through legislation. Moving from "pay as clear" to "pay as bid," as many have proposed, will not change it. This would only lead to inefficiencies in the merit order because market participants would try to assess the eventual clearing price and somehow adjust their bids to it instead of bidding their marginal cost. In practice, in the best scenarios, the result would be the same.[11]

Figure 4.1 The Supply and Demand Curves for a Given Hour in a Marginal Spot Market and the Usual Depiction of Windfall Profits

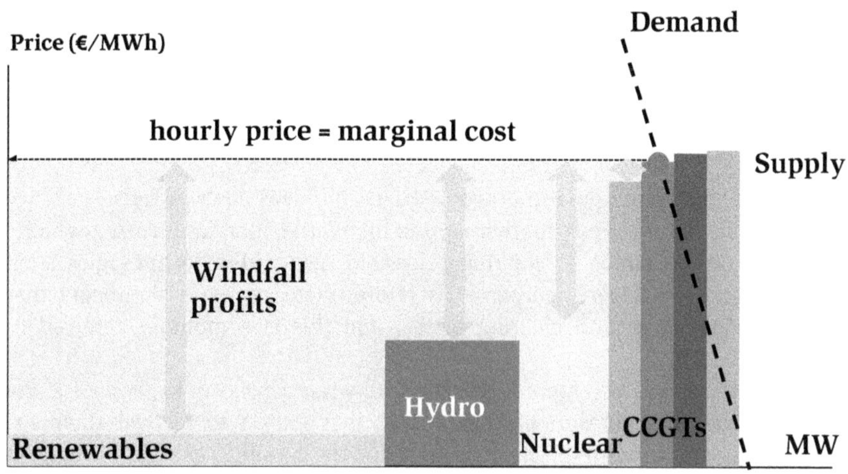

Note: The intersection of both curves defines the hourly price.

10. Interestingly, when there are periods of low spot prices (such as in 2020, during the COVID lockdowns, or in the many hours of prices close to zero in hours of high photovoltaic production), this criticism is not present.
11. There is plenty of scientific literature on this topic. An early and authoritative paper is Kahn, A.E., et al., July 2001, *Uniform Pricing or Pay-as-Bid Pricing: A Dilemma for California and Beyond*, The Electricity Journal. ACER's Final Assessment of the EU Wholesale Electricity Market Design, April 2022 also discusses this point.

Is the spot price relevant for consumers?

Much of the attention during this crisis has focused on the high prices in the wholesale spot market. This market is used to ensure a cost-efficient operation of the electricity system and to exchange energy on a day-ahead horizon. It is extremely important to ensure an efficient dispatching of generation facilities, to make adequate use of the interconnections, and to manage the operations of suppliers, traders, and generators. However, most energy is not traded in the spot market. Most suppliers buy, and most generators sell, their energy in advance in forward markets through contracts that typically are one year long. Even in cases such as the Iberian or Nordic markets, where most of the electricity is physically traded in the spot market, a large part of that electricity is covered by financial contracts, settled by differences against the spot price. The combined effect of the spot market and these financial contracts is that the suppliers pay (and generators receive) a fixed, previously agreed, price for their energy, independently of the latest fluctuations of the spot market. Because of this, when spot prices started increasing in mid-2021, most suppliers (and thus most consumers, according to their contracts) continued to pay the fixed prices that they had arranged months before.[12]

Therefore, forward markets are more relevant than spot markets for the "real economy." Nevertheless, there is certainly a relationship between them: forward markets reflect the expectations that market participants have about spot prices and therefore are influenced by marginal principles. When those contracts that kept fixed prices during 2021 were renewed at the beginning of 2022, they typically increased their prices to reflect the new market conditions.

Do marginal markets generate windfall profits?

The usual criticism of marginal markets is based on ideas such as those depicted in Figure 4.1. Bids in the spot market approximate the marginal costs, which are comparatively low, relative to clearing prices, for generation technologies such as wind, photovoltaic, nuclear, or hydro. Therefore, there can be a significant margin between marginal costs and clearing prices, and this is sometimes referred to as "windfall profits."

This simplistic analysis ignores that the reality is much closer to Figure 4.2. Power plants have fixed and investment costs,[13] and they expect to recover them in the market. The margin between the clearing price and the variable costs should contribute

12. As mentioned before, there was an important exception: the Spanish regulated tariff, the so-called PVPC, is a direct pass-through of the hourly spot price. Because of this, millions of Spanish domestic consumers immediately felt the pain of high spot prices as soon as the crisis started. This justifies the attention that Spanish media and society have paid to the spot market, as well as the early reactions of the Spanish government when the crisis started.

13. Strictly speaking, investment costs are fixed and could be incorporated in the concept of fixed costs. However, we will separately use both terms, to emphasize that the controversies about cost recovery and windfall profits are usually focused on investment costs.

to the recovery of these fixed and investment costs. Critics of the marginal market go as far as sustaining that these investment costs sometimes do not exist, wrongly assuming, for instance, that nuclear or hydro facilities are fully amortized and do not require additional investments every year. However, the reality, although quite heterogeneous across Europe (and very much influenced by different levels of taxation), is quite different from that. If we compare the full costs of nuclear and hydro facilities with the historic wholesale electricity prices, it can be shown that, most of the time, the full costs are above the wholesale prices (this was certainly not the case in 2021-2023 but has been a frequent situation in many European markets for most years before the current crisis, very specially in 2020 under the COVID pandemic).[14] With the deep penetration of intermittent renewables, wholesale spot prices (and forward markets that reflect expected future spot prices) are increasingly volatile and captured prices are so low that investors—especially in renewable power—are very unlikely to recover their investment costs without additional revenue sources.

Do interventions distort the market? Should they evolve into a permanent feature of the market design?

The European electricity markets have witnessed many interventions by governments in 2021 and 2022. A very popular design of intervention has been the introduction of clawbacks[15] or price caps on the revenues of inframarginal generators. The justification behind these clawbacks is that the increase in gas prices drives up spot electricity prices, "unfairly" increasing the revenues of inframarginal plants (such as nuclear, wind, hydro or photovoltaic units) whose costs have not actually increased. Politicians argue that these clawbacks help to correct an unfair situation, protect customers, and do not distort the market, since they are "*ex post*" adjustments that do not affect the dynamics of price formation. But the reality is much more complicated.

First, clawbacks are extremely complex to implement. Since most electricity sales are done at forward prices and frequently to end consumers, applying a clawback to theoretical spot revenues that have not materialized would not be fair. Therefore, the implementation of the clawback would require a very intrusive monitoring of all wholesale and retail transactions.

14. There is not much public information about current nuclear costs. A rare exception are the reports of the French authorities about the costs of the French nuclear fleet. Endesa has commissioned several economic and audit reports on the costs of its nuclear facilities that have been referred to in the International Energy Agency Spain 2021 Energy Policy Review. This material can be provided by the author, please contact him at juan.alba@endesa.es.
15. We will call "clawback" a mechanism to capture perceived excess revenues (the so-called windfall profits) of generators above a certain value (that should in theory correspond to the "actual" cost of the generator). The simplest way is to impose some kind of payment obligation or tax when for the difference between the spot price and the price considered "reasonable". Things get more complicated if we acknowledge that most energy is not sold at spot prices, but in forward markets, or to end consumers, sometimes through retail subsidiaries, etc. Sometimes they are called "price caps" although this term is probably not too accurate (the actual price does not change).

Figure 4.2 A More Accurate Representation of a Marginal Spot Market

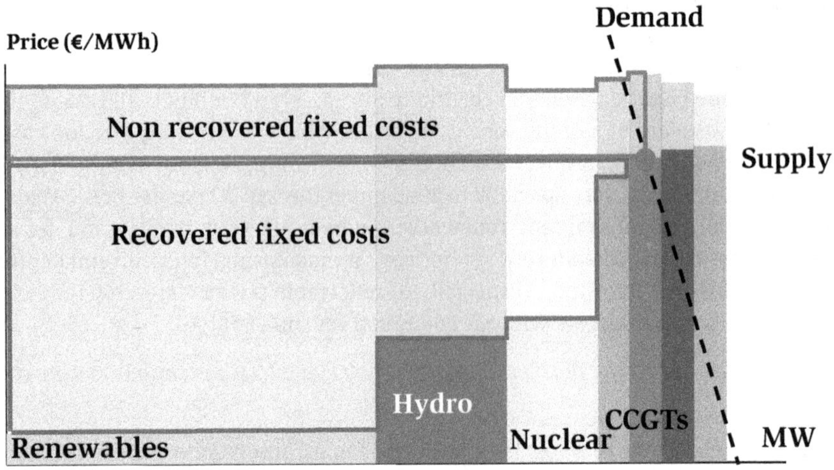

Second, clawbacks do affect the behavior of generators. They frequently affect differently the spot, intraday and balancing markets, and can distort the way generators operate in these markets. Moreover, they are a new cost that generators must face, therefore influencing their bidding strategies. The experience in some EU countries shows how the clawback has led to some inframarginal plants being stopped, leading to renewable resources not being used.

Third, they also affect the retail market: for instance, because of the clawback, Spanish vertically integrated generators are strongly incentivized to sell the production of their own inframarginal plants at 67 EUR/MWh,[16] and independent suppliers cannot replicate these offers, resulting in a deterioration of the competitive dynamics of the Spanish retail market.

Last, but not least, clawbacks are retroactive interventions that affect the legitimate expectations that generators had when they made their investment decisions.[17] A market prone to clawbacks has a much higher level of regulatory risk, and this negatively affects the business case of future investments and capital allocation across geographies and projects. This has a negative impact on the feasibility of the

16. The clawback is applied to the revenues obtained by generators beyond a threshold value. This includes revenues coming from the sales to end customers by vertically integrated companies. Therefore, the clawback acts as a de facto cap on the end user prices charged by these vertically integrated companies.
17. Those who support clawbacks sometimes say that most inframarginal generators (especially hydro and nuclear facilities) were built before market liberalization, and therefore their owners do not have any legitimate expectations about the operation in a market environment. This simplistic argument forgets the significant investments that have been carried out after the liberalization. In the case of Endesa's nuclear and hydro plants, the liberalization of Spain's electricity market took place in 1998, but the investments made after 2005 are higher than the value pending amortization in these assets.

enormous volume of investments that the energy transition must mobilize in all European countries.

Experience shows that all interventions in the wholesale market have unexpected consequences and produce inefficiencies.[18] They should certainly not be included as permanent features of the electricity market design.

Are there alternative market models?

In the last months of 2022 different proposals for new market designs were circulating in Europe. Some of them had an academic origin, such as the "two-markets" models proposed by Capros or Keay & Robinson.[19] These approaches are based on dividing the market into two:[20] a market for "as available" energy (i.e., renewable energy that is subject to the availability of resources such as wind or sun), and another market for "on demand" energy (i.e., energy that is available whenever needed, such as the production of thermal or storage units). However, numerous technical criticisms have been leveled against those models, questioning their feasibility (how to allocate demand to each market? How would this structure affect international exchanges? etc.)

There were also "nonpapers" proposed by governments, such as France, Spain, and Greece. They sometimes involved significant levels of re-regulation, such as the introduction of compulsory contracts for differences at regulated prices for certain existing power plants.

Indeed, there is an alternative to marginal markets. However, it is not a "non-marginal" market, as there is no such thing but a fully regulated system.

4 THE MARKET DESIGN PROPOSALS

The European Commission launched a public consultation in January 2023, which had a massive response from stakeholders. After the noisy debate that took place in 2022, a consensus emerged, in the view of the main protagonists, with wide agreement on some key principles:

- The short-term marginal market should be preserved and improved. It is critical to optimize the dispatching of power plants, storage systems and demand side

18. An interesting case of intervention is the "Iberian exception," already mentioned. This has arguably worked as a mechanism to limit wholesale prices (reducing "windfall profits" in the electricity market) but has maintained (or even increased) "windfall profits" in the gas market. Additionally, because of the way the cost of the subsidies has been passed through to customers, it has negatively affected many of them, distorting the price signal and frequently imposing an exposure to gas prices to customers who had contracted their supply at fixed prices. A discussion of the details and effects of the Iberian exception is beyond the scope of this chapter. A detailed description of the measure and a quantitative analysis of some if its effects can be found in Robinson, D., et al., November 2023, *The Iberian Exception: An Overview of Its Effects over Its First 100 Days*, The Oxford Institute for Energy Studies, OIES paper EL-50.
19. Keay, M. and Robinson, D., June 2017, *The Decarbonised Electricity System of the Future: The "Two Market" Approach*, Oxford Institute for Energy Studies, Energy Insight 14.
20. There are relevant differences between the two proposals, however, it is beyond the objective and limits of this chapter to discuss them.

response, to efficiently manage cross-border exchanges and to manage the portfolios of traders and suppliers.
- There is a need to foster liquidity in the forward markets. Most forward markets present very limited liquidity beyond one or two years. The low availability of long-term cross-border transmission rights limits the possibility of hedging risks across borders. And support schemes for renewable generation (RES) such as feed-in-tariffs or contract for differences (CfD), which disincentivize trading in forward markets to many generators, have created a structural imbalance between generators willing to sell forward and consumers/suppliers willing to buy forward. The rules concerning collateral requirements have made things worse in the current market environment, since high market prices have led to enormous increases in the amounts of cash needed as collateral, driving away many market participants, and reducing liquidity. However, increased liquidity in forward markets will facilitate risk hedging for consumers and producers alike.
- Long-term contracts[21] should be facilitated. Long-term contracts are a market-friendly way of delivering the benefit of low-cost renewable generation to end consumers, protecting them against price crises such as those of 2021-2022. Through long-term contracts with renewable generation, consumers can partially isolate their energy supply from volatile short-term markets influenced by gas prices. And they also facilitate investing in new generation. If (and this is a big "if") properly designed and implemented, long-term contracts can be fully compatible with a liquid forward market, and a virtuous circle can be created involving these elements: well-designed long-term contracts can be divided into pieces and traded in forward markets, and liquid forward markets can facilitate the management of long-term contracts.

However, this basic consensus leaves plenty of space for different views on many controversial topics included in the proposal, such as:

- The reaction to the crisis in 2021/2022 has mostly been improvised. Should a toolbox of crisis measures be introduced in legislation to have them readily available in the next crisis? Which criteria should be used to determine that a crisis has arrived, and who should make that decision?
- Should the interventions adopted in 2022 be extended into the future or even incorporated as an intrinsic part of our market design?
- Should priority be given to private contracts between producers and consumers (the so-called PPAs) or centralized contracting arrangements between producers and public entities (the so-called CfDs)? Can both elements coexist? Are they compatible with a liquid forward market or detrimental to it?
- Should CfD be the instrument of choice for public support for investments in generation? Should they be applied to new generation only, or to existing capacity as well?

21. Although the definition of "long term" is not always clear, this term refers to contract duration well beyond the usual one-three years, reaching time horizons like those of generation projects.

- How can PPAs be facilitated? Through standardization? Public guarantees?
- How can liquidity in forward markets be increased?
- What kind of mechanisms are needed to increase the protection of consumers?
- Many suppliers have gone bust during the crisis. Do we need mechanisms to increase the resilience of suppliers?

The proposal that the European Commission presented in March 2023 (in a record time since the debate started and the public consultation took place) was a reasonably well-balanced set of answers to these questions in the view of the main protagonists. This proposal must now evolve into a legal text, which must be adopted by the two co-legislators, the European Parliament and the Council. These two institutions already agreed to their respective positions and, while this chapter is being written, are involved in the Trilogue process with the Commission to reach the final agreement. This process will probably be over when this chapter is published.

In the following pages, we will give an overview of some of the issues under discussion and the range of solutions that are being explored. This discussion will still be relevant once the text has been finalized for the interpretation, implementation, development, and eventual evolution of the resulting legislation.

Section 5 focuses on different aspects of long-term contracting: PPAs, CfDs, forward markets and capacity mechanisms. The topics of section 6 are the retail market and the network. Section 7 deals with emergency market interventions: the market design proposal started as a response to the energy price crisis, and the new market design will probably incorporate some built-in crisis-response mechanisms.

Due to the limited space available, we will not cover all the elements present in the market reform proposal, but only those that, from the perspective of the author, are more relevant for the future success of this reform and can decisively contribute to an efficient and successful electricity market.

5 LONG-TERM CONTRACTS, INVESTMENTS, AND CUSTOMERS

The most notorious characteristic of the market design proposal is its focus on long-term contracts. The proposal of the Commission (as well as the amendments proposed by Parliament and Council) deal with different aspects of long-term contracts (such as PPAs, CfDs, forward markets and capacity mechanisms), not only from the point of view of their impact on investment, as usually, but also considering their effect in the stability and level of the prices paid by end consumers. As the Explanatory memorandum of the legislative proposal says, it includes measures aimed at creating "a buffer between short-term markets and electricity bills paid by consumers, in particular by way of incentivizing longer term contracting."

5.1 The Challenge of PPAs

PPAs are long-term contracts between a producer and a consumer, frequently linked to a specific generation asset, with a long duration, sometimes like the expected life of the asset. They can be quite complex since they can involve the allocation of a variety of construction, operational and market risks. They can take very different forms (physically versus financially settled, "pay-as-produce" versus "pay-as-consumed," covering 100% of the asset vs partial coverage, etc.)

The total volume of PPAs is relatively small. The accumulated amount of capacity contracted under this type of contract in the EU + UK + Norway reached 32.8 GW this year, while, as a reference, the installed generation capacity in the same area is greater than 1,150 GW.

The development of PPAs across Europe is quite heterogeneous, as shown in Figure 4.3. The volume of PPAs in countries such as Spain or Sweden is relatively high, while large markets like Germany, France and Italy have comparatively few PPAs. If we look at the data by sector, the ICT industry is dominant. Out of the six largest PPA buyers, four of them are Amazon, Google, Microsoft and Meta, while the traditional electrointensive consumers (steel producers, chemical industry, etc.) are underrepresented. This could indicate that the appetite for PPAs is not only linked to the relevance of the electricity costs in the accounts of a given company but also to other factors more related to corporate commitment to sustainability.

Figure 4.3 PPA Volume in the European Countries (in GW Accumulated 2013-2023)

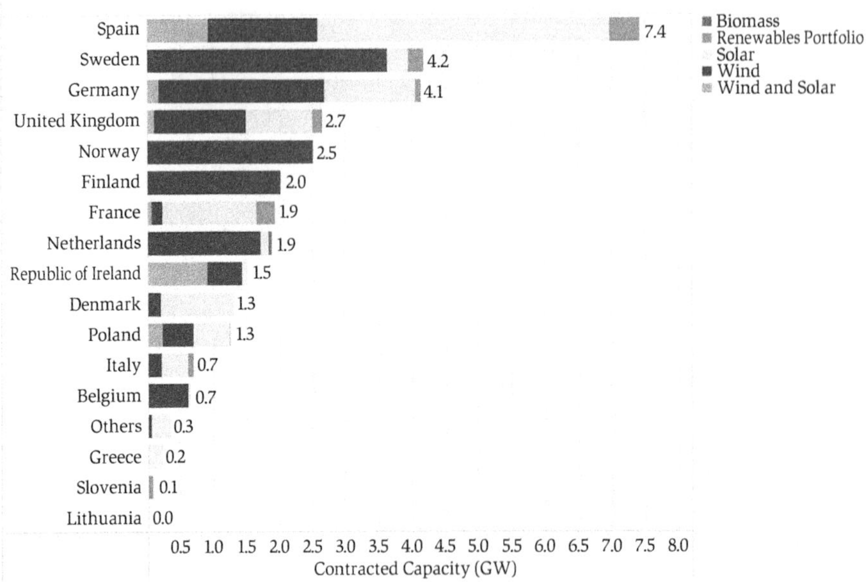

Source: RE-Source, European Platform for Corporate Renewable Energy Sourcing, https://resource-platform.eu/.

Probably a relevant factor until now has been that many customers had the expectation of decreasing prices in the long term.[22] Moreover, electrointensive consumers were sometimes reluctant to enter into long-term contracts that could be different from those of their competitors, bringing a competitive risk. Nevertheless, the price crisis of 2021-2023 has changed the expectations and attitudes of many energy users. However, increases in the cost of equipment have driven the price that generators expect upwards, making the PPAs less attractive to consumers than in the recent past.

Other factors can contribute to explain the relatively low development of PPAs. One of the key characteristics of these contracts is that they are custom-made. Producers use them because they allow a perfect cover of the specific risks of a concrete generation unit; this custom-made character might not be the most convenient for consumers, but the advantage that PPAs usually offer is that this complexity allows a more competitive price. In any case, entering a PPA is too complex for many corporate buyers for whom energy is not the main business.

Counterparty risk can be a relevant barrier for PPAs. When a producer signs a contract for fifteen or twenty years with a consumer, the position of the producer is backed by the asset. But how can the producer trust that the consumer will continue to take the energy and pay for it after such a long time? In many cases, signing a PPA involves posting costly guarantees for most corporate buyers, and this limits access to this market to companies with extremely solid credit ratings.

Because of this, PPAs are difficult to extend to small consumers. In theory, a retailer could be interested in signing a PPA to secure a competitive sourcing of energy in the long term. However, this would be a significant cost in terms of guarantees for most suppliers, as well as a risk: how can the retailer trust that its portfolio of customers will still be there ten years later? Because of that, when retailers sign a PPA, they cover a relatively small share of their expected demand, and PPAs are nowadays almost exclusively a tool for large corporate buyers.

Finally, the heterogeneous situation across Europe probably indicates that there are local legal, tax or accounting specificities that can make signing a PPA easier or more difficult depending on the country.

This situation explains that the facilitation of PPAs is a central element of the market design proposal presented by the European Commission, which advocated for reducing barriers and facilitating access to credit guarantees, and both the Council and the Parliament share this view and have proposed their own improvements, sometimes with more emphasis on standardization or on providing more transparency to this market.

Things are certainly moving in Germany, which in one year has increased PPA capacity by 70 % and escalated from fifth to third position in the RE-Source ranking. But it is still unclear what can be done to facilitate PPAs (and, especially, how to make this

22. Market prices often reflect expectations of system marginal prices, while PPAs are reflecting full costs, so some consumers could bet on low but volatile prices rather than on relatively higher but stable prices.

tool more accessible to smaller consumers) without distorting the energy market and ensuring that the State does not assume excessive risks.

5.2 Are CfDs the Answer?

CfDs are financial derivative contracts that pay the difference between a fixed price and an index such as the spot electricity price (when this difference is settled in both senses, positive and negative, we have a Two-Way Contract for Differences). So, a generator that has sold a contract for differences at 60 EUR/MWh can sell its production in the spot market, receiving the spot price, *p*. Simultaneously, the settlement of the contract for differences will pay the generator *[60 – p]*. The combined settlement of the spot market operations and the CfD will be *p + [60 – p] = 60*. In this way, the CfD will guarantee the generator a fixed revenue of 60 EUR/MWh.

CfDs are used in many financial and commodity markets. However, in the context of the market design reform, the term CfD refers specifically to a financial derivative contract between a producer and a central (typically state-owned) entity, that is usually allocated through a competitive process, such as an auction. CfDs have replaced feed-in-tariffs as one of the preferred designs for support schemes for renewable generation, and there is considerable experience in their implementation across the EU. The draft market design proposal presented by the European Commission proposes to establish CfDs as the default design for price-support schemes for new renewable generation.

The debate about CfD in the market design reform has focused on several issues, which are reflected in the Commission's proposal and in the amendments discussed by Parliament and Council:

- CfDs are presented as a "state-controlled" alternative to PPAs. PPAs are certainly less transparent since they are negotiated individually according to specific circumstances and, as we discussed earlier in this chapter, are difficult to extend to small consumers. CfDs, on the other hand, are fully transparent and their settlement can be allocated to all the demand, including small consumers. So, they are a useful (some would say "dangerous") tool for the State to control the development of the generation system.
- Because of this, if State planning is too optimistic, CfDs can lead to an excessive and inefficient development of generation. PPAs, by definition, lead to balanced demand and supply, since for every seller we need a buyer. Market-based development of renewable generation will automatically slow down when investors perceive that there is too much generation in the pipeline since market prices will reflect this excess. CfDs, on the contrary, are prone to an excess of generation: producers under CfDs are not exposed to market risks, so they might have an incentive to continue investing as long as there are more CfD auctions, even if demand does not grow at the same pace.
- There is a large variety of CfD designs with very different advantages, problems, and impacts. The simplest CfD is a pay-as-produced contract that guarantees a fixed price. As happens with feed-in-tariffs, these simple CfDs

remove all incentives for generators to behave efficiently from the system's point of view[23] and remove the need for generators to hedge their positions in the forward markets, since they are already protected by the CfD. The design of these contracts has led to different improvements: the settlement can be interrupted when prices are zero or below a certain threshold; the settlement can be applied to a limited volume of energy or to a pre-determined profile (increasing the incentive to react to market conditions); the contract can be settled against a forward price index, providing an incentive to hedge in the forward markets, etc.

PPAs are obviously settled between producer and buyer, but things are not so simple for CfDs. The producer side of the settlement is clear, but how does the buyer-side settlement work? In a first stage, the central entity that acts as a counterparty for the CfDs is the recipient of the buyer-side settlement, but this should be passed through to consumers. This can be done in a variety of ways, such as through levies associated with the network tariffs or added to the energy price. This means that CfD will create a financial settlement that will affect some or all consumers, potentially distorting their exposure to market conditions. For instance, when market prices are higher than the CfD price, the CfD will generate a surplus that can be used to reduce the price of energy for end consumers, acting as a hedge. However, what happens if a consumer has already contracted a hedge? The CfD can end up increasing the risk that the consumer is exposed to, crowding out other contract alternatives and slowing down the development of PPAs and the forward market.

Because of these problems, many people in the industry think that CfDs should be a last resort option to be used in case the market alone is not able to develop enough renewable generation capacity in line with EU decarbonization goals.

- The settlement of CfD has been one of the most controversial aspects of the negotiations in the Council. Some countries (including France) wanted to have the possibility of using the funds generated by CfDs to subsidize some consumers, while others, such as Germany, were concerned about the potential distortions of competition that this could cause.
- Interestingly, the wording of the proposal and the negotiations seem to have focused exclusively on a scenario in which the price of the CfD is below market prices, so the CfD generates a surplus. This is the situation that we have become used to, after two years of energy price crisis. However, chances are that, in the mid-term, if there is a large development of renewables, CfD prices can end up above market prices, and the CfD will not be a source of revenue, but a cost. Allocating this cost to end consumers can be tricky, as was the case with Feed-in-tariffs not so long ago.
- The "natural" application of CfDs is to support the development of new generation facilities and sometimes the refurbishment or enlargement of existing ones. However, some Member States, such as Spain, proposed to

23. For instance, they will have an incentive to produce even when there is a clear excess of supply over demand.

apply CfD at pre-determined prices to existing generators, not as a way of supporting investments, but as a tool to capture excessive revenues and control prices. Nevertheless, this possibility has been excluded from the final texts agreed in the Council and the Parliament that clearly establish the "voluntary" character of these contracts. No generator should be obliged to accept a CfD. At the same time, CfDs are perceived, for instance, as a tool to be used in France to support the restructuring of the existing nuclear fleet.

The wording of the proposal and the amendments, in general, go in the right direction, correctly identifying many of the problems. However, the devil is in the details, and the implementation of CfDs must be done cautiously to ensure an effective cohabitation with PPAs and forward markets and a balanced development of renewable generation. Future guidance of the Commission and ACER in this regard will be necessary to ensure a harmonious development at the European scale.

5.3 How to Increase Liquidity in the Forward Market

Despite the visibility of the spot or day ahead market, and its relevance for optimizing the dispatching of power plants, the supply of energy to end consumers and the cross-border exchanges, the forward market is arguably the most important element of the electricity market (as happens in all commodity markets). The forward market allows producers, suppliers, traders, and large consumers to hedge risks and buy and sell electricity in advance. It is fundamental for a competitive retail market since it allows suppliers to source the energy they sell. It offers generators the possibility of managing their risks and facilitates their access to finance. Many generators sell most of their production at forward prices, and consumers buy a large fraction of their energy needs at prices related to the forward market.

The ideal forward market should be very liquid, i.e., it should offer the possibility of buying and selling significant amounts of energy in different time horizons, ideally relatively long, without significantly affecting the prices. But forward markets are far from being as liquid as we need them to be. There are several reasons for that:

- Trading in forward markets involves credit risk. To manage such risk, market operators require collateral in amounts that depend on market conditions. In periods of high and volatile prices, the volumes of requested collateral can increase quickly, and this can drive out of the market those market parties who cannot afford the collateral, reducing liquidity. This situation is aggravated by the regulatory requirement to use cash as collateral.
  This issue is not included in the market design proposal, but it is dealt with in the ongoing review of the EMIR[24] regulation.
- Spot markets are today coupled across borders, allowing day ahead trading beyond national borders. A single algorithm jointly considers all bids for the

24. Regulation (EU) No. 648/2012 of the European Parliament and of the Council of 4 July 2012 on OTC derivatives, central counterparties, and trade repositories.

whole of Europe. Forward markets are connected as well, through long-term transmission rights, which are periodically auctioned for different maturities. However, the connection of forward markets is not as seamless as the coupling of spot markets. The volume and duration of long-term transmission rights are limited, so the possibilities for cross-border hedging in the forward market are restricted.

This topic was not included as such[25] in the Commission's market design proposal, but the Parliament has proposed an amendment mandating TSOs to auction long-term transmission rights up to three years ahead.

- Regulation and support schemes frequently contribute to limiting market liquidity. Many generators are totally or partially remunerated through support schemes (such as feed-in-tariffs, feed-in-premia, or CfD) that usually remove the incentive to trade in the forward market.[26] These producers would increase their risk, rather than reduce it when selling in the forward market. Unlike PPAs, which by definition are balanced between supply and demand, these support schemes do not necessarily have such a balance. For instance, a generator that is paid a feed-in-tariff does not have a customer counterpart who pays for it. Therefore, these schemes create a structural imbalance in the forward market:[27] there are more consumers seeking to buy energy forward than generators willing to sell.

  No attention was paid to this subject in the Commission's market design proposal. The proposal establishes CfD as the instrument of choice for price support schemes for renewable generation but does not impose any conditions on them related to this problem. However, the parliament has agreed to a helpful amendment asking for the minimization of the negative impact of CfD on forward markets and tasking ACER to monitor the impact of CfD on competition among suppliers and the functioning of the electricity markets.
- Last, but not least, regulatory and political uncertainty have a very negative effect on market liquidity. The emergency interventions (price caps, new taxes, clawbacks, retroactive measures, etc.) and the uncertainty of 2021-2022 have led to a significant reduction of the liquidity of all European forward markets.

However, the Commission seemed to ignore these issues and put forward its own proposal to increase liquidity through the creation of virtual trading hubs. The purpose

25. The Commission's proposal includes the offer of transmission rights with maturities of up to three years as part of the virtual trading hub that we discuss later in this section.
26. Intermittent renewable generators cannot hedge 100% of their production because of its uncertainty, so it could be argued that this effect of the support schemes is not significant. However, experience shows that renewable producers that are exposed to market prices usually hedge part of their production in the forward markets to manage their exposure, thus adding liquidity. Most current support schemes, linked to the day ahead prices, reduce or even remove all incentive to hedge forward.
27. In theory, these support schemes can be designed in ways that do not remove the incentive to trade forward, for instance, using CfDs that are settled against the forward price instead of the spot price, but such advanced schemes are not perfect and are still a rarity in Europe.

of this proposal is to move away from the current trading model, in which trading is concentrated in bidding zones, with a single price each, and market parties can hedge across the border by buying long-term transmission rights between bidding zones.

The new model would be based on pooling all the liquidity of several bidding zones into a single virtual trading hub, which would have a higher liquidity (in theory). The problem is that generators and consumers continue to operate in the bidding zones where the price is not necessarily the price of the trading hub, so there is a need for contracts between the trading hub and each bidding zone ("zone to hub transmission rights"). Therefore, the liquidity issue will shift from the hub to the "zone to hub" and "hub to hub" transmission rights.

The virtual trading hub model is certainly feasible: a similar scheme has been applied for many years in the Nordic countries. However, moving a large part of the EU from the current model to the virtual trading hubs will be complex and costly, and it is far from proven that this change will increase liquidity. Because of that, a large part of the industry is asking for a thorough assessment and cost-benefit analysis to be carried out before making a binding decision on this matter.

In any case, a central requirement for a liquid forward market is the harmonious development of PPAs and CfDs. If properly designed, these instruments can offer different ways of joining the market for different market participants and can create a virtuous circle that promotes liquidity. And a liquid forward market will help the parties of PPAs and CfDs to manage their risks and operations.

5.4 The Missing Capacity Markets

Capacity markets were first included in the European electricity legislation in the Clean Energy Package,[28] but they were defined as temporary, last-resort tools, implemented under very restrictive conditions, and approved by DG Competition applying State aid criteria. Design of capacity market across Europe is not homogeneous, and cross-border participation is limited. Their approval and implementation require a considerable time, while their temporary character is not well suited to a mechanism that is intended to provide long-term investment signals.

Capacity markets are mostly relevant to facilitate investment in generation, storage, and demand-side management, by providing a stable source of revenue that makes these market participants less reliant on price peaks. But some capacity mechanisms, notably the so-called reliability options,[29] are also intended to hedge consumers against high prices, so they are very relevant to the objective of this reform.

Therefore, it is surprising that the Commission did not include anything about capacity markets in its proposal, probably considering that this was too complex a

28. However, several capacity mechanisms had been authorized as State-aid by the Commission prior to the approval of the Clean Energy package.
29. Pérez-Arriaga, I.J., 1999. *Reliability and Generation Adequacy*. IEEE Power Eng. Rev. 19, 6–10; Vazquez, C., Rivier, M. and Perez-Arriaga, I.J.J., 2002. *A Market Approach to Long-Term Security of Supply*. IEEE Trans. Power Syst. 17, 349–357. https://doi.org/10.1109/TPWRS.2002.1007903; Bhagwat, P.C. and Meeus, L., *Reliability Options: Can They Deliver on Their Promises?*, EUI Working Paper RSCAS 2019/21.

subject for the limited time available. However, the proposal does introduce a pseudo-capacity market to support resources delivering short-term flexibility (mainly storage and demand-side response) through payments for the available capacity.

There is growing evidence about the role that capacity markets play in the development of new sources of firm and flexible carbon-free capacity (storage and demand-side management, as well as assets providing long-term flexibility that might be needed in the future), and there are arguments to consider capacity markets as an integral part of the market, on equal footing with the intraday or the balancing markets. Therefore, both the Parliament and the Council have put forward amendments to mandate the Commission to explore the possibilities of streamlining the approval process for capacity markets, including them as an integral part of the market design and even presenting a legislative proposal on this subject.

Treating capacity markets as an integral part of the market design could require the introduction in legislation of more detailed design criteria, probably aiming at a somehow harmonized design across Europe. But this will certainly be challenging, considering that Member States want to keep control of security of supply and are likely to argue that the design of capacity mechanisms depends too much on national factors. In any case, it looks certain that once this reform is approved, arguments about capacity markets will continue.

6 CUSTOMERS, SUPPLIERS, AND DISTRIBUTORS

Most of the market design proposal deals with the wholesale market. However, given the focus of the reform on protecting consumers, it is natural that the proposal includes many elements related to the retail market. Moreover, the text does not forget the grid, especially the distribution grid. It is more and more frequent to mention the important role of the grid in the energy transition because it is needed to integrate a growing amount of renewable generation. But we cannot forget that the grid is also critical for electrification: replacing equipment and processes based on fossil fuels, such as boilers and furnaces, with electric equipment, in the many applications where it is technically and economically possible, will require increasing the capacity of the distribution network.

6.1 The Retail Market

The energy price crisis started in the wholesale market, which was impacted by high gas prices, but it affected the retail market. If a retailer is committed to selling electricity to its customers at fixed prices, but its sourcing is not secured in the same way, the consequences can be catastrophic. Even if the retailer has its procurement hedged, imbalances caused when customers' consumption is different from the expected profile can also cause significant costs. The price crisis of 2021-2023 has caused several suppliers across Europe to go bankrupt.

The draft regulation proposed by the Commission has addressed suppliers' risk exposure, by including an article asking regulators to ensure that suppliers implement "appropriate hedging strategies," and even allowing Member States to require suppliers to hedge a certain share of their position using renewable PPAs. This level of intervention can be counterproductive. Hedging strategies must be adapted to the characteristics of each supplier's portfolio, and their design is a key aspect of a supplier's differentiation from competitors. Imposing some kind of harmonization is unlikely to be effective. And mandating the use of PPAs can lead to more risk, not less: PPAs are long-duration contracts; they can last ten or fifteen years or even longer. Customers' contracts, however, are typically one or two years long, and in most cases can be rescinded at the customer's will without any penalty. Requiring a supplier to hedge for ten or fifteen years, when it doesn't know whether its customers will still be around for that long, could be counterproductive. At the same time, these obligations would increase liquidity in the PPA and forward market, and the risks could be managed in a sufficiently liquid forward market (where the retailers could unwind their positions). Moreover, this would be an alternative to vertical integration for retailers that would increase their resilience and their ability to compete with incumbents.

However, it makes sense to carry out some kind of standardized stress tests to assess the resilience of suppliers, while leaving them the necessary flexibility to decide how best to respond. In any case, it is necessary to reach an adequate balance between ensuring suppliers' resilience and not introducing barriers to entry into the retail market, which could be detrimental to competition.

The draft regulation includes other issues related to the retail market, such as:

- Imposing an obligation on suppliers to offer fixed-price offers (surprising, considering that previous legislation had already introduced an obligation to offer dynamic-price offers).
- Prohibiting the disconnection of vulnerable consumers.
- Allowing several meters for one single consumer.
- Facilitating energy sharing.

Most of the industry considers that these measures will be unlikely to bring a real improvement to the retail market, but some of them will significantly increase the complexity of the operations of suppliers and distribution companies, with uncertain impacts.

Unfortunately, the so-called affordability options,[30] a market-based mechanism to protect some consumers, proposed by ACER in its assessment of the wholesale market, do not seem to have received much consideration as a possible element of the proposal.

Last, we cannot forget that Governments' interventions in the wholesale market, trying to protect consumers from the impact of the crisis, have sometimes caused collateral damage in the retail market. For instance, as mentioned at the beginning of this chapter, in September 2021, Spain introduced a clawback on its inframarginal

30. Batlle, B., Schittekatte, T. and Knittel, C.R., *Power Price Crisis in the EU: Unveiling Current Policy Responses and Proposing a Balanced Regulatory Remedy*, February 25, 2022, MITEI-WP-2022-02 and *Power Price Crisis in the EU 2.0+ Desperate Times Call for Desperate Measures*, March 31, 2022, MITEI-WP-2022-03.

generators[31] (nuclear, hydro, renewable), imposing a payment obligation roughly equivalent to the wholesale price increase above "normal levels". Since a significant part of the inframarginal production is sold by vertically integrated companies to end customers, this measure implies that when a vertically integrated company sells its production to end consumers at prices above 67 EUR/MWh, it must pay most of the difference.

This has led to vertically integrated companies selling significant volumes of energy to end customers at 67 EUR/MWh, something that independent suppliers, who source their energy in the wholesale market, could not do. The independent suppliers loudly complain that the clawback damages competition in the retail market. However, this has not prevented other countries from adopting similar measures, and even the EU itself has passed the regulation on emergency interventions[32] with a similar effect (although the "cap" price was 180 EUR/MWh, well above the Spanish value). The lesson is that, besides trying to design legislation to improve the health of the retail market, we need to apply the "do not significant harm" principle to any measure taken to reduce the impact of the crisis.

6.2 The Grid

The market design proposal does not pay much attention to the grids. However, there is a novelty that will have a significant impact on the ability of the electricity grid to supply new customers. There is a mandate to national regulators to adapt the remuneration schemes for transmission and distribution, among other things, to foster the so-called anticipatory investments. To understand the potential impact of this measure, we need to consider that most grid regulation schemes are focused on efficiency and on preventing unnecessary investments. Because of this, the development of the grid is mostly reactive:[33] it follows the needs of consumers. Frequently, when a customer wants to connect to the grid (or to increase the capacity of its connection), some network components must be reinforced well beyond the connection itself. Depending on the national regulation, this reinforcement can be an additional cost for the customer or be paid by the grid tariffs, but a common problem is that this approach is usually a source of significant delays (up to years). Because of this, the grid has sometimes become an obstacle to the energy transition. There are industries that have tried to electrify their processes by, for instance, replacing a gas boiler with a heat pump, but this idea had to be abandoned because increasing the connection took too long or proved impossible due to lack of capacity in the grid.

The introduction of "anticipatory investments," i.e., trying to anticipate the needs of the customers, so that the network is ready when the customer needs it, could be the

31. This was introduced by Royal Decree-Law 17/2021.
32. Council Regulation (EU) 2022/1854 of 6 October 2022 on an emergency intervention to address high energy prices.
33. This is frequently the case for distribution networks. Transmission grids are normally subject to official public planning processes (this is the case in Spain) that allow for some anticipation of system needs. However, these processes are far from flexible enough: they do not guarantee an efficient adaptation to the needs of the grid's users.

beginning of a major shift in the regulation of grids, that could facilitate electrification and the energy transition, and obviously have a major impact on the retail electricity market. However, this is a complex challenge: the brief mention of this concept in a European regulation will not be sufficient, since significant changes in national regulation on access and connection to the grid, as well as network planning, will be needed.

7 THE FUTURE OF EMERGENCY MARKET INTERVENTIONS

Since the summer of 2021, governments have introduced a variety of interventions, subsidies and tax measures trying to alleviate the impacts of the energy price crisis on consumers.[34] Just a minority of these interventions have been approved by the European Commission,[35] while the majority have been adopted in an uncoordinated way. The Commission issued communications in Spring 2022 (*see* footnotes 3 and 4) discussing possible approaches to intervention, and finally, a Council regulation on emergency interventions (*see* footnote 7) establishing a set of European temporary emergency interventions for the current crisis. However, it did not attempt to harmonize the measures adopted by Member States, and even the regulation on emergency interventions allowed almost complete leeway for Member States to deviate from the European design by maintaining or introducing their own national interventions.

From the beginning, discussions about market design also involved temporary emergency market interventions, with proposals to turn some of these interventions into permanent features of the wholesale market or to introduce apparently minor changes that were conceptually in line with the assumptions behind the interventions (mainly, the lack of trust on marginal markets). A clear example of this was the proposal of the Spanish government,[36] whose main element was the introduction of CfDs at regulated prices for most infra-marginal generation. However, already in the initial proposal of the European Commission, the most "innovative" solutions were discarded, and the debates in the Parliament and the Council made clear that there was neither enough support for making substantial changes to the current market design nor for introducing "regulated CfDs": both Parliament and Council consider that CfDs must be voluntary and used only for new or refurbished generation capacity.

Therefore, the discussions about emergency market interventions are focused on two issues:

(i) The conditions to declare an electricity price crisis. The market design regulation will include a provision setting several objective conditions to

34. ACER, 20.03.2023, *ACER's Inventory of 400+ Energy Emergency Measures Seeks to Aid Policy Makers Going Forward*, https://www.acer.europa.eu/news-and-events/news/acers-inventory-400-energy-emergency-measures-seeks-aid-policy-makers-going-forward.
35. An example is the so-called Iberian exception, introduced in Spain by Royal Decree-Law 10/2022 and in Portugal by Decree-Law 33/2022 and its associated Direitiva 11/2022 of ERSE, and approved by the European Commission in "State Aid SA. 102454 (2022/N)—Spain and SA.102569 (2022/N)—Portugal—Production cost adjustment mechanism for the reduction of the electricity wholesale price in the Iberian market."
36. Proposal to reform the EU's wholesale power market, Non-paper by Spain.

declare a price crisis (increases in wholesale and retail prices above a threshold, impact on the economy). In case a price crisis is declared, Member States will be allowed to apply targeted interventions to price setting for certain categories of consumers and, specifically, will be authorized to set prices below costs (eventually compensating the affected suppliers).

(ii) The extension until June 2024 of the mandatory cap on market revenues established by the regulation on emergency interventions.

The definition of objective criteria for declaring a price crisis intends to prevent a repetition of the events that have developed in 2021/2022: Member States and the EU were taken by surprise by the crisis, and measures were improvised and implemented in a heterogeneous way. However, there are not many reasons to be optimistic about the eventual success of this new approach, since its implementation could largely diverge among different Member States. Furthermore, the next crisis is likely to be different from the last one, and the only measure foreseen in the regulation (price interventions in the retail market) is likely to be considered insufficient or inappropriate by the Member States if the new crisis is serious enough. In the last crisis, the European Commission did not have the willingness or the authority to prevent a patchwork of national measures, and this is likely to happen again if there is another crisis.

The extension of the regulation on emergency interventions presents similar challenges. As previously mentioned, Member States had almost complete flexibility to implement different measures, and it is likely that they will take advantage of this point in the market design regulation to extend those other measures as well. There are reasons to argue that the extension is no longer justified in the current market conditions, but, if an extension is introduced, it would make sense to aim at a harmonization of the measures, not allowing the flexibility for Member States that has accompanied the Regulation on emergency interventions.

8 FINAL THOUGHTS

When this chapter was written, the trilogue negotiations had just started. There seems to be significant agreement in the cornerstones of the proposal among the Commission, the Parliament and the Council, and the final choices among these two texts and the Commission's proposal should not make a big difference. We are likely to have a new regulation and directive on the internal electricity market at the beginning of 2024.

For some people, the market design regulation is a disappointment because there are no revolutionary changes: the future electricity market will not be very different from the current one, after all. Many of them think that the modest reforms are not addressing the major problems that lie ahead and that the EU will be having to rethink market design very soon, a repeat of the recognition that the 2019 reform was inadequate to the task. For others, the soon-to-be-approved regulation is a success precisely because it respects the fundamental elements of the current market design and adds some focus on long-term contracts and price signals, which have received less attention than they should in the past. Most of the energy industry certainly has a positive view of the text, and the author shares this opinion.

However, the experience of the last two years proves that we cannot consider this process finished. There are important topics that have not been closed with this proposal, such as capacity markets, network regulation, regulated prices, or demand-side response. So, there is still a significant legislative and regulatory effort to be done before the electricity market design can be considered finished. Let us hope that the next stages of this process can develop in a more peaceful context.

CHAPTER 5

Energy Prices, Consumers and Market Stability: In Search of a Viable Equilibrium – A Synthetic Approach to the Greek Market Case Study

Marios Andrikopoulos[*]

1 INTRODUCTION

It has been my pleasure and honour to have been included among the participants of the annual Global Competition Law Center Annual Conference, this year – 2023 – dedicated to the '*future of energy markets*'.

My personal experience derives from my position as Legal Director of ELPEDISON SA, which I have held since 2013.

ELPEDISON is a leading company in Greece, active in electricity production and supply, gas supply, energy and gas trading and energy efficiency services.[1] The Company runs two privately owned natural gas (NG)-fired combined cycle power plants and represents over 350,000 clients in the supply of electricity and NG. The presentation during the conference and this chapter focus on the Greek electricity market example.

2 SEEING THE CRISIS APPROACHING FROM ATHENS

Greece a full member of the at the time EEC, since 1981 – being its 10th Member State, has equally been a full-scale part of the EU energy market, with the Target Model

* Based on the presentation to the 18th GCLC Annual Conference – 'The future of energy markets' (20-21 April 2023) – with the inclusion of recent developments.

1. The shareholding structure of ELPEDISON SA is: HELLENiQ ENERGY HOLDINGS SA 50%, EDISON SpA 50%.

mechanisms being active since 1 November 2020. In this sense, it has equally been part of the European-scale energy crisis.

As of 2021, the rapid increase in LNG prices brought the first signs of the energy crisis to appear, with energy companies facing increased wholesale prices. It has to be noted that most of the supply contracts with clients/consumers were bearing clauses of variable pricing. The variable pricing, known as the 'readjustment clause', had led for many years to a framework of low-cost energy bills. Now the turn had been to practically non-affordable prices.

The above impasse has considerably worsened due to the Russian invasion of Ukraine and due to the global uncertainty for the NG routes such development provoked. The whole mixture led to a practically uncontrollable increase of the bills – leading to a systemic crisis, as the consumers wouldn't be in place to cover the bills, i.e., a bad debt crisis was threatening to accompany the energy crisis, with the risk of default for the market participants.

It was evident that the State would have to intervene, balancing between the EU Law obligations and the need to stabilize the internal front, granting significant aid to consumers, bearing variable pricing contracts.

The situation was further worsened as, at the domestic level, 'easy solutions' and even populist voices appeared in the public debate.[2] Rational pro-European argumentation struggled[3] to explain that the problem was not national – that it had a pan-European effect – as the energy market developed at the European level and the Member States interconnected and interacted.

2. It has to be emphasized that to date, the legality of the re-adjustment clause contracts has been recognized by crucial case law of the Greek Courts.
3. I have actively participated in the public debate by intervening within the framework of specialized conferences and publishing articles in the press and on the internet.

Indicative tables:

Figure 5.1 2019-2022 Day-Ahead Electricity Prices Evolution GR, ITA, GER, FR (Period Between January 2019 to September 2022): A Pan-European Problem

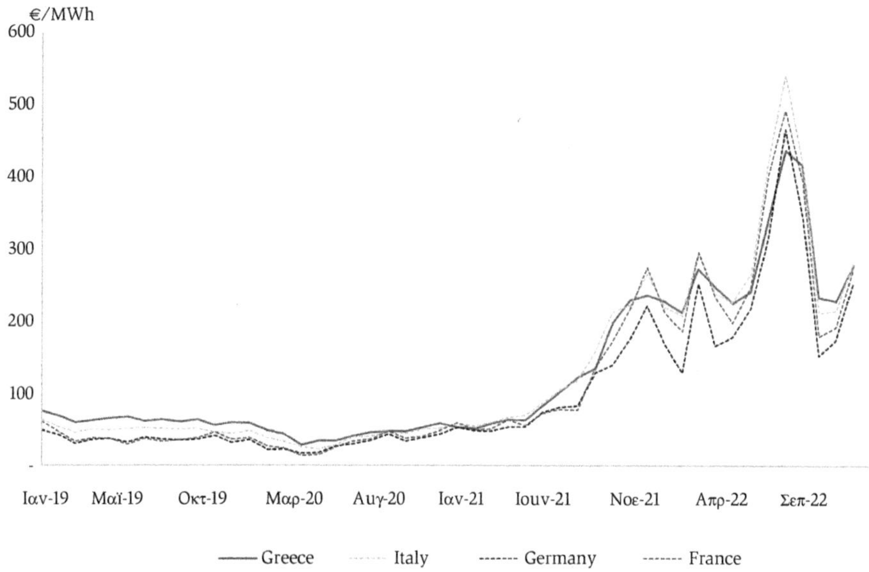

Figure 5.2 2019-2022 NG Day Ahead Prices in TTF: Conclusion – Similar Fluctuation with the Electricity Prices Evolution

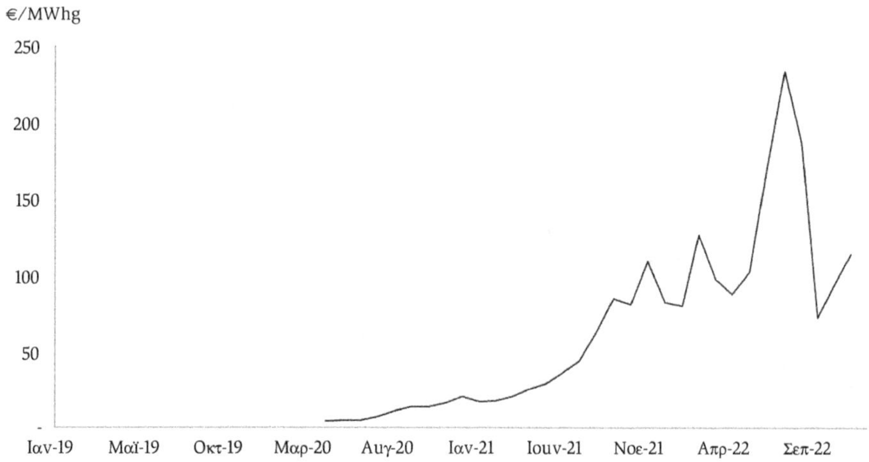

3 THE FIRST WAVE OF MEASURES

In order to confront the situation and provide the needed aid scheme, the Government used the 'Energy Transition Fund' – known in Greek (and hereinafter) as '*TEM*' ('*Tamio Energiakis Metavasis*'), created under Law 4839/2021. The *TEM* has been granted considerable resources, namely the '*Special RES Account*', a state account funded by a special levy imposed on renewables production, regulatory levies imposed on the electricity production market (a special levy on the gas used in gas turbines[4]), as well as the state budget. The purpose has been to be in a position under the form of an aid scheme, to cover part of the energy bills – a construction compatible with EU Law and the Commission's toolbox (then REPowerEU plan) to tackle the exceptional situation that has occurred.

Further funding of the TEM has been provided by Law 4951/2022, which introduced a cap in the wholesale electricity markets (day-ahead, intra-day). The Regulator calculated the cap per technology on a monthly basis and the surplus of the production activity has been an equal source of funding for the TEM.[5]

The above framework has been constructed using the technique of *legislative authorizations*, allowing either the Minister of Energy or the Energy Sector Regulator (RAEYY for Greece) to adopt more specific measures under administrative decisions.

4 FURTHER MEASURES IMPOSED

Trying to further control this critical situation, in August 2022, the Greek legislator intervened in the contractual link between companies and clients imposing a mandatory temporary system pursuant to Article 138 of the above Law 4951/2022, establishing a transitional emergency mechanism in the electricity supply sector to mitigate the economic consequences of the energy crisis.

The logic of the system has been the suspension of the so-called re-adjustment clause and the obligation for each supplier to announce by the 20th of each month, its pricing for the next month. By the same Law has been adopted the suspension of the re-adjustment clause. This system had initially been scheduled to last until 1 July 2023; however, following extensions it has been valid until 31 December 2023.

Critics have been emitted from market participants – as it has been sustained that the price volatility and the risk undertaken by the suppliers led to the inclusion of a risk premium in each pricing policy – thus leading to higher pricing. As a consequence, the subsidies scheme had to be higher, leading to a potential vicious circle. However, it has to be considered that extraordinary situations probably need extraordinary measures,

4. Initially pursuant to Law 4994/2022, a 10 EUR/MWhg levy on natural gas used for electricity production has been imposed. On 2 March 2023 pursuant to Law 5027/2023, the above levy has been replaced by a 5% on the TTF month-ahead price, corresponding to the NG volumes consumed.
5. Pursuant to Art. 122 of Law 4951/2022 has been created a Temporary Mechanism for the Return of Part of the Day Ahead Market Revenue, from 1 July 2022 until 1 June 2023. The mechanism may expire earlier.
   A price cap is set per technology, based on production costs and a reasonable profit margin.

non-previously tested. In any case, the combination of the above system, along with the subsidies to customer bills, brought back to an extent a certain balance.

5 EXTRAORDINARY TAXATION TO ELECTRICITY PRODUCERS AND SUPPLIERS

A point of further tension has been the decision of the Government to impose a 90% taxation on the alleged extraordinary/also called windfall profits initially of the electricity producers and then on suppliers.

More specifically, on 27 May 2022 has been adopted Law 4936/2022 (National Climate Law) – where within its framework, Article 37 has introduced the adoption of an excise tax levy imposed on the electricity producers (thermal and RES) – having as a base the increase of the gross profit margin from the participation in energy markets for the period 1 October 2021-30 June 2022.

Pursuant to the results of the adopted methodology, the profits considered extraordinary have been taxed by 90%. The final import has reached EUR 344 m, as announced in March 2023.

Furthermore, on 18 November 2022, Law 4994/2022 established a Temporary Mechanism for Returning Part of Revenues of Electricity Suppliers (Article 40). This has been defined as an extraordinary tax levy based on 'excess revenues' in the domestic retail electricity market. On 2 March 2023, Law 5027/2023 amended the provisions for the extraordinary taxation of electricity supply with improvements to the Law's provisions. The critical period has been set for the time frame between 1 August 2022 and 1 July 2023 (same as the quasi-regulated operation of the retail market).

The Law introduces the concept of the '*Reasonable Maximum Retail Price (RMRP)*' based on the average cost of electricity supply, plus a reasonable maximum profit margin. The RMRP took into account the percentage of power system losses, operating costs and contingencies. The methodology and the technical details of the mechanism have been finalized pursuant to a Joint Ministerial Decision issued on 1 November 2023.

Critics have been emitted regarding the compatibility of the framework with the Constitution, as well as with principles of the EU Legislation and the respective frame set by the REPpower EU plan.[6] The mechanism concerning the producers has been challenged before the Hellenic Council of State by part of the market participants. The judgment has not been issued to date. Regarding the mechanism concerning the suppliers, the time bar for a similar recourse before the Council of State expires on January 2024. It is estimated that recourses will be filed.

6 RECENT DEVELOPMENTS

The Greek legislator, in view of the expiration of the previous scheme and the impossibility under EU Law principles to further pursue the aid scheme, proceeded to

6. In respect to the taxation of NG power plants.

the adoption of a new system, in place as of 1 January 2024. Practically, the Ministry designed a methodology for pricing, which obliges Suppliers to announce on the 1st day of each month their prices for this supply programme. In parallel, each supplier may offer fixed pricing programmes, variable programmes (*ex post* billing) or smart metring programmes.[7]

The above system is complicated and remains to be evaluated within the framework of its application. Competition appears to be fierce between suppliers – a rather positive sign. More conclusions will be derived in Q1 and Q2 of 2024.

At the level of the wholesale and production market, it is estimated as very positive the lifting of all extraordinary measures.

7 THE AFTER CRISIS (?) ERA

The energy crisis has been an extraordinary situation, which unavoidably has needed the implementation of extraordinary measures. The Hellenic Republic has shown rapid reflexes and Prime Minister Kyriakos Mitsotakis had a very constructive presence and participation at the European level.

The measures managed to maintain pricing at affordable levels. Within the first year of operation of the TEM, EUR 8.5 billion have been granted as aid to customers, out of which only EUR 1.6 billion has been provided by the State Budget.

In parallel, the whole European market has proven to be resilient, and policies perhaps long-needed such as the reexamination of the diversification of NG supply have been implemented.

In any case, the crisis has also been an occasion to rediscover the EU energy law fundamentals, i.e., security of supply and consumer protection, with a just balance.

A just balance in my opinion has also to be sought between thermal units with flexibility and environment-friendly technologies and standards and RES. Modern NG power plants offer precious flexibility, crucial to the security of supply.

At the end of 2023, we need to be optimistic. Estimations and analysis present that the critical situation regarding energy supply stability has passed. However, tensions and threats persist. The war in Ukraine is ongoing, whereas the Middle East crisis and the risk for vessels crossing the Suez Canal, along with uncertainty for the Persian Gulf stability, form a volatile framework.

Overall, we need to be in constant search of a just balance of long-medium and long-term policies – in constant search of the *viable equilibrium*.

7. More specifically pursuant to Art. 17 of Law 5066/2023, an amendment has been brought to 138A or Law 4951/2022 concerning the implementation of provisions to the electricity supply for the period 1 January 2024-31 December 2024. According to the provisions of the above article, all the customers who were submitted to the framework of Art. 138 of Law 4951/2022 (*see* above the per month fixed price system, replacing the re-adjustment clause contracts) will automatically fall to the Special Pricing Program designed by the Ministry of Energy unless they have opted for a different scheme.

   Pricing programmes have been classified as 'green' for the methodology designed by the Ministry of Energy, 'blue' for fixed pricing programmes, 'yellow' for *ex post* billed variable programmes and 'orange' for smart metring 'dynamic' programmes.

Part III EU Energy Infrastructures and Solidarity Amongst Member States

CHAPTER 6

Complete Markets to Complete the Energy Transition

Albert Riera[*]

In 2021 and 2022, Europe experienced a price crisis in the natural gas market, chiefly due to a reduction in the supply of natural gas from Russia. Throughout the previous decade, natural gas prices fluctuated within the range of 5 EUR/MWh to 35 EUR/MWh, while during 2022, natural gas was traded at an average price of 123 EUR/MWh.[1] The sharp increase in natural gas prices spread to electricity markets across the EU, as gas-fired power plants tend to mark the wholesale electricity price in most Member States. For example, in Germany, the daily spot price in 2022 averaged 235 EUR/MWh, representing an increase of 540% with respect to the average over the 2017-2020 period.[2]

The unprecedented surge in electricity prices had profound social and economic effects: Households lost purchasing power, industries lost competitiveness, and inflation skyrocketed, forcing the European Central Bank to raise interest rates, further impoverishing households and undermining economic recovery.

As the effects of the price crisis persisted, an increasing number of Member States, academics, institutions, and other stakeholders highlighted the need to reform the design of the electricity market. Most of the debate, particularly in the early stages, focused on whether the current market design was over-exposed to natural gas prices, with some stakeholders, including the President of the European Commission, calling for the need to decouple electricity prices from natural gas prices.[3] As discussions on

* This article benefited greatly from discussions with Néstor Cortés. All opinions expressed in the article are exclusively my own.

1. Based on day-ahead trades at Title Transfer Facility (TTF), the largest virtual trading point for natural gas in the EU, located in the Netherlands, which serves as a key reference point for pricing natural gas in the EU.
2. Based on daily spot prices at EPEX.
3. https://ec.europa.eu/commission/presscorner/detail/ov/SPEECH_22_5493.

market reform progressed, it was also questioned whether the existing market design was fit to deliver the investments needed to continue the green transition and meet decarbonisation objectives.

This chapter addresses some of those concerns. First, it seeks to respond to the question of whether the current wholesale market design can effectively procure the necessary investments to reach the highly demanding renewable targets needed to decarbonise the EU's electricity markets which, as shown in Figure 6.1, will require massive investments in intermittent renewables, mostly wind -both onshore and offshore- and solar technologies.

Figure 6.1 Wind and Solar Installed Capacities in EU-27, Historical and Expected

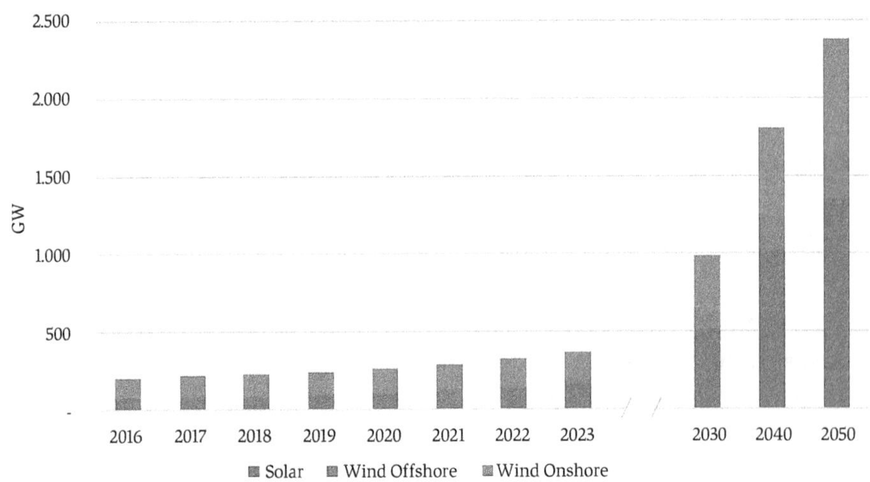

Note: Based on data from ENTSOE. Expected capacities for 2030, 2040 and 2050 are presented as the average between the two scenarios considered in TYNDP, that is 'Global Ambition' and 'Distributed Energy'.

Second, the chapter also discusses whether an energy-only market will be able to deliver the necessary investments in firm and flexible capacity needed to ensure security of supply during the decarbonisation process of the electricity system.

The chapter originates from a presentation I delivered at the 18th Annual Conference of the Global Competition Law Centre (GCLC) in April 2023. At that time, the European Commission had recently introduced a legislative proposal aimed at revising the prevailing electricity market design. Subsequent to negotiations within, and between, the European Council and the European Parliament, a provisional legislative agreement was reached in December 2023. Due to my direct involvement in those negotiations, my presentation refrained from delving into the specifics of the legislative proposal, and similarly, this chapter does not address such content. At any rate, and despite the already-achieved agreement to reform the electricity market, I believe that the insights presented in this chapter will continue to be relevant for several years to come.

The chapter begins with an overview of the economic foundations that led to the current wholesale market design, which will hopefully serve to introduce and understand the remaining sections.

1 THE ECONOMIC FOUNDATIONS OF THE EXISTING WHOLESALE ELECTRICITY MARKET DESIGN

The liberalisation of wholesale electricity markets in the EU aimed to lower the cost of electricity supply through static efficiency gains by improving the operation of generation assets and dynamic efficiency gains from better investment decisions.

Many believed that properly functioning short-term organised markets, such as day-ahead, intraday and balancing markets, were sufficient to achieve those efficiencies. In short:

- Static efficiencies on the supply side would materialise as competition in short-term markets incentivises firms to minimise the variable costs of their generation assets. Furthermore, such a competitive process would also reveal the opportunity costs of generation plants, enabling efficient dispatch based on merit-order. On the demand side, the price resulting from short-term markets would provide the right signal for demand to make efficient consumption decisions.
- Dynamic efficiencies would be gained because the resulting price from short-term markets, which under free-entry and free-exit conditions reflects the long-run incremental cost of generating electricity, provides the right signals for the efficient exit and entry of generation plants.[4]

In addition, there was a belief that nothing would prevent producers and consumers from developing long-term markets, by entering into price hedges to reduce capital costs for the former and provide price stability for the latter.

It is undisputed that some of those expectations, such as the development of long-term markets, have not materialised. Indeed, forward products with maturities exceeding two years exhibit minimal liquidity, and there has been limited growth in Power Purchase Agreements (PPAs) as well.

However, to a large extent, and for a long time, many of those founding beliefs have proven correct. Certainly, short-term markets have generally succeeded at optimising the dispatch of the increasingly interconnected European generation fleet. In addition, the price signals generated by short-term markets over the last twenty years have, by and large, attracted investment in new generation, such as combined-cycle gas turbine (CCGTs) – a type of gas-fired power plant –which not only helped to

4. If there are no barriers to entry exit the market, the long-run market equilibrium price must be equivalent not only to the long-run incremental cost (LRIC) of generating electricity, which includes variable, but also investment costs.

meet growing electricity demand but also displaced less efficient and more polluting technologies such as coal.

However, today's electricity system and its investment needs are completely different from that of twenty years ago. On the supply side, the market has evolved, and continues to evolve, from a market structure characterised by vertically integrated companies operating a limited number of large capacity thermal plants, to a market with a larger number of companies operating plants of varying capacity sizes, often with intermittent output. In addition, the cost structure of the investments required today is radically different from those required twenty years ago. Whereas thermal power plants were characterised by high variable costs in relation to their investment costs, renewables are characterised by the opposite. In a market where investment costs have historically been recovered through short-term market revenues, and the prices in these markets have reflected variable costs, this is certainly a paradigm shift.

On the demand side, consumers participate more actively in the electricity system. In the past, most consumers' relationship with the electricity system was limited to the simple act of turning their switches on and off. Today, an increasing number of consumers generate their own electricity, then consume it, store it, or pour it into the electrical grid, depending on their needs. In addition, technological advances and investments have greatly reduced the frequency of blackouts, which in today's digitalised economy entail very high costs and are hardly tolerated by society.

Honouring the EU's commitment to decarbonisation, particularly the growing presence of intermittent renewables, will only intensify the consequences of these structural changes, prompting the query of whether the existing market design remains suitable for steering the energy transition. This is the focus of the rest of the chapter, which is structured around two questions:

(i) Can the existing market design deliver sufficient and efficient investment in renewable generation?
(ii) Will an energy-only market incentivise the investment needed to guarantee security of supply?

2 CAN THE EXISTING MARKET DESIGN DELIVER SUFFICIENT AND EFFICIENT INVESTMENT IN RENEWABLE GENERATION?

This section argues that the existing wholesale electricity market lacks sufficient access to long-term contracts and, as a result, is unlikely to deliver the renewable investments needed at a low cost. It is, therefore, necessary to complement the spot market with long-term contracts, such as PPAs and Contracts for Differences (CfDs) that provide the necessary investment signals for renewable entry. However, the design of long-term contracts, such as CfDs, is key to obtaining the efficiencies that can emerge by complementing short-term markets with long-term contracts.

2.1 Short-Term Wholesale Price Signals Are Not Unlikely to Deliver Sufficient and Efficient Renewable Energy Investment

Electricity markets are incomplete, in particular, long-term markets are generally missing. The liquidity of forward products with maturities beyond two years is practically inexistent, even in the most liquid contracts for European power, such as the EEX German Power Future.[5] However, PPAs have not experienced substantial development either. As of 2023, less than 7% of the installed wind and solar capacity in the EU was covered by a PPA.[6]

Debates persist regarding the factors hindering the development of long-term markets, with no definitive consensus reached. Some of the possible explanations include:

- The high risk of contract default, particularly on the demand side, can lead to high transaction costs, such as costly banking guarantees.
- The potential for regulatory market intervention during times of high prices that might disincentive demand to pay for price hedges.
- Coordination issues on the demand side might imply that the best hedging strategy for a consumer is to remain exposed to the spot price.[7]
- Measures to promote competition in retail markets prevent retailers from signing contracts with their clients beyond a specific duration, which can lead to a lack of demand for futures.[8]
- Vertically integrated utilities, which enjoy a natural hedge between generation and retail activities, might not have incentives to offer price-hedging contracts to competing retailers.

Be as it may, the fact is that sufficiently deep and liquid long-term markets have not developed since the liberalisation of the EU electricity markets. The electricity market of the past managed to navigate through such market incompleteness without any major consequences. On the demand side, policymakers did not acknowledge the necessity to electrify extensive sectors of the economy. At present, however, the absence of access to stable electricity prices represents a significant barrier to investment in electrification, in addition to a substantial consumer welfare loss.

On the supply side, investments in fossil fuel generation were naturally hedged against spot price risk, as spot prices were highly correlated with fuel prices. Today,

---

5. *See* ACER 2023, 'Progress of EU electricity wholesale market integration. 2023 Market Monitoring Report'.
6. Based on data from windeurope.org. However, there are substantial differences in PPA development among countries. The reason for such heterogeneity in PPA development are not clearly understood.
7. For example, when the competitors of an industrial consumer are not hedged and exposed to the pool price, the most prudent approach for the industrial consumer is to also stay exposed to the pool price. This ensures that it will encounter the same production costs as its rivals.
8. To foster retail competition, some Member States prohibit retail suppliers from presenting contracts with binding commitments extending beyond a specified duration (e.g., one year) to households and SMEs. Consequently, retail agreements ensuring price stability beyond that timeframe are not viable, leading to a lack of demand for futures.

however, most of the investments needed to decarbonise the electricity sector, such as wind and solar, have variable costs close to zero. Hence without access to long-term contracts, they face great exposure to the uncertainty of pool prices.

In addition, as the share of renewables increases in electricity systems, periods with zero or very low prices will be more frequent in short-term markets. This effect, predicted years ago and sometimes referred to as cannibalisation, is no longer a theoretical hypothesis but an empirical observation that is increasingly frequent in those countries with a high share of intermittent renewables. One example is the Spanish day-ahead market. In 2017, there were merely two hours with prices below 5 EUR/MWh. Fast forward two years to 2019, and that number rose to 68 hours. Another two years later, in 2021, the count further increased to 195 hours. During 2023, there have been 527 hours with prices below 5 EUR/MWh.

As renewable projects tend to capture the lower tail of the price distribution in the pool market, their profitability is largely exposed to cannibalisation. If low-price events are frequent enough, renewable projects might not reach grid parity and recover their investment, thus putting at risk meeting decarbonisation objectives.

Some pundits argue that such concern is unjustified, as the EU Emission Trading Scheme (ETS) will guarantee that emission reduction targets are met across the sectors it covers, including the electricity sector. Furthermore, they argue, that as the ETS establishes a uniform carbon emission price across the sectors it covers, it attains emission reductions from those sectors and technologies that can achieve it more efficiently.

Such a conclusion applies to markets that are perfectly competitive, characterised by complete information and full rationality, and where buyers and sellers face no restrictions in signing contracts that account for all conceivable contingencies. Such idealistic conditions are what some authors define as an Arrow-Debreu economy.[9]

In practice, however, the assumptions behind that theoretical framework represent an oversimplification of electricity markets. Once those assumptions are relaxed and aligned with the existing frictions of electricity markets, it becomes clear that the ETS alone is not sufficient to guarantee meeting emission reduction targets, nor that the targets will be achieved at the lowest possible cost.

First, unlike in the Arrow-Debreu economy, and as explained above, electricity markets are incomplete, as long-term markets are generally missing. Without access to long-term markets, the profitability of renewable investments depends on the revenues that the project will obtain from selling its production in short-term markets, particularly in the day-ahead market. As electricity systems converge towards full decarbonisation, the distribution of pool prices will depend on many factors with highly uncertain evolution.

A salient example is the penetration of storage and demand response, which could have a key impact on the distribution of pool prices and on mitigating the effects of cannibalisation. However, predicting storage and demand response deployment with sufficient accuracy is difficult, if not impossible, as it depends on technological

9. P. Joskow 2021. 'From hierarchies to markets and partially back again in electricity: responding to decarbonization and security of supply goals'. Journal of Institutional Economics (2022), 18, 313–329 DOI: 10.1017/s1744137421000400.

change, the existence of support schemes, or the introduction of market design changes, all of which are highly uncertain. Another factor is future gas prices, which have become volatile and difficult to predict due to increasing geopolitical instability and a decreasing share of long-term contracts in the European gas market.

Thus, if renewable energy projects do not have access to long-term contracts, exposure to short-term market prices implies a large financial risk that translates into higher costs of capital, and thus a more expensive decarbonisation path.

Second, the Arrow-Debreu argument above requires the volume of emission allowances in the EU ETS to remain unaffected by its price. In practice, this might not be the case. A surge in the price of ETS has negative effects on the economy, which can induce policymakers to intervene in the EU ETS market, for example, by increasing the amount of emission allowances, and therefore jeopardising meeting emission targets. This phenomenon has already been observed in several Member States, but notably in Poland, which in August 2022 proposed to suspend the ETS market, as a result of a surge in electricity prices.[10]

Finally, the ETS encompasses approximately 45 % of the EU emissions, leaving the remaining 55 % generated by sectors not included in it, commonly referred to as diffuse sectors. In many instances, diffuse sectors lack a carbon tax reflecting the cost of the negative externality that emissions generate to the environment. The lack of a carbon tax in diffuse sectors puts electricity supply, which does include the ETS carbon price, at a competitive disadvantage with respect to other fuels such as natural gas or petroleum products, leading to emission levels above the optimal. Of course, the technical solution to such a problem would be to introduce a carbon tax for diffuse sectors. In practice, however, carbon taxes have encountered significant challenges in achieving widespread implementation, primarily attributed to strong public opposition.[11] In the absence of a carbon tax in diffuse sectors, promoting renewable deployment is the second-best solution.[12]

2.2 The Relative Merits of PPAs and CfDs to Incentivise Renewable Investment at Minimum Cost

One of the main consensuses that have emerged from the European debate on electricity market reform is the need to foster long-term contracts. In this regard, two instruments have been discussed at length: CfDs and PPAs. Conceptually, the only difference between a PPA and a CfD, is that the off-taker of the CfDs is a public entity designated by the government, while the off-taker of PPAs is a private consumer.

CfDs can have slightly different interpretations. However, in the context of the European debate on electricity market reform, CfDs typically refer to long-term

10. https://www.ft.com/content/6123bda2-12d7-48ae-a139-efd89f4a1034.
11. S. Carattini, M. Carvalho, S. Fankhauser 2017. How to make carbon taxes more acceptable. Centre for Climate Change Economics and Policy, Grantham Research Institute on Climate Change and the Environment.
12. D. Newbery 2018. 'Polices for decarbonizing a liberalized power sector'. Economics: the Open-Access, Open-Assessment E-Journal, 12 DOI: 10.5018/economics-ejournal.ja.2018-40.

contracts for the supply of electricity, where the seller is a generation unit, such as a new renewable plant, and a public entity acts as the off-taker.[13] The CfD establishes a reference price (e.g., the spot price) and a predetermined fixed level known as the strike price. If the reference price exceeds the strike price, the generator compensates the off-taker by paying the difference; conversely, if the reference price falls below the strike price, the generator receives the difference from the off-taker.[14] The strike price of the CfD is typically determined through competitive auctions, where generators compete on it to be awarded the CfD.

PPAs are bilateral long-term contracts for the supply of electricity between a generator and a consumer, typically a large industrial consumer or a retailer. PPAs can have different designs but ultimately, they will provide price insurance to both parties. Again, the only conceptual difference between a PPA and a CfD, is that the off-taker of the CfDs is a public entity designated by the government, while the off-taker of PPAs is a private consumer.

Some stakeholders argue that PPAs serve as a more effective tool than CfDs for promoting renewable energy investments. The primary reason is that as being a market-based instrument, PPAs are not susceptible to regulatory errors. CfDs, however, require the policymaker to make error-prone decisions, such as: (i) deciding how much renewable capacity to contract, (ii) for how long, and (iii) under which conditions.

In the best-case scenario, the policymaker does not have sufficient information, such as consumer preferences or investment costs, to make the best decisions. In the worst-case scenario, beyond facing a deficiency in information, the policymaker might also be subject to regulatory capture, or be influenced by political considerations that do not necessarily aim to maximise social welfare.

Moreover, in contrast to CfDs, the versatility in design provided by PPAs enhances overall welfare. That is, each PPA can be tailored to meet the unique requirements and preferences of both the buyer and the seller. In contrast, CfDs typically require a standardised design that may not adequately capture the specific contractual needs of both buyers and sellers.

In summary, those who argue in favour of PPAs over CfDs consider that the market is better suited than a policymaker to assign risks among generators and consumers. Thus, they argue, policy efforts should focus on removing existing barriers to the development of PPAs, for example, by offering state-backed guarantee schemes to PPA buyers. Importantly, some argue that Member States should refrain from conducting

13. There are different ways in which the government, or the public entity acting as the off-taker, can allocate the costs and revenues arising from the settlement of the CfD. For example: (i) they can be directly allocated among final electricity consumers through network charges; (ii) they can be allocated to electricity suppliers, which then pass them through to final electricity consumers (the extent of the pass-through depends on several factors, including the competitive dynamics of the retail market); (iii) they might be allocated to the national budget, in which case the final off-taker of the CfD is the taxpayer, and not the electricity consumer.
14. Such symmetrical risk sharing is sometimes referred to as a two-way CfD. In principle, there are other CfD designs where risk sharing is not symmetrical. For example, the generator might receive payments when the strike price is above the reference price, but does not pay when the strike price is below the reference price.

CfD auctions, or at least limit them to very specific circumstances, such as to incentivise investments in technologies that are not mature enough to reach grid parity.

Conversely, other stakeholders argue that CfDs present several advantages in comparison to PPAs, for multiple reasons.[15]

First, CfDs reduce transaction costs, which results in a lower cost of renewable deployment and thus lower electricity prices for consumers. The reason is that PPAs entail large counterparty risks for the developer, as there is no guarantee that the off-taker will honour the terms of the contract, particularly for long-duration agreements. That is, an industrial consumer might cease its activity over the contractual period, or might find it tempting, or even a matter of corporate survival, to dispute the terms of the contract if the reference price falls below the strike price. In order to hedge against counterparty risk, developers require costly banking guarantees from off-takers, thus increasing the cost of electricity supply for the latter. Some authors estimate that, by steering clear of the extended commitments associated with PPA, CfDs can lead to an implicit reduction in the cost of electricity of around 20 %.[16]

On the other hand, the public entity acting as the off-taker of the CfD, typically enters into such contracts on behalf of all, or a large share, of consumers in the electricity system. Thus, by pooling risks among many different consumers, counterparty risk for developers is minimised, thus reducing financing costs. According to some estimates, this results in a reduction in electricity generation costs of around 10 % compared to PPAs.[17]

Second, banking guarantees, as well as the complexity and minimum volume requirements in PPA contracts are an entry barrier to the PPA market, particularly for small consumers. By pooling demand and risks across all consumers, CfDs guarantee small consumers, such as households or SMEs, access to competitive prices from renewable energy. In turn, this implies that deployed renewable energy capacity is not limited by the volume of consumers that are willing, or capable, to sign PPA contracts, thus providing a credible path for the decarbonisation of the electricity sector.

Third, CfDs can increase competition in the supply side, by attracting project developers that would otherwise face entry barriers in the PPA market. The barriers can be due to, among others, a lack of information resulting from the opacity of the PPA market, or a lack of pre-existing commercial relationships with potential PPA off-takers.

It can be concluded from the above discussion that neither CfDs nor PPAs can be deemed clearly superior to the other. Each instrument has its advantages and disadvantages, and they can be viewed as complementary instruments.

On the supply side, some investors, particularly new entrants or those with limited financial capabilities, may gravitate toward the financial security offered by CfDs. Conversely, more seasoned investors might prefer to generate value from the greater flexibility offered by PPA design. On the demand side, sophisticated electricity

15. S. Ambec et al. 2023: 'Electricity Market Design: Views from European Economists'.
16. Nils May and Karsten Neuhoff 2021. 'Financing power: Impacts of energy policies in changing regulatory environments.' The Energy Journal 42 (4) DOI: 10.5547/01956574.42.4.nmay.
17. Karsten Neuhoff, Nils May and Jörn C. Richstein. 2022. 'Financing renewables in the age of falling technology costs.' Resource and Energy Economics 70 (November) DOI: 10.1016/j.reseneeco.2022.101330.

consumers might prefer to engage in tailored PPAs to meet their specific hedging requirements. In contrast, CfDs can ensure that consumers who cannot participate in the PPA market gain access to stable and competitive electricity prices.

As each instrument plays a distinct role in the energy transition, it is advisable to eliminate regulatory obstacles hindering the growth of CfDs and market-related barriers that impede the expansion of PPA usage.

2.3 Balancing Trade-Offs: Designing CfDs for Efficient Dispatch and Investment Decisions

The preceding section has articulated that when appropriately structured, CfDs can significantly drive low-cost renewable investments. However, contractual design is crucial to ensure that dynamic and static efficiencies are attained.

This section provides an overview of the main challenges and available alternatives to design CfDs for renewable intermittent assets, such as wind and solar PV, which represent the bulk of the renewable investments in the EU for the next decade (*see* Figure 6.1).[18] It argues that optimal CfD design requires providing revenue certainty to generators while avoiding dispatch and investment distortions and that balancing these different objectives requires trade-offs and careful decision-making.

Start by considering a simple CfD design, whereby generators receive remuneration for the actual volume of electricity produced (i.e., often labelled an 'as produced' contract), and where the reference price against which the CfD is settled is the hourly spot price. This design completely eliminates the price risk for the generator, as it will always receive the CfD strike price per unit of output, independently of spot prices.[19]

The advantage of this design is that as price risk is eliminated, it results in a lower equity/debt ratio, hence a lower cost of capital, and hence a lower cost to decarbonise the electricity sector. However, as generators are not exposed to the spot price, several distortions are created:

- Generators have incentives to bid in the spot market below their variable costs, which distorts dispatch and artificially depresses pool prices.
- Locational investment decisions are distorted, as investors do not have the incentives to invest in those sites where the availability of renewable energy resources, such as wind or solar, is correlated with spot prices.
- Investors may not select the technologies that provide the greatest value to the electricity system, such as those with generation profiles strongly correlated with spot prices.

18. This section only addresses the supply side of CfD design. It does not discuss the demand side of CfD design (i.e., how the revenues or costs generated by CfDs should be allocated among consumers), as it is beyond the scope of the chapter.
19. That is, if the generator sells its production at the hourly spot market, which is also the reference price of the CfD, the generator is fully hedged against price risk, as it will always receive the strike price. Mathematically, the revenue received by the generator in this case is given by: $Q \times p + Q \times (s - p)$, where Q is the quantity produced, p is the hourly pot price and s is the strike price. This expression is equivalent to $Q \times s$, which is independent of the hourly spot prices.

- Liquidity in forward markets is jeopardised, as selling the production in the forward market generates additional price risk.

There seems to be a consensus among academics and stakeholders that the lower cost of capital that this design might achieve does not compensate for the costs resulting from the abovementioned distortions.

A more sophisticated alternative to the 'as produced' contract settled against hourly prices discussed above is to use a different reference price, such as the weighted average hourly spot price over one month, or one quarter, or even monthly or quarterly forward prices. In such a case, the generator has some exposure to the spot price, which limits dispatch and investment distortions. In addition, it may also increase liquidity in forward markets, as the generator has incentives to hedge its spot price exposure. The main disadvantage of this design alternative, however, is that although it limits dispatch distortions, it does not fully eliminate them.[20]

A third design alternative is what some academics refer to as yardstick CfDs.[21] The underlying principle is that the quantity of electricity remunerated by the CfD does not depend on the actual production of the plant, but rather on the generation profile of a reference plant. This design allows hedging against spot prices, while it preserves dispatch and investment incentives:

- It ensures efficiency of dispatch, as the best strategy for generation units when bidding in the spot market is to reveal their opportunity cost.[22]
- It incentivises investors to outperform the reference plant, and thus choose locations or plant designs that create an output profile that maximises value for the electricity system.

The main drawback of yardstick CfDs is that in order to preserve dispatch and investment incentives, it requires an accurate estimation of reference plant profiles, which can be a complex task. In addition, because different technologies have different production profiles, each technology typically requires its own reference plant profile. As a result, if different technologies compete on the strike price in the same auction, technological investment choice is distorted, as the auction will not necessarily select those technologies that add the highest value to the electricity system.

As a solution to the abovementioned problem, some authors suggest running technology-specific auctions.[18] However, this approach requires central planning and is therefore prone to regulatory failures, as policymakers might not have enough information to allocate the optimal amount of contracts across different technologies. In addition, central planning is subject to regulatory capture, which can lead to the over-procurement of some technologies.

20. For more details, *see* T. Schittekatte and C. Batlle 2023, 'Power Crisis in the EU 3.0: Proposals to Complete Long-Term Markets', Working Paper Series, MIT and CEEPR.
21. *See* D. Newbery 2021: Designing efficient Renewable Electricity Support Schemes. EPRG Working Paper 2107. University of Cambridge.
22. Provided that the output generation profile and the actual profile do not substantially diverge.

Most CfD design alternatives that have been implemented or discussed by the literature, such as those discussed above, try to hedge generators against price risk, but few designs hedge generators against volume risks. However, volume is likely to be a major risk factor for generators in the mid-term future.

Increasing shares of renewable generators will lead, inevitably, to more frequent and acute curtailments. Even in the best-case scenario, where investments in storage and demand response reach optimal levels, the incremental costs of avoiding additional curtailment will exceed its value, and hence curtailment will still be inevitable. In the worst-case scenario, suboptimal investments in storage and demand response will exacerbate curtailment.

In most electricity systems, the risk of curtailment is allocated proportionally among non-dispatchable renewable generators. In other words, when the combined output of these generators surpasses demand, the reduction in power output is distributed among them in accordance with their programmed electricity delivery volumes.

Such an approach has two implications. First, new renewable investments generate a negative externality on existing plants. That is, while new generation will cause additional curtailment, its cost is not fully internalised by new investments, as it is shared with existing renewable plants. The implication of such an externality is that it can induce inefficient entry and curtailment volumes above the optimal level.

Second, as new entrants are tomorrow's incumbents, the profitability of new entry will be affected by the curtailments generated by future entry, which increases volume uncertainty for new entrants, and hence implies a more expensive decarbonisation path.

A potential solution that could resolve both issues is to assign curtailment first to those renewable generators that enter the market at a later stage. This approach would eliminate the entry distortions generated by the negative externality that new generators impose on existing ones. In addition, it would also reduce curtailment volume uncertainty for new investments, as curtailment risk for a new entrant will no longer depend on uncertainty over future entry.

3 WILL AN ENERGY-ONLY MARKET INCENTIVISE THE INVESTMENT NEEDED TO GUARANTEE SECURITY OF SUPPLY?

This section argues that an energy-only market will not incentivise the investments in firm and flexible capacity needed to guarantee security of supply during the energy transition. The theoretical foundations under which an energy-only market could provide the right investment incentives do not hold in practice. As a result, attaining optimal levels of security of supply requires complementing energy markets with capacity markets, something which is at odds with existing EU regulation, and it should be revisited. Finally, it argues that in the near future the interplay between firm capacity and flexible capacity, and how to procure them both efficiently, will likely become increasingly important and challenging.

3.1 The Theoretical Foundations of the Energy-Only Market Paradigm

Under the right set of assumptions, it can be shown that an energy-only market will provide the optimal level of security of supply and the optimal generation mix.

To that end, consider a market with two generation technologies: peaker and baseload. The peaker technology has a higher variable cost, compared to the baseload technology, that is $VC^P > VC^B$. Conversely, the baseload technology has higher investment cost in relation to those of the peaker technology, $I^B > I^P$.[23]

In addition, there is a third 'technology', which is the possibility to ration demand. This technology does not require any investment, but its variable cost is the highest, and equal to consumers' willingness to pay not to have their supply interrupted, or the value of loss load (VoLL). In the EU, the estimations of VoLL performed by Member States fall within the range of several thousand euros.[24]

The efficient generation cost curve for this market is given by the envelopment cost curve for each of these technologies, shown in Figure 6.2.

Figure 6.2 Total Generation Costs

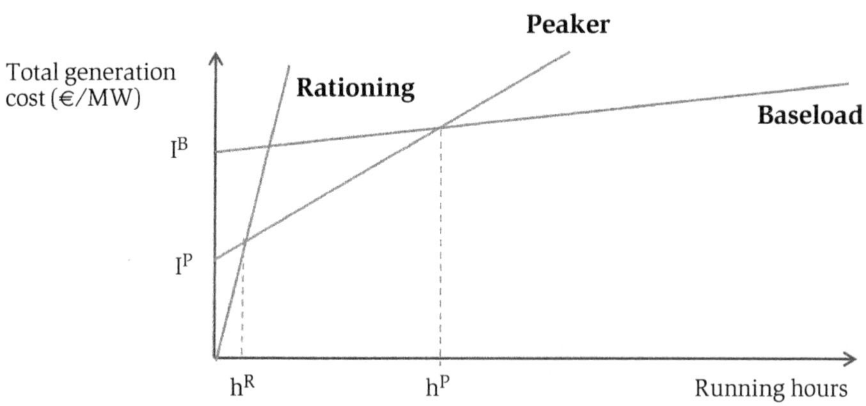

Note: For each technology, the cost curve is given by I + CV × h.

In other words, the optimal investment choice is as follows:

- invest in the baseload technology if it will operate for more than h^P hours;
- invest in the peaker technology if it is expected to operate between h^R and h^P hours, and;
- refrain from investing in any technology, if rationing is anticipated to be less than h^R hours.

23. For simplicity, assume that neither technology has any fixed O&M costs. The assumption has no effect on the main conclusions drawn.
24. *See* ACER (October 2022). 'Security of EU electricity supply in 2021: Report on Member States approaches to assess and ensure adequacy'.

From the efficient generation cost curve described above, it is possible to calculate the optimal installed capacity for the peaker and baseload technologies, C^P and C^B. As Figure 6.3 shows, they are given by the intersection between the optimal running hours for each technology, h^R and h^P, and the monotonic load curve.[25]

Figure 6.3 Optimal Electrical Mix

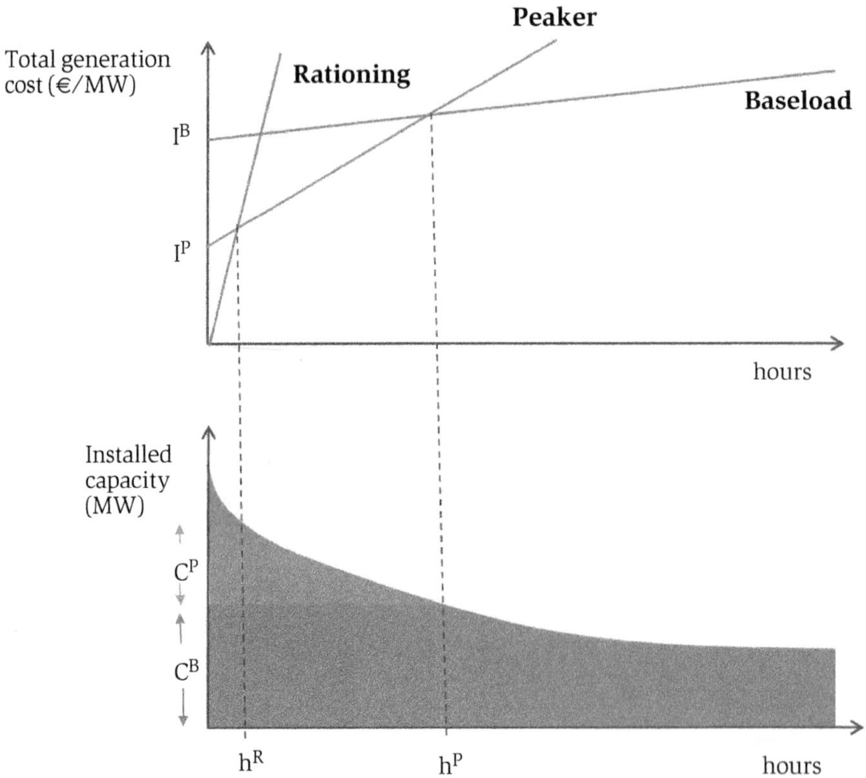

Note: The optimal installed capacity for the peaker and baseload technologies, C^P and C^B, are given by the intersection between the optimal running hours for each technology, h^R and h^P, and the monotonic load curve.

That is, the bottom diagram of Figure 6.3 shows that the optimal amounts of installed capacities C^P and C^B are such that:

- Rationing occurs during h^R hours.
- The peaker technology operates during h^P hours.
- The baseload technology operates continuously.

25. Each point in the monotonic load curve indicates the number of hours h in a year, in which demand D is larger or equal to D_h MW.

When certain assumptions hold, including unrestricted market entry and exit, and unrestricted wholesale prices, a competitive market will yield the optimal generation mix (C^P, C^B) and the optimal number of rationing hours (h^R).

Given the installed capacities C^P and C^B, a competitive market will show the following set of prices (P):

- P = VoLL during h^R hours when there is demand rationing.
- P = CV^P during h^P-h^R hours, when the peaker technology is the marginal technology.
- P = CV^B the rest of the time, when the installed capacity of the baseload technology is sufficient to meet demand.

Given this set of prices, it can be shown that as long as the installed capacities of each technology are equal to the optimal mix (C^P, C^B), each technology recovers its investment cost. In other words, the competitive market will procure the optimal capacity investment, and therefore the optimal amount of rationing hours.

The peaking technology only obtains a margin when there is demand rationing and the market price reaches the VoLL value. If there is no demand rationing, the peaking plant is either not generating, or it is generating and receiving a market price equal to its variable cost, and thus obtains no margin. Thus, mathematically, the margin obtained by it is given by (VoLL - CV^P) × h^R. If there is market-free entry and exit, the market equilibrium requires this margin to be equal to its investment cost. Only when the capacity installed is equal to the optimal capacity C^P, this condition is fulfilled.[26] Typically, this condition implies that the optimal amount of rationing is around three hours/year.[27]

Similarly, the margin obtained by the baseload technology is equal to (VoLL - CV^P) × h^R + (CV^P - CV^B) × (h^P - h^R). Again, in a competitive market with market-free entry and exit, this margin will be equal to its investment cost, and the installed capacity will be equal to the optimal capacity C^B.

In essence, given specific assumptions, the competitive market equilibrium in an energy-only market aligns with the optimal outcome, including the provision of security of supply. However, the energy-only model outlined above, while useful for understanding technological mix, market entry and exit incentives, and long-term price formation, relies on several oversimplified assumptions that diverge from the actual conditions in which electricity markets function.

The next section shows that when some of those assumptions are relaxed and better aligned with real market conditions, the energy-only market will procure a deficit of installed capacity and will not deliver sufficient security of supply.

26. The margin is higher than the investment cost when there are too many rationing hours h(R), which implies that the capacity installed is below the optimum C(P). Conversely, the margin can only be lower than the investment costs if there are there are too few rationing hours h(R), which implies that the capacity installed is above the optimum level C(P).
27. To see this, note that investment recovery by the peaker technology requires that hR = IP/(VoLL - CVP). Using a VoLL of 20,000 EUR/MWh, and the annualised investment cost for the peaking technology (IP) equivalent to 60,000 EUR/MW, this implies that hR = 3 hours/year. This calculation neglects the variable cost CVP, as it is negligible compared to the VoLL.

3.2 An Energy-Only Market Will Not Deliver Sufficient Security of Supply

The previous section has shown that under some assumptions an energy-only market will deliver the efficient level of installed capacities and security of supply.

The most fundamental assumption for that result to hold is that market prices should increase to the VoLL value when existing installed capacities are not enough to meet demand. In practice, however, there exist different market and regulatory failures that prevent those conditions from holding.

First, prices are capped by regulation. Price caps serve to mitigate market power and protect consumers, particularly during stress situations when supply is tight. In the EU, the level of the price cap is set following a methodology established by the European Agency for the Cooperation of Energy Regulators (ACER).[28] Currently, the price cap is set at 4,000 EUR/MWh in the day-ahead market.[29]

The level of the cap is several multiples below the VoLL of European consumers, which is at around 22,000 EUR/MWh.[30] The difference between the level of the price cap and the VoLL generates a missing money problem for generators.

That is, using the energy-only framework depicted above, it no longer holds that generators recover their investment when the amount of rationing hours is equal to the optimal amount h^R. If the wholesale price during rationing hours is suppressed by the price cap, generators require more hours of rationing to recover their investment. Thus, the price cap leads to underinvestment in capacity and demand rationing above the optimal level. In particular, if the level of the cap is around a fifth of the level of the VoLL, as is the case today, it follows that the energy-only market equilibrium will result in approximately 500 % more rationing hours compared to the optimum amount of rationing.

Second, even in the absence of explicitly regulated price caps, there are different ways in which generators' revenues during scarcity events can be implicitly capped.

Market prices increase to VoLL levels when demand is rationed, that is, at times of scarcity. However, scarcity events coincide with those situations when generators are more capable of exerting market power. That is, when supply is too tight to meet demand, generators become pivotal to meet demand, which enables them to increase prices through anticompetitive practices such as capacity withholding or excess pricing.

However, it is not always straightforward for competition authorities to identify such practices and differentiate them from legitimate competitive behaviour. Therefore,

28. ACER 2023. Harmonised maximum and minimum clearing prices for single intraday coupling in accordance with Article 54(1) of Commission Regulation (EU) 2015/1222 of 24 July 2015 establishing a guideline on capacity allocation and congestion management (CACM Regulation).
29. ACER initially set price cap of 3,000 EUR/MWh in the day-ahead market, with rules to increase it if necessary. Due to the price crisis that commenced in the latter half of 2021, in May, the threshold defined in the regulation was surpassed, leading to an escalation of the maximum price in the daily market from 3,000 EUR/MWh to 4,000 EUR/MWh.
30. The average Value of Lost Load (VoLL) for the EU is calculated based on the average of the 11 Member States that have estimated a VoLL, weighted by the population of each country. *See* ACER (October 2022). 'Security of EU electricity supply in 2021: Report on Member States approaches to assess and ensure adequacy'.

in times of scarcity, generators run the risk of facing unwarranted penalties from competition authorities, diminishing the expected revenues that generators could earn in such situations.

Regulatory intervention is another form of implicit price caps. Policymakers and System Operators tend to be wary of the repercussions of scarcity events, such as involuntary demand rationing and the accompanying sharp increases in electricity prices and thus may intervene in the market and do 'whatever it takes' to prevent either. A recent example of price intervention in the EU is the revenue cap introduced in October 2022 by Council Regulation 2022/1854 on emergency interventions.[31] It is beyond the scope of this chapter to analyse whether such a measure was justified or not. What is relevant, however, is that regulatory intervention, regardless of whether it is justified or not, is not a theoretical hypothesis, but a real and tangible risk that reduces investment incentives below the optimum.

To summarise, the energy-only market will only provide sufficient investment if generators are able to recover their investment in very few hours of high prices during scarcity events. Hence, the risk of having market revenues suppressed either by sanctions from competition authorities or by regulatory intervention precisely during those scarcity conditions constitutes a large risk, against which the only possible hedging strategy is to underinvest.

Third, the energy-only market paradigm considers the electricity market in isolation from other markets, and as such, it does not take into account the positive externalities that security of electricity supply generates to the wider economy.

To illustrate this, consider a firm that produces a given good or service at a cost c, and sells it into the market at a price p. The firm's private cost of reducing one unit of output, as a result of having its supply of electricity interrupted, is equivalent to the opportunity cost of not being able to sell that unit into the market, that is $p - c$.

However, the social cost of having the supply of that good or service interrupted is potentially much higher, as the value v that such product or service generates to society is typically substantially higher than its market price. That is, while the private cost of supply interruption (i.e., the VoLL) is given by $p - c$, the social cost of the interruption is given by $v - c$, with $v > p$.

In other words, the positive externality generated by security of supply is given by $v - p$. As this additional benefit to society is not internalised by private consumers, an energy-only market will deliver insufficient security of supply. That is, in the energy-only market setting, incentivising the optimal investment requires the wholesale price to reach $v - c$ during scarcity events. However, such a price level cannot be sustained, as consumers are only willing to pay up to p-c.

Fourth, the energy-only market will only procure the optimal amount of security of supply if generators are free to enter and exit the market. In practice, however, such conditions do not hold in many markets.

31. Council Regulation 2022/1854 established a cap up to 180 EUR/MWh on the market revenues that inframarginal generators could obtain from selling their production to the market.

In the long run, barriers to exit are the most problematic for security of supply.[32] Regulation might prevent some plants from exiting the market if security of supply is jeopardised.[33] In the short run, such exit barriers can prevent uncoordinated capacity retirement, and thus prevent black-outs. In the long run, however, barriers to exit depress pool prices and reduce investment incentives below the optimal level. Importantly, barriers to exit in combination with explicit or implicit price caps, can generate a vicious cycle of underinvestment, whereby price caps generate an investment deficit, as a result, regulators have to impose exit barriers to prevent black-outs, which further reduces investment incentives.

Finally, some authors have highlighted that due to investors' bounded rationality, such as the lack of perfect foresight or herd behaviour guiding investment decisions, an energy-only market is prone to exhibit construction cycles. These cycles involve phases of underinvestment, resulting in high prices and low security of supply, succeeded by periods of excessive investment, low prices and security of supply above the optimal level. In other words, unless a capacity market coordinates entry decisions, an energy-only market will not lead to the optimal levels of security of supply.[34]

3.3 Capacity Markets Should Be an Embedded Feature of Electricity Markets

The previous section has outlined different market and regulatory failures that prevent energy-only markets from delivering sufficient security of supply. Many of these failures will not disappear in the future, as they are structural, not temporary: Security of supply will always generate positive externalities to the wider economy, and regulators and policymakers will never be able to make a credible commitment not to intervene in the market during scarcity events. On the contrary, the increasing share of intermittent renewable energies in electricity systems will exacerbate the detrimental effect that energy-only markets have on security of supply.[35]

Achieving optimal levels of security of supply during the energy transition requires completing existing electricity markets with capacity markets. However, the existing EU regulatory framework contemplates the use of capacity markets as a last

32. If barriers to entry affect baseload technologies, they do have an impact on security of supply. That is, in the energy-only model depicted above, it can be shown that if the installed capacity of the baseload technology is limited below the optimal level, the market equilibrium implies a capacity expansion of the peaking technology to compensate for the gap. That is, the sum of the total installed capacity C(P) + C(B) remains unchanged, and hence the optimal number of rationing hours h(R) is unaffected. If barriers to entry affect peaker technologies, they do have a negative effect on security of supply.
33. In Spain, for example, CCGT owners submitted an appeal to the Spanish Supreme Court, seeking the closure of those plants following an unsuccessful response from the Spanish Administration on their closure request. *See* https://cincodias.elpais.com/companias/2023-11-10/el-supremo-autoriza-el-cierre-temporal-de-cinco-ciclos-combinados-que-pidio-naturgy-pero-rechaza-fijar-una-indemnizacion.html.
34. A. Ford 1999. Cycles in competitive electricity markets: a simulation study of the western United States. *Energy Policy* 27, 637, 658 DOI: 10.1016/s0301-4215(99)00050-6.
35. G. Llobet, J. Padilla 2018. Conventional Power Plants in Liberalized Electricity Markets with Renewable Entry. The Energy Journal 39(3) DOI: 10.5547/01956574.39.3.gllo.

resort and temporary measure, thus presuming that the structural market failures described above can somehow be eliminated. In addition, the approval process for a capacity market under EU legislation is cumbersome and prone to finding that a capacity market is not needed.

In contrast to other types of support schemes that only require compatibility with the EU State Aid Framework, the approval of a capacity market must additionally adhere to specific energy regulations. Member States are obligated to follow a predetermined methodology to substantiate the necessity of the capacity market under these regulations.[36]

In short, Member States are required to show that without the implementation of a capacity market, the expected number of rationing hours (h^R in Figure 6.3), often denoted as Loss of Load Expectation (LOLE), exceeds the optimal level. This optimal level of rationing hours is known as the reliability standard.

The expected LOLE is determined using a probabilistic model that spans a ten-year period. This model optimises dispatch and investment choices by considering crucial input assumptions, including projections for demand, fuel prices, investment and fixed costs, price caps, grid and generation capacity expansions, retirements, or climatic conditions.[37] This exercise is performed by ENTSO-E at the EU level, and it is known as the European Resource Adequacy Assessment (ERAA).

On the other hand, the optimal LOLE, or reliability standard, is calculated as the ratio between the cost of new entry (CONE) and VoLL, where CONE is typically equivalent to the annuity of the investment costs of the peaking technology (i.e., I^P in Figure 6.3). That is, the optimal amount of rationing hours is given at the point where the incremental cost of capacity additions (i.e., CONE) is equal to the incremental value added by it (i.e., VoLL).

It is beyond the scope of this chapter to provide a deep review of the abovementioned methodologies defined by EU regulation to calculate the optimal and expected rationing hours. However, it is important to highlight that such an approach presents two main problems.

First, it is inclined to conclude that an energy-only market will deliver sufficient adequacy. The main reason for it, beyond specific methodological details, is that among the different market failures outlined in the preceding section that prevent an energy-only market from providing sufficient investment incentives, the methodology employed only considers price caps and, to some extent, entry-exit barriers, as a potential market failure that could lead to identifying a capacity gap.

Key market failures such as positive externalities, regulatory intervention during scarcity events, or entry coordination problems are absent from the analysis. In other words, if one were to remove price caps from the assumptions employed in the resource adequacy assessment, the need for a capacity market would never be justified.

Second, the results of the resource adequacy assessment are extremely sensitive to the assumptions employed: Assume a high price cap, and expected LOLE plummets. Assume a low price cap and LOLE skyrockets. Assume adverse climatic conditions, and the

36. Articles 21, 23, 24, 25, and 27 of Regulation (EU) 2019/943.
37. ACER Decision (2020). Methodology for the European resource adequacy assessment.

ERAA will conclude that additional capacity is needed to prevent blackouts. Assume milder climatic conditions, and it will find that existing capacity should be retired.

The implication of this high variability of results is two-fold. On the one hand, it makes it difficult to extract meaningful conclusions on whether a capacity market is needed, given the test requirement to use a unique LOLE value.[38] On the other hand, because the results obtained are highly sensitive to the input assumptions, these are highly contested. This is the reason why since ACER published its ERAA methodology in 2020, Europe still lacks an ERAA. Due to disagreements on the assumptions employed, ACER decided neither to approve ENTSO-E's ERAA 2021, nor ENTOS-E's ERAA 2022 in the following year.[39]

As a result of these regulatory shortcomings, as of today, security of supply depends on highly contested methodologies and cumbersome models that overestimate the ability of energy-only markets to deliver it. Such a regulatory approach is problematic, especially considering that markets are better suited to extract such information.

In particular, a well-designed and competitive capacity market would itself determine whether generators require capacity payments to achieve sufficient security of supply. That is, competition among generators for capacity contracts drives capacity prices towards the opportunity cost for making capacity available.

For a new entrant, that opportunity cost is the gap between its investment cost and the margin it expects from selling electricity in the wholesale market.[40] When this gap is positive, indicating the existence of opportunity costs, the capacity market will exhibit positive prices. If the gap is zero (as assumed in the energy-only setting) or even negative, capacity prices will tend towards zero.

Because the information provided by the capacity price is clearly more reliable than the information provided by the ERAA or any other resource adequacy assessment, a competitive capacity market minimises the risk of overcompensating generators, while it guarantees that security of supply is not at risk.

Thus, instead of requiring excessive efforts to justify the need for a capacity market, regulation should focus on ensuring that capacity market design leads to prices that reflect the minimum cost of achieving security of supply.

3.4 The Increasing Interplay Between Adequacy and Flexibility

Until quite recently, maintaining security of supply was merely an adequacy problem. In essence, if the electricity system had enough installed firm capacity to meet peak demand, security of supply was guaranteed.

---

38. As explained above, the approval of a capacity market requires the expected LOLE to be higher than the reliability standard.
39. *See* 'ACER Decision No 04/2023 on the European Resource Adequacy Assessment for 2022'. And 'ACER Decision No 02/2022 on the European Resource Adequacy Assessment for 2021'.
40. For an existing generator, the opportunity cost is given by the difference between its fixed costs and the margin obtained by selling electricity in the market. Note that in this case fixed cost do not include investment costs already sunk, unless some of these can be recoup, for instance, by dismantling the asset and selling its parts.

To that end, different types of capacity mechanisms have been implemented in the EU and other jurisdictions, such as reliability options, capacity-wide mechanisms, decentralised capacity obligations, or strategic reserves. There is abundant literature that discusses the advantages and disadvantages of each of these mechanisms. Despite their differences, however, all these mechanisms ultimately pursue incentivising the availability of firm capacity during scarcity conditions.

Nevertheless, the increasing share of intermittent renewable energies implies that security of supply no longer relies solely on having adequate firm capacity. Now, it also needs capacity, or load, to be sufficiently flexible across different time horizons.

In time horizons of a few hours, flexible capacity is needed to rapidly increase or decrease its output to follow the net load,[41] which shows faster variations due to increasing renewable shares. This is illustrated in Figure 6.4, which displays the maximum ramps in Germany's net load for 1, 3, and 8-hour intervals in 2025 and 2030. These ramps increase in time and reach a substantial fraction of the total dispatchable capacity or even exceed it.

Figure 6.4 Expected Net Load Ramps in Germany in 2025 and 2030

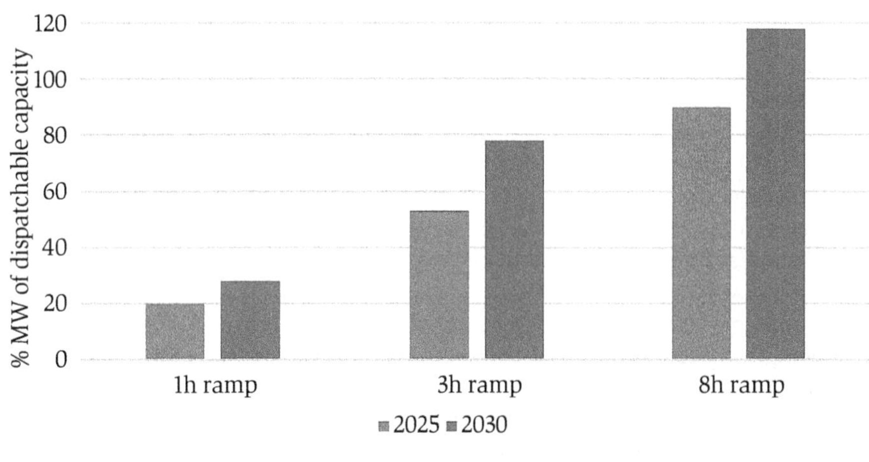

Source: ENTSOE-E 2021. Assessment of Future Flexibility Needs.

In shorter time horizons, flexible capacity also needs to be available for activation in a matter of minutes for balancing services, such as secondary or tertiary frequency control. As the share of intermittent renewables increases, so does the uncertainty over net load and hence demand for balancing services and operating reserves.

In even shorter time horizons, instantaneous intermittent renewable production generates high-rate frequency changes that require the activation of operating reserves in less than 30 seconds, usually known as primary reserve control. Large shares of

41. The net load is the difference between electricity demand and generation from variable renewable resources. It must be balanced by dispatchable resources, such as thermal units, dispatchable hydropower, demand side response or storage.

renewable penetration increase the need for such service, particularly in electricity systems that are not interconnected to a neighbouring country that is not part of the same synchronous grid.[42]

For similar reasons to the analysis provided at the beginning of this section, an energy-only market complemented by the traditional design of balancing markets will not deliver flexibility. Incentivising the necessary investments in flexible resources requires completing the existing design with additional markets for flexibility products that are currently missing. The need for new flexibility products is not homogenous across Europe. It depends on market and network specificities.

For example, peripheral countries with limited synchronous interconnection might prioritise the introduction of additional fast response services in order to ensure sufficient system inertia as the share of variable renewable generation increases. In recognition of such flexibility needs, Ireland, the United Kingdom, and Italy have introduced new ultrafast response frequency services, with activation times below one second. Due to the competitive advantage of batteries in providing ultrafast response services compared to other flexibility sources, these services have become important catalysts for investments in battery technology.[43]

However, the need for flexible resources with sufficient ramp-up (or down) capacity might prevail in countries with higher shares of solar PV production, where the daily imbalance between maximum solar production and peak demand generates a steep net load curve.

Different technologies provide different types of flexibility and different levels of firm capacity. For example, a nuclear plant can provide substantial firm capacity but limited flexibility, while batteries may provide substantial short-term flexibility but limited firm capacity, particularly in the case of short-duration storage. However, most technologies can contribute, with varying degrees, to both products. As a result, there exists substantial product substitution between flexibility and firm capacity that raises the question of whether the different products should be jointly or separately procured.

Separate procurement means, for example, that there is a market for firm capacity that is completely independent of markets for frequency products at different time horizons. Under such a scheme, the investment signal that incentivises entry is provided by the different market prices. However, separate procurement, particularly in the early stages of the development of markets for flexibility products, can lead to high uncertainty of revenue streams and high-risk premia.

To see this, consider an electricity market complemented with two additional markets: a capacity market, remunerating firm capacity, and a separate market (or markets) remunerating flexibility. How would a new entrant, like battery storage, bid in the capacity market? It would bid the difference between its investment cost and the discounted value of its expected margin from selling electricity and flexibility services. If there is substantial uncertainty over flexibility revenues, for instance, because flexibility markets are still in their infancy, the discounted value of those revenues will

42. IRENA 2018. Power System Flexibility for the Energy Transition.
43. Economic Consulting Associates, 2021: Fast & furious: fast frequency response services as the key to rev up battery investments.

be low. Consequently, the new entrant will place a high bid in the capacity market, leading to high capacity prices for consumers, or insufficient investment in flexible resources.

There are different potential solutions to such a problem. A potential alternative that has been discussed in the literature is to adjust the design of capacity markets to not only value firm capacity but also flexibility. In this sense, it is possible to design a capacity market that generates two different price signals: One price for firm capacity, and a different price for flexibility.[44] Under this framework, the different technologies compete in a single auction to procure both services, and each technology is valued accordingly. Unlike the traditional capacity market design, where all technologies compete to provide firm capacity at the lowest possible cost, thereby putting flexible resources at a competitive disadvantage, this alternative design grants a competitive edge to flexible resources over non-flexible counterparts, reflecting the added value of flexible resources to system reliability.

The interplay between firm capacity and flexibility and how to efficiently procure them both is still not understood. Further academic research and practical experience are needed to provide more clarity. At any rate, through this journey, one certainty remains: We must complete markets to complete the energy transition.

44. X. Fang et al. 2021. Redesigning capacity market to include flexibility via ramp constraints in high-renewable penetrated system. International Journal of Electrical Power & Energy Systems 128 DOI: 10.1016/j.ijepes.2020.106677.

CHAPTER 7

The Impact of the Recovery and Resilience Facility, REPowerEU and State Aid Rules in Ensuring a Level Playing Field Within the EU

Nicole Robins & Matteo Marengon

1 INTRODUCTION

The concept of a level playing field, whereby all economic actors are bound by the same set of rules and conditions to ensure fair competition, has been a core foundation of economic integration within the EU, particularly in relation to how economic interactions between Member States have been governed.[1]

In the energy sector, the concept of a level playing field is closely linked to the Energy Union. The EU energy package was introduced in early 2015 with the objective of creating an integrated energy system across the EU, with effective and harmonised regulation of energy markets at the EU level.[2] The aim was to move away from a fragmented system characterised by national regulatory frameworks that were not coordinated, retail markets that were not functioning appropriately, ageing energy infrastructure, and areas with limited access to the energy network ('energy islands').[3] In particular, the Energy Union was developed in 2015 to ensure energy security and

1. Zuleeg, F. (2020), 'The end of the level playing field?', Commentary, *European Policy Centre*, 1 October, available at: https://www.epc.eu/en/Publications/The-end-of-the-level-playing-field~377b20.
2. European Commission (2015), 'Energy Union Package', COM(2015) 80 final, 25 February, available at: https://eur-lex.europa.eu/resource.html?uri=cellar:1bd46c90-bdd4-11e4-bbe1-01aa75ed71a1.0001.03/DOC_1&format=PDF.
3. European Commission (2015), *supra*, p. 3.

solidarity across the EU with a fully integrated European energy market, in addition to supporting the EU's decarbonisation objectives (among other aspects).[4]

In 2020, the Commission adopted a set of proposals to make the EU's climate, energy, transport and taxation policies fit for reducing net greenhouse gas emissions by at least 55% by 2030 relative to 1990 levels.[5] At the end of March 2023, a provisional agreement was reached between the European Parliament and the Council that reaffirmed the aim to reach this target by 2030.[6] The provisional agreement also set out the EU's aim of achieving 45% renewables within the energy mix by 2030.[7]

The green transition poses challenges in terms of preserving the level playing field within the energy sector in the EU. As with the issues raised during the response to the COVID-19 pandemic, commentators have highlighted concerns that the more indebted Member States will not be able to progress as quickly with the green transition as the subsidies that they can provide are less generous.[8]

Following Russia's invasion of Ukraine, on 23 March 2022, the Commission introduced the Temporary Crisis Framework (TCF), which governs how Member States can provide State aid to companies in order to mitigate the impact of the economic crisis caused by the invasion.[9] Subsequently, as a result of feedback received from Member States in the context of a targeted consultation on the TCF,[10] and following the introduction of the 'Green Deal Industrial Plan',[11] the TCF has evolved into the Temporary Crisis and Transition Framework (TCTF).[12]

Meanwhile, the Commission has introduced various policies that are designed to reduce the gap between Member States in terms of progress with the green transition. In particular, on 12 February 2021, the European Parliament and Council adopted a

4. *Ibid.*, p. 4.
5. European Commission (2020), 'A European Green Deal', available at: https://commission.europa.eu/strategy-and-policy/priorities-2019-2024/european-green-deal_en.
6. European Commission (2023), 'European Green Deal: EU agrees stronger legislation to accelerate the rollout of renewable energy', press release, 30 March, available at: https://ec.europa.eu/commission/presscorner/detail/en/IP_23_2061. The revised Renewable Energy Directive, which incorporated these targets, entered into force in November 2023. See European Commission (2023), 'Renewable Energy Directive', available at: https://energy.ec.europa.eu/topics/renewable-energy/renewable-energy-directive-targets-and-rules/renewable-energy-directive_en.
7. *Ibid.*
8. Cornago, E. and Springford, J. (2023), 'Europe needs both fiscal and energy solidarity', Centre for European Reform, March, p. 2, available at: https://www.cer.eu/sites/default/files/pbrief_energy_solidarity_EC_JS_14.3.23.pdf.
9. European Commission (2023), 'Temporary Crisis and Transmission Framework', available at: https://competition-policy.ec.europa.eu/state-aid/temporary-crisis-and-transition-framework_en.
10. *See*: European Commission (2022), 'State aid: Commission consults Member States on proposal to prolong and amend Temporary Crisis Framework', press release, 6 October, available at: https://ec.europa.eu/commission/presscorner/detail/en/ip_22_6000; and European Commission (2022), 'State aid: Commission further consults Member States on prolongation and adjustment of Temporary Crisis Framework', press release, 26 October, available at: https://ec.europa.eu/commission/presscorner/detail/en/ip_22_6403.
11. On 1 February 2023, the Commission presented the Green Deal Industrial Plan with the aim of scaling up the EU's manufacturing capacity to meet the EU's net zero targets. *See*: European Commission (2023), 'The Green Deal Industrial Plan: putting Europe's net-zero industry in the lead', 1 February, available at: https://ec.europa.eu/commission/presscorner/detail/en/ip_23_510.
12. *Ibid.*

regulation establishing the Recovery and Resilience Facility (RRF).[13] The RRF is designed to mitigate the economic impact of the COVID-19 pandemic and focuses on a number of areas, including the green transition.[14] Moreover, following Russia's invasion of Ukraine, the Commission presented the REPowerEU plan with the aim of significantly reducing the dependency of EU Member States on fossil fuels from Russia before 2030.[15]

In this chapter, we discuss whether the design of the EU's recent policies contributes towards reducing the existing gap between Member States in terms of progress with the green transition. In particular, we first explore the current progress towards the energy transition before discussing the role of State aid in achieving this and looking at how the response to the energy crisis has differed across Member States. We then examine how funding has been allocated under the RRF and REPowerEU and whether these policies have the potential to mitigate any divergences.

2 PROGRESS TOWARDS THE GREEN TRANSITION AND DIFFERENCES ACROSS MEMBER STATES

There are significant differences across Member States in terms of their progress towards the green transition, and some evidence of a West-East divide. For example, all Eastern European Member States, with the exception of Estonia, Hungary and Latvia, are ranked towards the bottom of the World Economic Forum's Energy Transition Index, which benchmarks countries' readiness for the green transition as well as the performance of their energy systems.[16] For example, Sweden, Denmark and Finland are towards the top of the World Economic Forum's rankings, while Bulgaria, Romania, Cyprus and Malta are towards the bottom.[17]

A number of factors explain the differences in progress towards the energy transition, including different views regarding the benefits of renewable energy.[18] As illustrated in Figure 7.1, commentators, such as Mata Pérez, Scholten and Smith Stegen (2019), have highlighted that Eastern European Member States may be more concerned about achieving security of supply and diversifying their energy sources than Western European Member States, which may focus more on achieving the renewable energy targets.[19] Other commentators, such as Ćetković and Buzogány (2016), have

13. Regulation (EU) 2021/241 of the European Parliament and of the Council of 12 February 2021 establishing the Recovery and Resilience Facility, available at: https://eur-lex.europa.eu/legal-content/EN/TXT/PDF/?uri=CELEX:02021R0241-20230301.
14. *Ibid.*
15. European Commission (2022), 'REPowerEU: A plan to rapidly reduce dependence on Russian fossil fuels and fast forward the green transition', 18 May, available at: https://ec.europa.eu/commission/presscorner/detail/en/ip_22_3131.
16. At the time of writing this chapter in August 2023, this finding reflects the latest available rankings from the World Economic Forum. *See* World Economic Forum (2023), 'Fostering Effective Energy Transition 2023 Edition', *Insight Report*, June, p. 12, available at: https://www3.weforum.org/docs/WEF_Fostering_Effective_Energy_Transition_2023.pdf.
17. *Ibid.*
18. Mata Pérez, M., Scholten, D. and Smith Stegen, K. (2019), 'The multi-speed energy transition in Europe: Opportunities and challenges for EU energy security', *Energy Strategy Reviews*, 26, p. 5 DOI: 10.1016/j.esr.2019.100415.
19. *Ibid.*, pp. 2-3 and 5.

highlighted that the lack of the necessary infrastructure and the more limited collaboration between government and industry in Central and Eastern European (CEE) countries may adversely affect their progress towards the green transition.[20]

Figure 7.1 Classification of Member States' Priorities in the Energy Sector

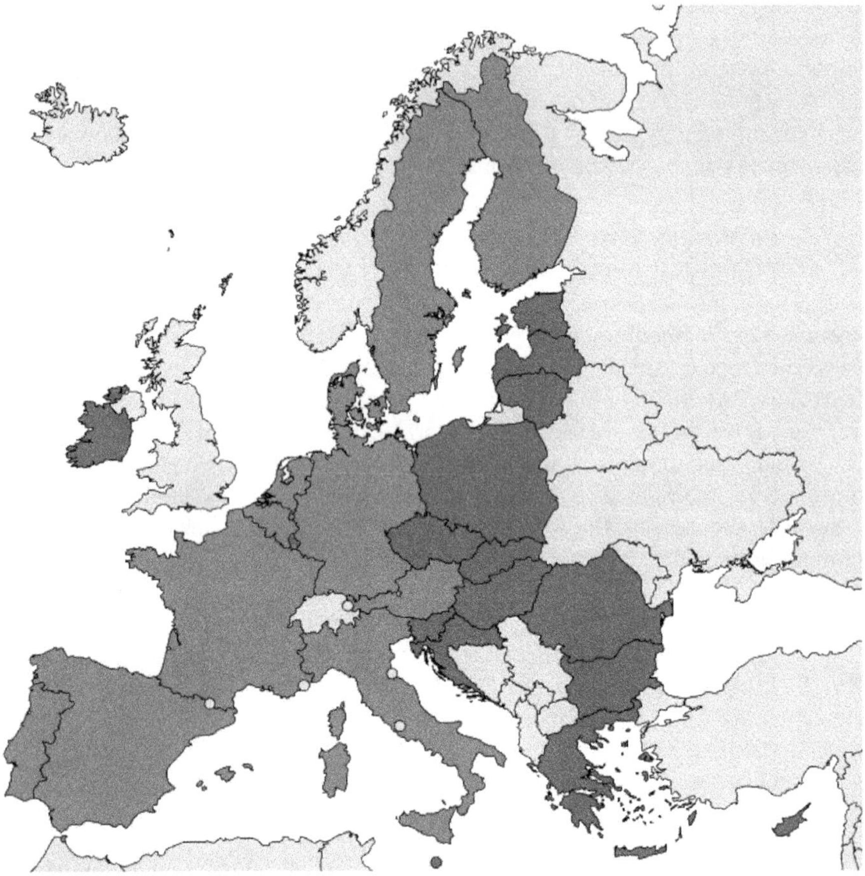

Note/Source: Green shading indicates those Member States that, according to Mata Pérez, Scholten and Smith Stegen (2019), may focus more on achieving the renewable energy targets set by the EU, while blue shading indicates those Member States that, according to the authors, may focus more on achieving security of supply. Oxera reproduction based on Mata Pérez, Scholten and Smith Stegen (2019), *supra*, Figure 1.

20. Ćetković, S. and Buzogány, A. (2016), 'Varieties of capitalism and clean energy transitions in the European Union: When renewable energy hits different economic logics', *Climate Policy*, 16(5):1–16, April, pp. 651-652 DOI: 10.1080/14693062.2015.1135778.

As shown in Figure 7.2, there are also significant differences in progress towards the green transition within Western Europe as well as within the CEE.

Figure 7.2 Energy Mix in the EU-27 Member States as of 2021 (%)

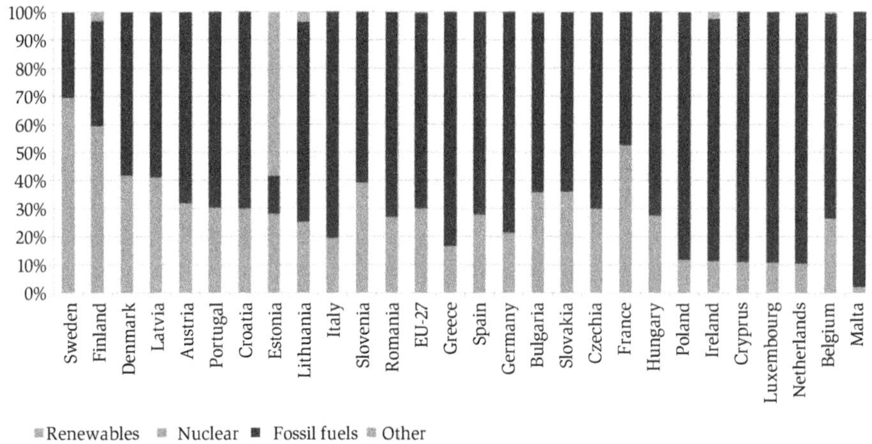

Notes/Sources: The energy mix is expressed as the share of the respective sources of energy relative to gross available energy (excluding net imports of electricity). Gross available energy refers to the overall supply of energy for all activities in a particular country, including energy transformation (i.e., electricity that is generated from combustible fuels). 'Other' refers to manufactured gases, peat and peat products, oil shale and oil sands, and heat. In Estonia, 56% of the gross available energy was from oil shale and oil sands. Oxera analysis, based on data from Eurostat (2023), 'Simplified energy balances', available at: https://ec.europa.eu/eurostat/databrowser/view/NRG_BAL_S/default/table?lang = en.

Within Western Europe, as of 2021, the share of renewables in the energy mix was highest in Sweden, Finland and Denmark, and lowest in Belgium and the Netherlands.[21] In the CEE, as of 2021, the share of renewables was highest in Latvia, Croatia and Estonia, and was lowest in Hungary and Poland.[22] Within the CEE, the differences might be explained by factors such as the degree of environmental awareness, financing constraints, and the extent of the State's involvement in the traditional power sector, as well as different strategies for ensuring the security of supply.[23] Furthermore, commentators have noted that the achievement of the EU's

21. Oxera analysis, based on data from Eurostat (2023), 'Simplified energy balances', available at: https://ec.europa.eu/eurostat/databrowser/view/NRG_BAL_S/default/table?lang = en.
22. *Ibid.*
23. Ćetković, S. and Buzogány, A. (2016), *supra*, pp. 651-652; and Fazle Rabbi, M., et al. (2022), 'Energy security and energy transition to achieve carbon neutrality', *Energies* 2022, 15, 8126, pp. 4-5 DOI: 10.3390/en15218126.

energy targets in some CEE countries such as Croatia and Estonia has been facilitated by structural changes to their economies that began in the 1990s.[24]

2.1 The Role of State Aid Prior to the Energy Crisis in Achieving the Energy Transition

State aid plays an important role in incentivising companies to undertake the necessary investments in green technologies and energy efficiency to achieve the energy transition, alongside regulation and competition policy. State aid may play a particularly important role in incentivising the development of renewable capacity, as well as encouraging the development of energy storage facilities and the phase-out of fossil fuels.

Figure 7.3 shows each Member State's expenditure on State aid for environmental protection as a percentage of its respective GDP, against the Member State's ranking on the World Economic Forum's Energy Transition Index. The figure shows that those EU countries that have spent the most on State aid for environmental protection in the past two decades have made greater progress towards the green transition, particularly Germany, Sweden and Denmark. However, while the share of renewables in the energy mix is high in Sweden and Denmark (towards the top of all EU countries as of 2021), as of 2021, it remained low in Germany at just over 15%. Therefore, although State aid is an important driver of the energy transition, significant differences across Member States do exist.

Figure 7.3 State Aid on Environmental Protection as a Percentage of GDP (2001-2021) and the 2023 Energy Transition Index

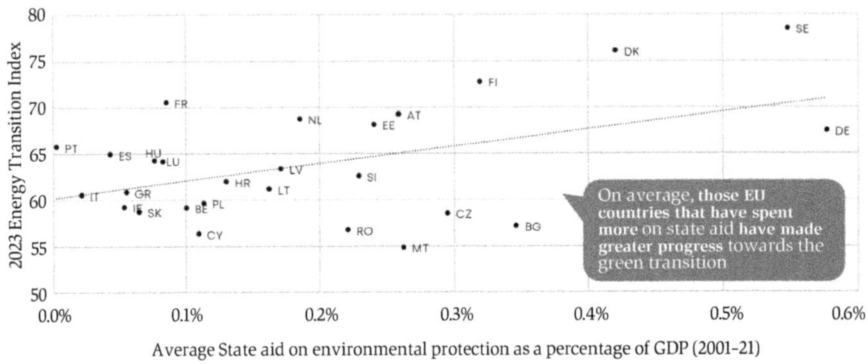

Notes/Sources: The Energy Transition Index as defined by the World Economic Forum. At the time of writing this chapter in August 2023, the figure is based on the latest data available for State aid

24. *See*: Wojtkowska-Łodej, G. and Lukaszewska, H.N. (2019), 'Convergence or divergence of the European Union's energy strategy in the Central European countries?', *CES Working Papers*, XI(2), p. 106.

expenditure on environmental protection, which is for 2021. *See* World Economic Forum (2023), 'Fostering Effective Energy Transition 2023 edition', Insight Report, June. Oxera analysis, based on data from Eurostat and the World Economic Forum.

Over the last two decades, there has been a substantial increase in State aid expenditure on environmental protection in the energy sector.[25] Figure 7.4 shows the average State aid expenditure on environmental protection in each Member State as a percentage of each Member State's GDP over the last two decades. This analysis shows that there are significant differences among Member States, with Germany, Sweden and Denmark spending the most on renewables as a percentage of their GDP, while Greece and some Eastern European countries, such as Slovakia, lag behind. It is noticeable that the four most indebted EU countries occupy positions within the bottom five of all Member States in terms of the amount spent on State aid for environmental protection. Based on average government debt as a percentage of GDP over the 2018-2022 period,[26] the four most indebted countries are Greece (188%), Italy (144%), Portugal (122%) and Spain (110%).

Figure 7.4 Average State Aid Expenditure on Environmental Protection as a Percentage of GDP (2001-2021)

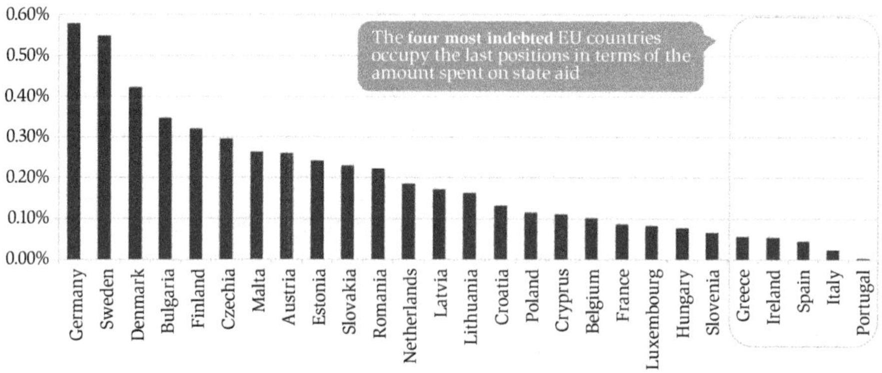

Notes/Sources: At the time of writing this chapter in August 2023, this figure is based on the latest data available for State aid expenditure on environmental protection, which is for 2021. The figure shows State aid that falls within the scope of the Commission's guidelines on State aid for climate, environmental protection and energy, based on Eurostat (2023), 'Government deficit/surplus, debt and associated data', 21 April, available at: https://ec.europa.eu/eurostat/databrowser/view/gov_10dd_edpt1/default/table?lang=en; and Eurostat (2023), 'State aid Scoreboard 2022', available at: https://webgate.ec.europa.eu/comp/redisstat/databrowser/explore/all/all_themes.

25. Eurostat (2023), 'State aid Scoreboard 2022', available at: https://webgate.ec.europa.eu/comp/redisstat/databrowser/explore/all/all_themes.
26. Government debt is defined by Eurostat as the 'total consolidated gross debt at nominal (face) value outstanding at the end of the year and consolidated between and within the sectors of general government'. *See*: Eurostat, 'General government gross debt (EDP concept), consolidated – annual data (tipsgo10)', available at: https://ec.europa.eu/eurostat/cache/metadata/en/tipsgo10_esms.htm.

Therefore, prior to the onset of the energy crisis triggered by Russia's invasion of Ukraine, there were significant differences among Member States in terms of progress towards the energy transition. State aid expenditure in the energy sector has played a significant role in determining each Member State's speed of progress towards net zero. In particular, differences in Member States' public budgets may explain the divergences observed within the EU by enabling less indebted countries to spend more.

2.2 The Energy Crisis and the Differences in the Response

Russia's invasion of Ukraine in February 2022 and its subsequent curtailment of gas supplies to Europe led to an unprecedented energy crisis for the EU, which has been characterised by persistently high and volatile energy prices.[27] Although energy prices in the EU started to rise in 2021 against the backdrop of the COVID-19 pandemic and growing international demand, they rose particularly sharply following Russia's invasion of Ukraine. In particular, the average index reflecting EU consumer prices for electricity, gas and other fuels increased by c. 29% between January 2021 and January 2022 – just prior to the invasion in February 2022 – and by a further 36% after it (between January 2022 and October 2022).[28]

In response to the energy crisis, EU governments have targeted funds mostly towards the following three broad categories of measures:

(1) price mitigation measures to reduce retail energy prices (e.g., reductions to energy taxes and the introduction of price caps);
(2) income support measures for households and businesses (e.g., cash transfers, tax credits and vouchers);
(3) investment support measures to decrease reliance on natural gas, particularly in order to reduce consumers' exposure to high prices through, for example, investments in energy efficiency and energy grid infrastructure.[29]

There are differences across Member States in the types of measures that have been introduced to tackle the energy crisis. According to the Centre for European Reform, some EU countries, such as Germany and Italy, have targeted greater subsidies towards lower-income households and small- and medium-sized enterprises.[30] Some countries, such as Germany, France and the UK, have provided public funds to support

27. European Commission (2023), 'EU action to address the energy crisis', available at: https://commission.europa.eu/strategy-and-policy/priorities-2019-2024/european-green-deal/eu-action-address-energy-crisis_en#: ~ :text = To%20reduce%20the%20risk%20and,incentivising%20consumption%20reduction.
28. Oxera calculations based on data from the Council of the European Union (2023). *See*: Council of the European Union (2023), 'Infographic – Energy price rise since 2021', 5 May, available at: https://www.consilium.europa.eu/en/infographics/energy-prices-2021/.
29. Cornago, E. and Springford, J. (2023), *supra*, p. 1.
30. For example, the authors note that '[f]or example, Germany has provided some heating subsidies only to recipients of housing benefits, and Italy has provided more generous discounts on energy bills to households under a certain income threshold.' *See*: Cornago, E. and Springford, J. (2023), *supra*, p. 1.

energy companies that have been particularly affected by the significant rise in wholesale energy prices.[31] According to the authors' calculations, while France has provided slightly greater support to households than to businesses, Italy and Spain have instead provided relatively more funding to businesses, with evidence of trade-offs between providing support to households and providing it to businesses in those countries with smaller public budgets.[32]

In response to the energy crisis, there have been significant differences across Member States in terms of the level of expenditure on State aid. As noted by the Centre for European Reform, the response to the energy crisis has shown that less indebted countries are able to provide greater subsidies to households and businesses.[33] The authors also raise concerns that, as the cost of borrowing by governments increases, investments in the more indebted EU countries could be severely affected by austerity programmes.[34]

Following Russia's invasion of Ukraine, on 23 March 2022, the Commission adopted the TCF to govern State aid provided by Member States, with the aim of mitigating the impact of the resulting economic crisis.[35] The TCF outlines the tools available to Member States to provide funding to companies to mitigate the economic effects of the invasion, the corresponding sanctions imposed by the EU and international partners and the countermeasures introduced by Russia.[36]

As shown in Figure 7.5, according to data provided by the Commission, as of January 2023, Germany and France together accounted for c. 77% of the c. EUR 672 billion of State aid approved by the Commission under the TCF.[37]

31. *Ibid.*, p. 5.
32. *Ibid.*, p. 7.
33. *Ibid.*, p. 2.
34. *Ibid.*
35. European Commission (2023), 'Temporary Crisis and Transition Framework', available at: https://competition-policy.ec.europa.eu/state-aid/temporary-crisis-and-transition-framework_en.
36. During 2022, Russia unilaterally decided to stop supplying gas to a number of EU countries, which led to a significant increase in gas and electricity prices. For example, in June 2022 Gazprom reduced gas deliveries flowing through the Nord Stream 1 pipeline to only 40% of the pipeline's capacity. *See*: Council of the European Union (2023), 'Energy prices and security of supply', 31 March, available at: https://www.consilium.europa.eu/en/policies/energy-prices-and-security-of-supply/; and Reuters (2022), 'Nord Stream 1 gas supply cut aimed at sowing uncertainty, Germany warns', 15 June, available at: https://www.reuters.com/business/energy/german-minister-accuses-russia-finding-excuse-cut-nord-stream-1-gas-2022-06-15/.
37. European Commission (2023), 'The use of crisis State aid measures in response to the Russian invasion of Ukraine', Competition State aid Brief N. 1/2023, July, p. 2, available at: https://competition-policy.ec.europa.eu/system/files/2023-07/state_aid_brief_1_2023_kdam23001enn_TCTF_survey_0.pdf. As at the time of writing this chapter in August 2023, this reflects the latest information available from the Commission regarding the breakdown of the measures approved under the TCF.

Figure 7.5 Share of State Aid Approved under the TCF

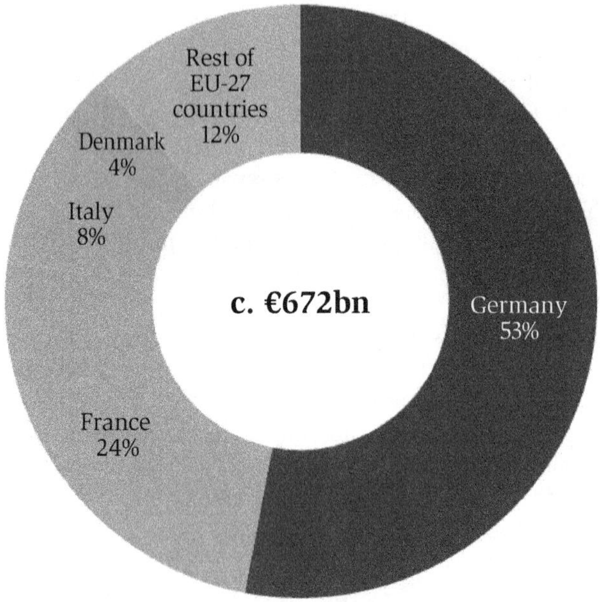

Source: At the time of writing this chapter in August 2023, the figure reflects the latest data available from the Commission regarding the breakdown of the measures approved under the TCF. Oxera analysis, based on European Commission (2023), 'The use of crisis State aid measures in response to the Russian invasion of Ukraine', *Competition State aid Brief N. 1/2023*, July, p. 2, available at: https://competition-policy.ec.europa.eu/system/files/2023-07/state_aid_brief_1_2023_kdam23001enn_TCTF_survey_0.pdf.

It has been widely reported that there are significant differences across Member States regarding the benefits of relaxing State aid control for green investments, with views differing, in particular, between the Netherlands and Italy on the one hand and France and Germany on the other.[38] On 23 December 2022, six Member States sent a joint non-paper to the Commission highlighting the risks of relaxing State aid rules for green investments, including the potential for subsidy races and a possible adverse impact on regional development.[39]

On 1 February 2023, the Commission presented the Green Deal Industrial Plan, which aims to provide a more supportive environment for scaling up the EU's manufacturing capacity for the net zero industry required to meet the EU's climate

38. Cornago, E. and Springford, J. (2023), *supra*, p. 2.
39. On 2 February 2023, the original joint statement by Denmark, Finland, Ireland, the Netherlands, Poland and Sweden was signed by Czechia, Hungary, Latvia and Slovakia. *See* Euractiv (2023), 'Eleven EU countries urge "great caution" in loosening state aid rules', 15 February, available at: https://www.euractiv.com/section/economy-jobs/news/eleven-eu-countries-urge-great-caution-in-loosening-state-aid-rules/.

targets.[40] The Plan builds on previous initiatives and complements the Green Deal and REPowerEU.[41] It is based on the following four pillars: (i) a predictable and simplified regulatory environment; (ii) speeding up access to finance; (iii) enhancing skills; and (iv) ensuring open trade in order to develop resilient supply chains.[42]

Taking into account feedback received from Member States[43] and in light of the introduction of the Green Deal Industrial Plan, a new State aid framework was adopted by the Commission in March 2023: the TCTF.[44] The Framework:

- extends the possibility for Member States to support measures needed for the transition towards net zero as outlined in the Green Deal Industrial Plan (such as schemes for accelerating the rollout of renewables and energy storage and the decarbonisation of industrial production processes);
- amends the scope of such measures with the aim of making schemes easier to design and more effective by: (i) simplifying the conditions for the granting of aid to small projects and less mature technologies, such as renewable hydrogen; (ii) expanding the possibilities of support for the deployment of all types of renewable energy source; (iii) expanding the possibilities of support for the decarbonisation of industrial processes switching to hydrogen-derived fuels; and (iv) providing for higher aid ceilings and simplified administrative procedures;
- introduces new measures to further accelerate investments in key sectors for the transition towards net zero, such as the manufacturing of strategic equipment (namely, batteries, solar panels, wind turbines, heat pumps, electrolysers and carbon capture usage and storage) as well as for the production of key components and related critical raw materials.

If there is a significant risk that investments in key sectors (as outlined above) could be diverted away from the EU, under the new framework Member States are allowed to provide the amount of support that the beneficiary could receive for an equivalent investment in the alternative location outside the European Economic Area (EEA) ('matching aid'), subject to certain conditions.

It has been reported that the introduction of the matching aid provision was explicitly requested by Germany and France in a joint paper published on 19 December

40. European Commission (2023), 'The Green Deal Industrial Plan: putting Europe's net-zero industry in the lead', 1 February, available at: https://ec.europa.eu/commission/presscorner/detail/en/ip_23_510.
41. *Ibid.*
42. *Ibid.*
43. European Commission (2022), 'State aid: Commission consults Member States on proposal to prolong and amend Temporary Crisis Framework', press release, 6 October, available at: https://ec.europa.eu/commission/presscorner/detail/en/ip_22_6000; and European Commission (2022), 'State aid: Commission further consults Member States on prolongation and adjustment of Temporary Crisis Framework', press release, 26 October, available at: https://ec.europa.eu/commission/presscorner/detail/en/ip_22_6403.
44. European Commission (2023), 'State aid: Commission adopts Temporary Crisis and Transition Framework to further support transition towards net-zero economy', press release, 9 March, available at: https://ec.europa.eu/commission/presscorner/detail/en/ip_23_1563.

2022[45] in order to mitigate the risks that European companies could relocate to the US following the introduction of the US Inflation Reduction Act (IRA).[46]

Under the TCTF, matching aid is subject to a number of conditions, including the following:

- the amount of aid must be less than the 'funding gap', defined as the minimum amount needed to incentivise the aid beneficiary to locate the investment in the EEA;
- investments must take place in assisted areas, or investments must occur cross-border with a significant element taking place in at least two assisted areas;
- the beneficiary should use state-of-the-art production technology from the perspective of environmental emissions; and
- the aid cannot trigger the relocation of investments between Member States.[47]

Figure 7.6 illustrates the calculation of the funding gap, and the possible impact of the matching aid provision.[48] If the expected profitability of the project without aid from the Member State concerned exceeds that of the project that would be undertaken in the counterfactual scenario (i.e., in the absence of aid), there is no funding gap and, as such, no aid can be granted (as illustrated in the diagram on the left). A matching aid clause, however, might allow the possibility of granting aid in the same circumstances but where state support from a jurisdiction outside the EEA is available (as illustrated in the diagram on the right).

45. Euractiv (2022), 'Germany and France seek to match US green industry subsidies', 19 December, available at: https://www.euractiv.com/section/economy-jobs/news/germany-and-france-want-to-match-us-subsidies/.
46. The US IRA of August 2022 aims to reduce inflation and to invest in domestic clean energy production. It represents the largest effort to address climate change in US history. For the full text of the IRA, *see*: congress.gov, 'H.R.5376 – Inflation Reduction Act of 2022, https://www.congress.gov/bill/117th-congress/house-bill/5376/text.
47. European Commission (2023), 'Remarks by Executive Vice-President Vestager on the proposal for a State aid Temporary Crisis and Transition Framework', 1 February, available at: https://ec.europa.eu/commission/presscorner/detail/en/speech_23_527; and European Commission (2023), 'State aid: Commission adopts Temporary Crisis and Transition Framework to further support transition towards net-zero economy', press release, 9 March, available at: https://ec.europa.eu/commission/presscorner/detail/en/ip_23_1563.
48. The funding gap is calculated as the difference between the net present value (NPV) of the expected cash flows of the aided investment and that of the counterfactual investment in a non-EEA jurisdiction which the aid beneficiary would credibly carry out in the absence of aid in the EEA (notably including any funding from public authorities that the beneficiary would be likely to receive in the non-EEA jurisdiction). Sufficient evidence must be provided to demonstrate the credibility of both scenarios, i.e., using realistic assumptions as part of a credible business plan. According to the Commission, in principle, it is unlikely that aid that exceeds the capital investment costs necessary to locate the project in the area concerned would be considered compatible. *See*: European Commission (2023), 'Temporary Crisis and Transition Framework for State Aid measures to support the economy following the aggression against Ukraine by Russia', Communication from the Commission, 2023/C 101/03, 17 March, para. 86, available at: https://eur-lex.europa.eu/legal-content/EN/TXT/PDF/?uri=CELEX:52023XC0317(01).

Figure 7.6 Illustration of the Possible Impact of the Matching Aid Provision on the Calculation of the Funding Gap

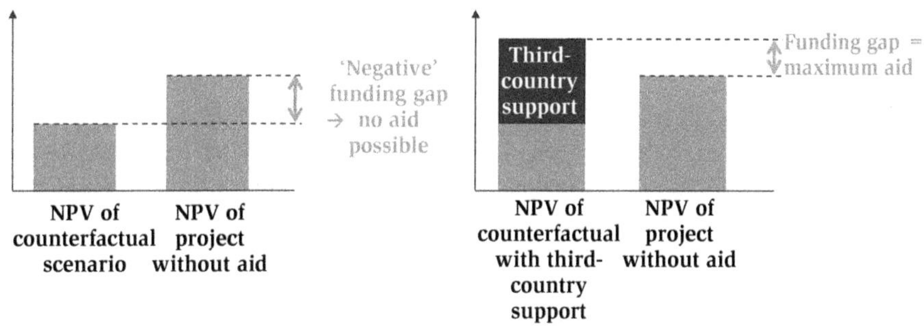

Note: NPV denotes the net present value, which is a measure of the profitability of the project, taking into account the inherent uncertainty associated with future cash flows.
Source: Oxera illustration.

At the time of the introduction of the TCTF in March 2023, Commissioner Vestager acknowledged that the potential for 'matching aid' creates 'a serious risk to competition and the integrity of the Single Market.'[49] The Commissioner went on to acknowledge that: '[t]hat's why we need to make this possibility temporary, well targeted in size and scope, and pending real benefits for people and the European economy at large'.[50]

While the matching aid provision has been welcomed by industry associations, some have also indicated that it is not sufficient to ensure the competitiveness of some elements of the supply chain that are needed to facilitate the necessary investments to achieve the Green Deal, such as investments in the solar PV manufacturing industry in the EU, given the structural disadvantages of manufacturing in Europe – in particular, high energy costs.[51]

3 THE RECOVERY AND RESILIENCE FACILITY

The RRF is an EU-wide source of funding, comprising grants and loans to support reforms and investments in EU Member States. The RRF is the centrepiece of the

49. European Commission (2023), Remarks by Executive Vice-President Vestager on the proposal for a State aid Temporary Crisis and Transition Framework, 1 February, available at: https://ec.europa.eu/commission/presscorner/detail/en/speech_23_527.
50. *Ibid.*
51. Hemetsberger, W. (2022), 'Delivering the ambition of the Green Deal Industry Plan for solar PV', *SolarPower Europe*, 22 May, available at: https://api.solarpowereurope.org/uploads/Solar_Power_Europe_NZIA_letter_May_2022_6a59e60336.pdf?updated_at=2023-05-19T13:47:20.624Z; and Solar Power Europe (2023), 'Record-low solar PV prices risk EU's open strategic autonomy', 11 September, available at: https://api.solarpowereurope.org/uploads/Solar_Power_Europe_Price_Crisis_Letter_11_September_2023_16ce4c88fa.pdf?updated_at=2023-09-11T08:02:41.696Z.

'NextGenerationEU' (NGEU), a temporary instrument that is designed to help mitigate the economic and social impact of the COVID-19 pandemic and to prepare EU economies for the green and digital transitions.[52] The funds available under the RRF amount to approximately EUR 724 billion in total, which is composed of loans (c. EUR 386 billion) and grants (c. EUR 338 billion).[53] The Commission has introduced a target that at least 37 % of each Member State's RRF funding should be dedicated towards the green transition.[54]

Studies have found that coordinated action at the EU level is more effective due to significant spillover effects across Member States.[55] Due to the high level of integration of EU economies, a large part of the economic benefit in a given Member State spills over to other Member States and assuming a coordinated expansion through the NGEU, each Member State benefits from the increase in economic activity in other EU countries.[56] In particular, studies undertaken by the Commission have found that taking into account spillover effects leads to EU-wide GDP effects that are approximately one-third larger.[57] Furthermore, the results show that spillover effects account for the majority of the impact on GDP in small economies with smaller NGEU allocations (e.g., Ireland and Luxembourg).[58] Conversely, for several countries with larger allocations under the RRF and more limited international trade (e.g., Bulgaria, Croatia, Greece and Italy),[59] a greater part of the increase in output is expected to result from their own allocations.[60]

Under the RRF, Member States with the lowest GDP per capita and those that have been most affected by the COVID-19 pandemic receive greater funds (in GDP terms).[61] As shown in Figure VII below, the Member States receiving the most from the RRF (in the form of both grants and loans) as a percentage of their respective GDP in

52. European Commission (2023), 'Recovery Plan for Europe', available at: https://commission.europa.eu/strategy-and-policy/recovery-plan-europe_en.
53. European Commission (2023), 'Recovery and Resilience Scoreboard', 9 August, available at: https://ec.europa.eu/economy_finance/recovery-and-resilience-scoreboard/.
54. Regulation (EU) 2021/241 of the European Parliament and of the Council of 12 February 2021 establishing the Recovery and Resilience Facility.
55. Pfeiffer, P., Varga, J. and Veld, J. (2021), 'Quantifying spillovers of Next Generation EU investment', *Discussion Paper 144*, July, available at: https://economy-finance.ec.europa.eu/system/files/2021-07/dp144_en.pdf; and Picek, O. (2020), 'Spillover effects from Next Generation EU', *Intereconomics*, 55, 24 October, pp. 325-331, available at: https://link.springer.com/article/10.1007/s10272-020-0923-z.
56. *Ibid.*
57. Pfeiffer, P., Varga, J. and Veld, J. (2021), *supra*, p. 3.
58. *Ibid.*, p. 8.
59. The authors refer to those economies characterised by relatively low levels of international trade. *See*: *ibid.*, p. 10.
60. *Ibid.*
61. In particular, the allocation of grants among EU Member States takes into account the following metrics: (i) the Member State's population; (ii) the inverse of its GDP per capita; (iii) its average unemployment rate over the 2015-2019 period relative to the EU average; (iv) its reduction in real GDP observed over 2020 and its observed cumulative loss in real GDP over the period 2020-2021. *See*: European Commission (2021), 'Questions and answers: The Recovery and Resilience Facility', 22 April, available at: https://ec.europa.eu/commission/presscorner/detail/en/qanda_21_1870.

2019 are Greece (over 16%), Romania (c. 12%), Croatia (c. 11%) and Italy (c. 11%).[62] In contrast, Denmark, Ireland and Luxembourg receive the lowest amounts at less than 0.5% of their respective GDP.[63]

Figure 7.7 Total RRF Amounts (Grants and Loans) by Member State as a Percentage of GDP in 2019

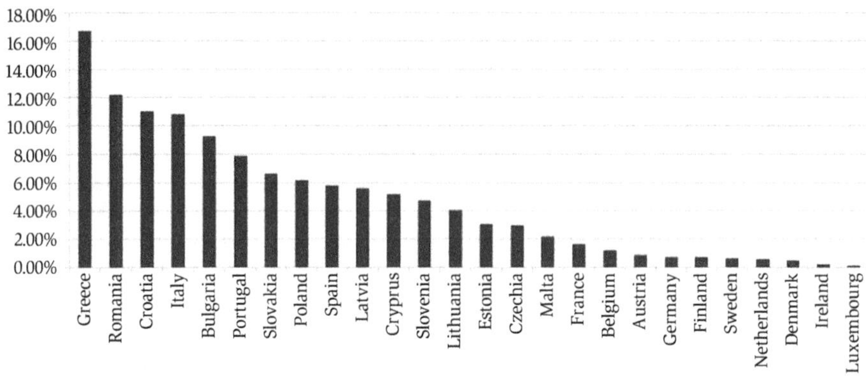

Note/Sources: Data refers to all funding under the RRF, based on the latest data available from the Commission at the time of writing this chapter in August 2023. Data is not available for Hungary. European Commission (2023), 'Recovery and Resilience Scoreboard, Country Overview', available at: https://ec.europa.eu/economy_finance/recovery-and-resilience-scoreboard/country_overview.html?lang=en.

In line with the design of the allocation of grants among Member States, those EU Member States with the lowest GDP per capita received more funds (in GDP terms) under the RRF, as shown in Figure 7.8.

62. European Commission (2023), 'Recovery and Resilience Scoreboard, Country Overview', available at: https://ec.europa.eu/economy_finance/recovery-and-resilience-scoreboard/country_overview.html?lang=en.
63. *Ibid.*

Figure 7.8 GDP Per Capita as a Percentage of Average GDP per Capita Across the EU-27 in 2019 and RRF Grants as a Percentage of Each Member State's GDP in 2019

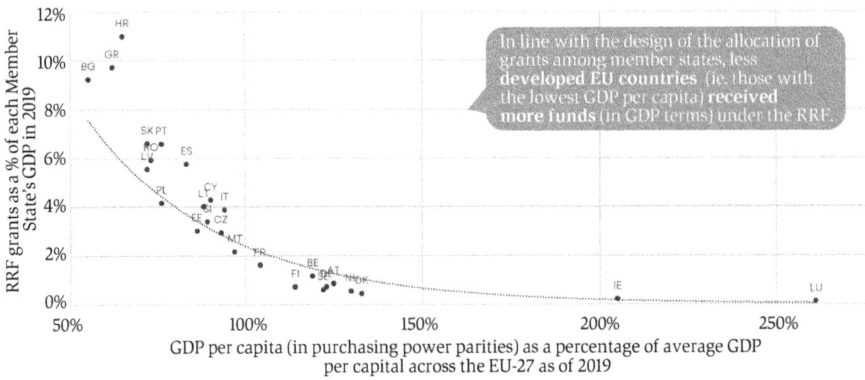

Note/Sources: GDP per capita has been adjusted for differences in price levels using Purchasing Power Parities. Data is not available for Hungary. Oxera analysis, based on the latest available data from Eurostat and the Commission at the time of writing this chapter in August 2023. *See* European Commission (2023), 'Recovery and Resilience Scoreboard, Country Overview', available at: https://ec.europa.eu/economy_finance/recovery-and-resilience-scoreboard/country_overview.html?lang=en.

Studies have also confirmed that the greatest impact of the RRF on growth in the forthcoming years is likely to be in economies with GDP per capita below the EU average, as well as those economies that have been most affected by the COVID-19 pandemic, thereby helping to reduce disparities within the EU.[64] For example, Pfeiffer, Varga and Veld (2021) estimate that the increase in Member States' real GDP due to the RRF will reach its peak in 2024 at more than 4% in Greece, around 3.75% in Bulgaria, Croatia and Romania, and around 3% in Italy and Portugal.[65]

The RRF can also help significantly to achieve the green transition. Those countries that plan to allocate the greatest share of their RRF plans to the green transition are below the EU-27 average in terms of their share of renewable energy as of 2021.[66] As shown in Figure 7.9, the share of the RRF plan allocated to the green transition (as a percentage of their respective GDP) is highest in those countries that are currently lagging behind in terms of the energy transition (according to the World Economic Forum's 2023 Energy Transition Index).

64. Afman, E., et al. (2021), 'An overview of the economics of the Recovery and Resilience Facility', *Quarterly Report on the Euro Area*, December, p. 15, available at: https://economy-finance.ec.europa.eu/system/files/2023-03/ip167_en_chapter%20I.pdf; and Watzka, S. and Watt, A. (2020), 'The macroeconomic effects of the EU Recovery and Resilience Facility', *IMK Policy Brief No. 98*, October, pp. 10–11, available at: https://www.imk-boeckler.de/fpdf/HBS-007880/p_imk_pb_98_2020.pdf.
65. Pfeiffer, P., Varga, J. and Veld, J. (2021), *supra*, p. 24.
66. European Commission (2023), 'Recovery and Resilience Scoreboard, Country Overview', available at: https://ec.europa.eu/economy_finance/recovery-and-resilience-scoreboard/country_overview.html?lang=en.

Figure 7.9 Amount of the RRF Plan in Each Member State Allocated to the Green Transition as a Percentage of the Member State's GDP in 2019

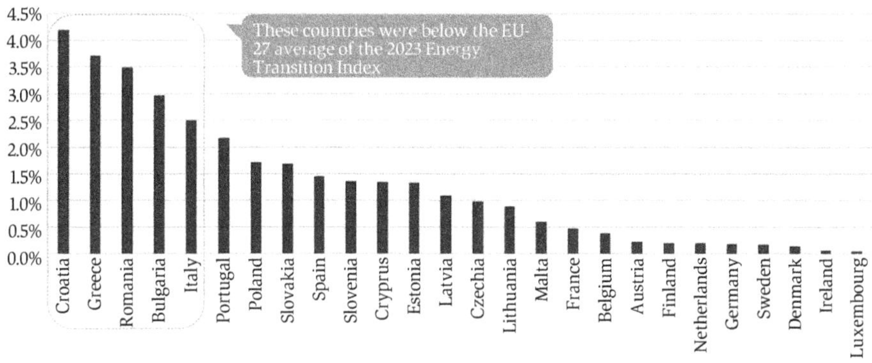

Note/Sources: Oxera analysis, based on the latest available data from the Commission at the time of writing this chapter in August 2023. Data is not available for Hungary. *See* European Commission (2023), 'Recovery and Resilience Scoreboard, Country Overview', available at: https://ec.europa.eu/economy_finance/recovery-and-resilience-scoreboard/country_overview.html?lang=en.

It is noticeable that Greece and Italy have spent particularly low amounts on State aid for environmental protection as a percentage of their respective GDP compared with most other EU Member States.[67] In contrast, some countries that have spent the most on State aid for environmental protection as a percentage of their GDP, such as Germany, Sweden and Denmark, are towards the low end in terms of the share of funding allocated to the green transition. Therefore, the design of the RRF can help to reduce disparities among Member States.

4 REPowerEU

On 8 March 2022, the Commission introduced REPowerEU with the aim of tackling the climate crisis and ending the EU's dependence on Russian fossil fuels.[68] The measures in the REPowerEU plan include energy savings, the diversification of energy supplies, and the accelerated rollout of renewable energy to replace fossil fuels in the home, industry and power generation.[69]

The EU has become more dependent on energy imports (i.e., net imports of energy relative to gross available energy) over the last three decades due to trends in production and consumption and due to the shift in the energy mix. At the EU level,

67. *See* Figure 7.4.
68. European Commission (2023), 'REPowerEU', available at: https://commission.europa.eu/strategy-and-policy/priorities-2019-2024/european-green-deal/repowereu-affordable-secure-and-sustainable-energy-europe_en.
69. *Ibid.*

Russia accounted for c. 41 % of all imports of natural gas in 2021.[70] Reliance on natural gas imports in the EU from Russia has steadily increased in the last ten years, from c. 30 % in 2012 to c. 41 % in 2021.[71] However, as shown in Figure 7.10, there are significant differences among Member States. As of 2021, the Czech Republic (100 %), Latvia (100 %) and Hungary (95 %) were the most dependent on natural gas imports from Russia, while Sweden, Spain and Luxembourg were the least dependent.[72]

Figure 7.10 Natural Gas Imports from Russia as a Percentage of Total Natural Gas Imports in the EU as of 2021 (%)

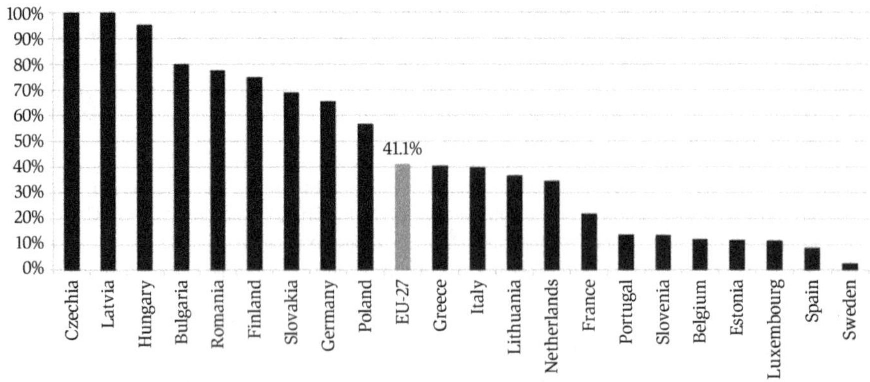

Notes/Sources: Data is not available for Austria, Croatia, Cyprus, Denmark, Ireland or Malta. Oxera analysis, based on the latest data from Eurostat at the time of writing this chapter in August 2023 is available at: https://ec.europa.eu/eurostat/web/energy/database.

In 2022, the EU significantly reduced its gas imports from Russia. In particular, the share of natural gas imports from Russia relative to total EU imports of natural gas decreased from c. 41 % in 2021 to c. 13 % by November 2022.[73]

Under REPowerEU, the allocation of the EUR 20 billion grants among EU Member States takes into account a number of metrics, including a country's GDP and the share of fossil fuels in each Member State's gross inland energy consumption.[74] The share of gas imports from Russia in each of the eight countries that will receive the most under REPowerEU exceeded 40 % of their total gas imports in 2021.[75]

70. Eurostat (2022), 'EU energy mix and import dependency', 4 March.
71. *Ibid.*
72. Oxera analysis, based on data from Eurostat, available at: https://ec.europa.eu/eurostat/web/energy/database.
73. European Council and Council of the European Union (2023), 'Infographic – Where does the EU's gas come from?', available at: https://www.consilium.europa.eu/en/infographics/eu-gas-supply/.
74. Regulation (EU) 2023/435 of the European Parliament and of the Council of 27 February 2023.
75. Based on data from Eurostat and the European Parliament. *See* European Parliament (2022), 'Provisional agreement resulting from interinstitutional negotiations', Committee on Budgets, 20 December, Annex Ia, and Eurostat (2023), 'Gross domestic product at market prices', available

On average, countries lagging behind in terms of the energy transition will receive the most under REPowerEU. This is shown by the negative relationship between the allocation of funds from REPowerEU and the score on the World Economic Forum's Energy Transition Index shown in Figure 7.11. In particular, Bulgaria, Romania, Poland and Hungary will receive some of the highest amounts under REPowerEU. It is noticeable that these countries were among the Member States most dependent on Russian natural gas imports as of 2021.[76] This illustrates how EU-wide sources of funding can help to reduce disparities across Member States.

Figure 7.11 2023 Energy Transition Index and the Allocation of the EUR 20 Billion Grants under REPowerEU as a Percentage of 2021 GDP

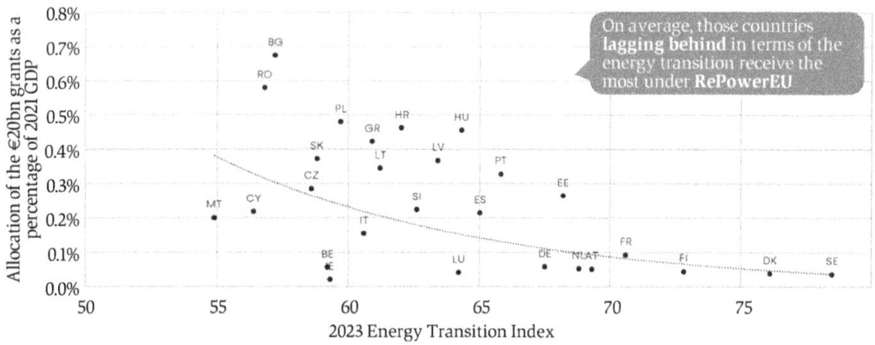

Sources: Oxera analysis, based on the latest available data from Eurostat, the European Parliament and the World Economic Forum at the time of writing this chapter in August 2023. *See* European Parliament (2022), 'Provisional agreement resulting from interinstitutional negotiations', Committee on Budgets, 20 December, p. 38; and World Economic Forum (2023), 'Fostering Effective Energy Transition 2023 edition', Insight Report, June.

5 CONCLUSIONS

There are significant differences across Member States in terms of progress towards net zero, with some evidence of a West-East divide in the EU, driven by different political priorities. Although we cannot yet assess the full impact of the RRF and REPowerEU, there are some indications that these policies have the potential to narrow the existing gap between Member States in terms of the energy transition.

Member States with the lowest GDP per capita have received more funds (relative to their GDP) under the RRF than others. Under REPowerEU, Member States lagging behind in terms of the energy transition (i.e., with the lowest rankings on the World Economic Forum's Energy Transition Index) will receive more grants than those EU

at: https://ec.europa.eu/eurostat/databrowser/view/TEC00001/default/table?lang=en&category=na10.nama10.nama_10_ma.

76. *See* Figure 7.10.

Member States that are leading the green transition. The allocation of REPowerEU resources prioritises those Member States that are more dependent on gas imports from Russia, thereby showing that progress towards the energy transition is not inconsistent with ensuring security of supply.

However, differences in Member States' expenditure on State aid lead to questions about how to maintain a level playing field, as recently shown by the substantial differences in the level of public spending notified by Member States under the TCF. In particular, expenditure on State aid in the energy sector has played a significant role in determining Member States' progress towards net zero. The significant differences in terms of the levels of State aid expenditure across Member States pose a challenge going forward.

It has been highlighted that the EU needs to invest substantially more to achieve its emissions targets. Indeed, the Centre for European Reform has highlighted that the EU needs to invest an additional EUR 250–EUR 300 billion a year to meet its 2030 emissions reduction targets.[77] Without greater investment from EU funds, more indebted countries could struggle to fund the transition away from fossil fuels.[78] The Commission's proposal for the Strategic Technologies for Europe Platform (STEP) might represent a first step by making available approximately EUR 160 billion for investments in the digital and green transition in the coming years, 'thus contributing to a level playing field for investments throughout the Single Market'.[79] In particular, the STEP, which, according to the Commission, will be the precursor to a future European Sovereignty Fund,[80] will reinforce and leverage existing EU instruments to quickly deploy financial support towards the development or manufacturing of critical technologies in the fields of digital technologies, clean technologies and biotechnologies.[81]

Based on the observed data, it appears that coordinated actions at the EU level are potentially more effective than national measures in achieving the twin objectives of accelerating the green transition in the EU while ensuring a level playing field.

77. Cornago, E. and Springford, J. (2023), *supra*, p. 2.
78. *Ibid.*
79. European Commission (2023), 'EU budget: Commission proposes Strategic Technologies for Europe Platform (STEP) to support European leadership on critical technologies', press release, 20 June, available at: https://ec.europa.eu/commission/presscorner/detail/en/ip_23_3364.
80. In September 2022, the Commission announced its intention to create a European Sovereignty Fund. According to the Commission, the Fund will be designed to provide budgetary support to well-identified projects for EU sovereignty. *See*: European Commission (2022), 'A European Sovereignty Fund for an industry "Made in Europe" I Blog of Commissioner Thierry Breton', Statement, 15 September, available at: https://ec.europa.eu/commission/presscorner/detail/en/STATEMENT_22_5543.
81. European Commission (2023), 'EU budget: Commission proposes Strategic Technologies for Europe Platform (STEP) to support European leadership on critical technologies', press release, 20 June.

Part IV The Reform of the Electricity Market Design and Competition Enforcement

CHAPTER 8

The Return of Long-Term Contracts for Electricity Purchase: Implications for Competition Policy

Fabien Roques & Guillaume Duquesne

The liberalisation of the electricity industry in the 1990s/2000s led to the vertical unbundling of formerly integrated activities of generation, transport and distribution, and supply. In the early years of liberalisation, many regulatory and competition authorities considered that long-term contracts for the supply of electricity should be restricted because of their potential to prevent the development of effective competition.[1] Through a number of landmark cases in the second part of the 2000s, the European Commission defined its approach for assessing the potential effects of long-term contracts on competition. This assessment consists of a balancing test of the positive and the negative effects of such contracts.

Many of the arguments that tilted the balancing test toward the potential negative effects of long-term contracts in the 2000s were related to the market structure prevalent at the time. The entire industry was undergoing restructuring, with one of the main priorities being to introduce competition along the unbundled value chain. Long-term contracts were identified as one of the issues undermining progress toward competitive markets.

The context is markedly different today. Many markets have become more competitive. Further, long-term contracts are identified as important enablers for the coordination and financing of capital-intensive clean technologies investments in the context of the energy transition. In other words, the pro-competitive effects of long-term contracts are likely to play a greater role in the context of the acceleration of

1. The 2007 European Commission Energy Sector Inquiry actually identified long-term contracts as one of the main priorities for antitrust enforcement in the electricity industry. *Source*: DG Competition Report on Energy Sector Inquiry, SEC(2006) 1724, 10 January 2007.

the energy transition, given efficiency gains associated with the facilitation and coordination of investments.

In this chapter, we analyse these evolutions and their implications for the need to revisit the historical approach adopted by the European Commission to assess the potential competitive effects of long-term contracts in the electricity industry.

This chapter is structured as follows. We first describe the potential pro- and anti-competitive effects of long-term contracts and the way in which the context influences the balancing of these effects. We then introduce the historical approach followed by the European Commission to assess long-term contracts for the supply of electricity. We then analyse the evolution of the context in the electricity industry, both in terms of market structure, technologies cost structure, and policy objectives. We draw implications for the balancing test of the anti- and pro-competitive effects of long-term contracts. We conclude that the change in context justifies a change of appreciation of long-term contracts, as the pro-competitive effects are more likely to outweigh their potential negative effects on competition in many cases.

1 THE ANTI- AND PRO-COMPETITIVE EFFECTS OF LONG-TERM CONTRACTS

The use of long-term contracts as an intermediate organisational form between vertical integration and short-term market trade has been extensively discussed in the economic literature.[2] The positive effects of such contracts relate to risk- and/or uncertainty mitigation and thereby induce efficiency gains for the financing and coordination of investments, whereas the main negative effects are related to the reduction in the size of the addressable market and the potential foreclosure of rivals.[3]

The potential *anti-competitive effects* of long-term contracts have been well documented in the literature:

- *Long-term contracts can support the foreclosure of actual or potential rivals.*[4] If a significant part of the demand is tied in the long term, this may foreclose rival electricity suppliers, which may fall below scale and exit the market, or not enter the market in the first place. Long-term contracts may thus lead to foreclosure and act as a barrier to entry.
- *Long-term contracts can dry up spot market liquidity.* By reducing the size of traded markets, long-term contracts may reduce liquidity and induce greater volatility. The absence of competitive and liquid spot markets is detrimental in

2. Glachant, Jean-Michel, Dominique Finon and Adrien De Hauteclocque, eds. *Competition, Contracts and Electricity Markets: A New Perspective*. Edward Elgar Publishing, 2011.
3. De Hauteclocque, Adrien and Jean-Michel Glachant. 'Long-Term Energy Supply Contracts in European Competition Policy: Fuzzy Not Crazy.' *Energy Policy* 37.12 (2009): 5399-5407 DOI: 10.1016/j.enpol.2009.07.054.
4. Aghion and Bolton, 'Contracts as a Barrier to Entry', *American Economic Review* 77 (1987): 388-401. Rasmusen, Ramseyer and Wiley, 'Naked Exclusion', *American Economic Review* 81 (1991): 1137-1145. Segal and Whinston, 'Naked Exclusion: Comment', *American Economic Review* 90 (2000): 296-309.

several ways. Competitive spot markets allow more transparency than bilateral contracting on the evolution of supply and demand and current production costs of the firms in place, which facilitates entry. The possibility to trade efficiently on the spot markets also limits the opportunity for dominant incumbents to abuse their market power when they contract bilaterally with smaller players. It also mitigates the risk that long-term contracts could lead to tacit collusion on spot markets by stabilising the market shares of an oligopoly of collectively dominant suppliers.[5]

However, long-term contracts can also have *pro-competitive effects*. In particular, long-term contracts are often considered efficient substitutes for vertical integration, and the literature highlights a number of potential positive effects on competition:

- *Long-term contracts can limit double marginalisation.*[6] Double marginalisation occurs when several firms at different levels of the supply chain concurrently exercise market power. Long-term contracts, like vertical integration, can allow the total single margin to be lower than the sum of the margin in the de-integrated case.
- *Long-term contracts may allow an efficient hedging of risks.* Long-term contracts can make revenues and expenses on both sides of the contract more stable and predictable. They can induce different types of efficiencies depending on the precise design of the contract. The most common types of long-term contracts allow the supplier to sell and the customer to buy a quantity of electricity at a fixed, pre-determined, price. On the buy side, this induced stability allows for a better predictability in conducting business, which makes industrial customers more likely to invest in electrifying their processes to decarbonise if they can benefit from more stable and predictable energy costs. On the supply side, this induced stability and predictability allows for suppliers to finance their investments at a lower cost of capital. Long-term contracts can therefore facilitate investment and entry. If spot prices are volatile, then long-term contracts can also facilitate investments and thus contribute to long-term generation adequacy.[7] Long-term contracts may also contribute to fuel mix diversity by facilitating investments in high-fixed-cost technologies. Indeed, the greater the fixed costs are, the greater the price and quantity risks are[8], and thus the higher the hedging benefits of long-term contracts are.
- Relatedly, *long-term contracts can allow efficient coordination of investments.* By internalising possible externalities, buyers and sellers can benefit from

5. C. Le Coq. Long-Term Supply Contracts and Collusion in the Electricity Market. SSE/EFI Working Paper Series in Economics and Finance No. 552, 2004.
6. L. Onofri. 'Electricity Market Restructuring and Energy Contracts: A Critical Note on the EU Commission's NEA Decision'. *European Journal of Law and Economics* 20 (2005): 71–85.
7. D. Newbery. 'Competition, Contracts and Entry in the Electricity Spot Market.' *RAND Journal of Economics* 29 (1998): 726-749.
8. F. Roques, D. Newbery and W. Nuttall. 'Fuel Mix Diversification Incentives in Liberalised Electricity Markets: A Mean-Variance Portfolio Theory Approach.' *Energy Economics* 30(4) (2007): 1831-1849.

co-optimising their business and therefore take coordinated investment decisions with the same long-term horizon.
- *Long-term contracts can mitigate the risk of market power abuse in the spot market*, by reducing the incentive to withhold capacity in the short-term market.[9] Long-term contracts may limit the incentives of dominant operators to abuse their market power on the spot markets as increases in prices in the spot markets would only be profitable on the un-contracted part of their supplies. As such, long-term contracts tend to increase traded volumes in the spot market, especially when supplier concentration is low.

Whether a long-term contract is pro- or anti-competitive depends on the balancing of these effects, which ultimately depends on the specific market conditions and the specific characteristics of the contract. In particular, the level of concentration in the market and the materiality of the positive effects associated with de-risking and coordinating investments are critical factors affecting the result of the balancing test.

2 HOW DID THE CASE LAW SHAPE THE CURRENT APPROACH TO LONG-TERM CONTRACTS?

Long-term contracts fall under Article 101 or 102 of the TFEU. Article 101 and Article 102 TFEU, which deal with anti-competitive practices[10] and abuses of dominance[11] respectively, together with relevant guidelines, notices and regulations, do not a priori allow or ban long-term contracts. They provide a framework of analysis based on market share thresholds defining which situations must be fully investigated. This framework is designed to provide predictability to firms and allow competition authorities to focus their enforcement resources on the most substantial potential infringement cases.

The European Commission conducts an in-depth case-by-case assessment of the potential anti-competitive effects of the contract only if some conditions are met, and has defined its approach through a number of milestone cases in the late 2000s. Unless a contract includes hardcore restraints (including, for example, resale price maintenance or certain territorial/customer restrictions), whether it is investigated by the European Commission or not typically depends on the parties' market shares. If the market share of one of the contracting parties falls below 15%, or if it is between 15% and 30% when the duration of the contract is below five years, the contract is in a 'safe harbour' where the Commission will not assess the potential effect of the contract.[12,13]

9. Blaise Allaz and Jean-Luc Vila. 'Cournot Competition, Forward Markets and Efficiency.' *Journal of Economic Theory* 59(1) (1993): 1-16.
10. https://eur-lex.europa.eu/LexUriServ/LexUriServ.do?uri=CELEX%3A12008E101%3AEN%3AHTML.
11. https://eur-lex.europa.eu/legal-content/EN/TXT/HTML/?uri=CELEX%3A12008E102.
12. Communication from the Commission Notice on agreements of minor importance which do not appreciably restrict competition under Article 101(1) of the Treaty on the Functioning of the European Union (De Minimis Notice) (2014/C 291/01) https://eur-lex.europa.eu/legal-content/EN/TXT/PDF/?uri=CELEX:52014XC0830(01).

Only cases where there is a strong presumption that the long-term contracts would result in substantial anti-competitive effects typically lead to an analysis of potential efficiency gains attached to the long-term contracts and a balancing test assessment. In such cases, the analysis typically proceeds in two steps:

(i) *The European Commission first assesses the potential anti-competitive effect of long-term contracts*. In its assessment, the European Commission considers both market conditions and the contract characteristics. Two landmark cases outline the main factors for the assessment, namely the *Distrigas* case (2007)[14] in the gas sector and its translation to the electricity sector in the *EDF Long-term contracts case* (2010).[15] Most prominently, the European Commission conducts a combined analysis of the following factors: contract features, competitive position of the parties, share of customer demand tied, duration of the contract, and overall share of the market covered by the contract. Past case law shows that the European Commission systematically banned exclusivity clauses for long-term contracts, as well as resale price fixing, fidelity rebates and tacit renewal. Further, any contract shorter than a year is generally not considered problematic, and an assessment is carried out beyond this threshold, with more leniency towards new entrants. The competitive position of the supplier, as well as the position of the buyer, are also considered. If either of them is too strong or if a significant portion of the market is already covered by a parallel network of long-term contracts, the contracts may be considered problematic.

(ii) *Whenever the European Commission considers that a long-term contract, or a portfolio of long-term contracts, is likely to create significant anticompetitive effects, it will analyse the potential efficiency gains leading to potential pro-competitive effects and then proceed to a balancing test*. For long-term contracts with substantial anti-competitive effects to be cleared by competition authorities, they should substantially improve economic efficiency, give a fair share of benefits to final consumers, be indispensable or at least proportional to the achievement of the efficiency gains and not grant contracting parties the possibility of eliminating competition in respect to a substantial part of the products in question. In case efficiency gains do not seem to clearly offset anti-competitive effects, a long-term contract might still be accepted if satisfactory remedies can be imposed.

13. COMMISSION REGULATION (EU) 2022/720 of 10 May 2022 on the application of Article 101(3) of the Treaty on the Functioning of the European Union to categories of vertical agreements and concerted practices https://eur-lex.europa.eu/legal-content/EN/TXT/PDF/?uri=CELEX:32022R0720.
14. Case COMP/B-1/37966 – *Distrigaz*, https://ec.europa.eu/competition/antitrust/cases/dec_docs/37966/37966_639_1.pdf.
15. Case COMP/39.286 – *EDF Long-Term Contracts*, https://ec.europa.eu/competition/antitrust/cases/dec_docs/39386/39386_1536_3.pdf.

The outcome of the balancing test is therefore highly influenced by the specific market conditions and the contract characteristics. The same long-term contract signed in a distinct market context may indeed result in different effects on competition and customers' welfare.

When State resources are involved, long-term contracts must comply with State Aid rules. First, the aid must facilitate the development of an economic activity deemed positive for society at large and must foster the creation of an incentive effect. As for the negative criterion test, the aid must not unduly affect trading conditions to an extent that would be harmful to society. Once this has been established, the European Commission carries out a case-by-case assessment of the positive and negative consequences of the aid.[16]

3 THE HISTORICAL APPROACH OF THE EUROPEAN COMMISSION TOWARDS LONG-TERM CONTRACTS IN THE ELECTRICITY SECTOR

Prior to liberalisation, long-term contracts were not a priority for the European Commission who rather focused on removing legal monopolies over imports and exports. A few decisions in the early to mid-1990s nonetheless concerned long-term power purchase agreements between independent power producers and national incumbents.[17] They mainly aimed at limiting their durations so that these long-term contracts would not jeopardise the forthcoming opening of markets.

A decade after the start of liberalisation in 1996, the European Commission 2007 Energy Sector Inquiry identified long-term contracts as one of the main priorities for antitrust enforcement.[18] At this time, against the background of the effort to restructure and liberalise the electricity markets, the European Commission identified long-term contracts as one of the issues undermining progress toward competitive markets. The Commission took a series of decisions against the portfolio of long-term contracts of several incumbents (Repsol,[19] E.ON Rurhgas,[20] RWE,[21] Distrigaz,[22] EDF,[23] Electrabel,[24]

16. Communication from the Commission Guidelines on State aid for climate, environmental protection and energy 2022, https://eur-lex.europa.eu/legal-content/EN/TXT/PDF/?uri=CELEX:52022XC0218(03).
17. Prior to liberalisation, in the early- to mid-1990s, a few decisions concerned long-term power purchase agreements between independent power producers and the national incumbents. The EC aimed to limit their durations, so that the contracts would not jeopardise the forthcoming opening of markets. A. De Hauteclocque. 'Legal Uncertainty and Competition Policy in European Deregulated Electricity Markets: The Case of Long-Term Exclusive Supply Contracts.' World Competition 32.1 (2009) DOI: 10.54648/woco2009006.
18. DG Competition Report on Energy Sector Inquiry, SEC(2006) 1724, 10 January 2007.
19. Case COMP/B-1/38.348 – *REPSOL C.P.P.*, https://ec.europa.eu/competition/antitrust/cases/dec_docs/38348/38348_998_1.pdf.
20. Case COMP/39.317 – *E.ON Gas*, https://ec.europa.eu/competition/antitrust/cases/dec_docs/39317/39317_1942_3.pdf.
21. Case COMP/39.402 – *RWE Gas Foreclosure*, https://ec.europa.eu/competition/antitrust/cases/dec_docs/39402/39402_576_1.pdf.
22. Case COMP/B-1/37966 – *Distrigaz*, https://ec.europa.eu/competition/antitrust/cases/dec_docs/37966/37966_639_1.pdf.

GDF[25]). The European Commission also intervened in Poland[26] and Hungary[27] to terminate long-term contracts under State Aid rules.

To understand the Euroepan Commission stance against long-term contracts at the time, in light of the assessment framework described in the previous section, it is necessary to look closer at the market context and policy priorities. In the early 2000s, the EU energy policy priorities were centred around making the market more competitive by increasing short-term competition. Former national incumbents entering long-term contracts to replicate vertical integration was working directly against this objective. The 2007 Energy Sector Inquiry concluded that the long-term contracts were cementing the dominant position of the incumbents and drying up the short-term markets liquidity, with no clear outweighing efficiencies, for the following reasons:[28]

- *Long-term contracts prevented the development of effective competition.* Before the restructuring of the markets, the electricity sector was both vertically and horizontally integrated. This integration arose from two factors. First, economies of scale in building long and complex projects allowed to bring down the complete cost of building generation assets and networks. Second, this allowed coordination across timeframes because of the centralisation of information. Integrated utilities are able to forecast the demand growth, which allows them to plan for the building of new generation assets and simultaneously plan for the corresponding expansion of network and flexibility assets. When the market was liberalised, incumbent suppliers and retailers entered long-term contracts, partly to replicate the benefits of vertical integration and partly because the market was not liquid and deep enough to allow efficient hedging. This gave rise to a situation where incentives were low to join the newly restructured markets, and several countries saw their incumbents enter long-term contracts with suppliers, which left the competitive structure of the market largely unchanged.
- *Long-term contracts were drying up short-term market liquidity.* The demand served through a long-term contract was not traded in the spot markets, which further contributed to reducing short-term markets liquidity.
- *Long-term contracts were not needed to support investments in generation assets and networks.* The generation fleet was already largely built and new entry typically relied on gas-fired generation that has low upfront capital costs

23. Case COMP/39.286 – *EDF Long-Term Contracts*, https://ec.europa.eu/competition/antitrust/cases/dec_docs/39386/39386_1536_3.pdf.
24. https://ec.europa.eu/commission/presscorner/detail/en/MEMO_07_313.
25. Case COMP/39.316 – *Gaz de France*, https://ec.europa.eu/competition/antitrust/cases/dec_docs/39316/39316_2298_3.pdf.
26. Commission Decision on the 25.09.2007 STATE AID awarded by Poland as part of Power Purchase Agreements and the state aid which Poland is planning to award concerning compensation for the voluntary termination of Power Purchase Agreements, https://ec.europa.eu/competition/state_aid/cases/202115/202115_763620_97_1.pdf.
27. Commission Decision of 4 June 2008 on the State aid C 41/05 awarded by Hungary through Power Purchase Agreements, https://eur-lex.europa.eu/LexUriServ/LexUriServ.do?uri=OJ:L:2009:225:0053:0103:EN:PDF.
28. DG Competition Report on Energy Sector Inquiry, SEC(2006) 1724, 10 January 2007.

and large fuel-induced variable costs. Against this background, long-term contracts were perceived unfavourably, especially for assets already amortised and /or for new assets that, because of their cost structure, did not incur substantial financing risk.

4 THE EVOLUTION OF THE ELECTRICITY INDUSTRY AND EU POLICY OBJECTIVES AND IMPLICATIONS FOR THE ASSESSMENT OF THE COMPETITIVE EFFECTS OF LONG-TERM CONTRACTS

The electricity market context, technology cost structure, and energy policy objectives have drastically evolved in the past decade. Many markets have become more competitive. Besides, long-term contracts are now identified as important enablers for the financing of capital-intensive clean technologies investments in the context of the energy transition.

In this section, we analyse these evolutions and their implications for the need to revisit the historical approach adopted by the European Commission to assess the potential competitive effects of long-term contracts in the electricity industry. We argue that the pro-competitive effects of long-term contracts are likely to play a greater role in the context of the acceleration of the energy transition, given efficiency gains associated with the facilitation and coordination of investments. This in turn means that this new context should in many cases tilt the balancing test.[29] We set out the key arguments supporting our analysis below:

First, against this new context, long-term contracts are less likely to have anti-competitive effects for the following reasons:

- *Electricity markets have generally become more liquid, competitive and integrated regionally both upstream and downstream.*[30] The electricity market has become more competitive in many countries, with former incumbents facing more intense actual or potential competition. Following the restructuring of the electricity markets across Europe, the transmission capacities between Member States have greatly increased through the building of interconnectors.[31] The integration of the electricity market has led to some harmonisation of operating rules.[32] This has resulted in the emergence of regional markets, with further integration planned in the future as cross border transmission

29. Dominique Bureau, Jean-Michel Glachant and Katheline Schubert. 'The Reform of the European Electricity Market: A Triple Challenge'. Notes du conseil d'analyse economique 76.1 (2023): 1-12.
30. ACER 2023. Progress of EU electricity wholesale market integration, https://www.acer.europa.eu/sites/default/files/documents/Publications/2023_MMR_Market_Integration.pdf.
31. TYNDP 2022, Opportunities for a more efficient European power system in 2030 and 2040, https://eepublicdownloads.blob.core.windows.net/public-cdn-container/tyndp-documents/TYNDP2022/public/system-needs-report.pdf.
32. Regulation (EC) No. 714/2009 of the European Parliament and of the Council of 13 July 2009 on conditions for access to the network for cross-border exchanges in electricity and repealing

capacity continues to develop.[33] In practice, incumbents now have reduced market shares in many countries.[34] Further, the liquidity in the spot markets has significantly developed.[35] The development of competition and liquidity makes any potential anti-competitive effects of long-term contracts less likely material.

- Some *customers have countervailing buyer power, which further reduces the likelihood of unfair terms in long-term contracts.*[36] The market power of consumers has evolved as well, with larger buyers having some form of negotiating power, which puts further pressure on suppliers to offer competitive offers.[37]

Second, long-term contracts are more likely to have pro-competitive effects in this new context. This is because the price level and volatility have increased as a result of, notably, the development of renewables as well as policy and regulatory uncertainty.[38] The volatility is expected to remain high at a time when significant coordinated investments are needed for the energy transition. Long-term contracts have the potential to fulfil market participants' hedging needs, supporting coordinated investments in the energy transition, shielding customers and industrials from price volatility and signalling Member States' commitment to decarbonisation, for the reasons explained below:

- *The cost structure of electricity production has typically changed toward relatively more fixed costs, increasing exposure to volume and price risks.*[39] The technologies corresponding to most investments in the next years are, renewables, nuclear, carbon capture and storage, as well as batteries and other storage technologies and are all capital intensive. In the traditional market design, the gas and coal-fired generation are supposed to bid their marginal costs in equilibrium, which they hope would cover their fuel and operating costs. Their relatively low capital costs are recovered in periods of scarcity when the price spikes whereby they earn large profits. For renewables and

---

Regulation (EC) No. 1228/2003, https://eur-lex.europa.eu/LexUriServ/LexUriServ.do?uri=OJ:L:2009:211:0015:0035:EN:PDF.

33. Clean Energy Package, https://energy.ec.europa.eu/topics/energy-strategy/clean-energy-all-europeans-package_en.
34. Mattia De Rosa et al. 'Diversification, Concentration and Renewability of the Energy Supply in the European Union.' *Energy* 253 (2022): 124097 DOI: 10.1016/j.energy.2022.124097. Eurostat (2023). 'Shrinking market shares for largest EU energy companies', https://ec.europa.eu/eurostat/web/products-eurostat-news/w/ddn-20230314-1.
35. ACER-CEER Market Monitoring Report, https://www.acer.europa.eu/electricity/market-monitoring-report.
36. S&P Market intelligence, 'New renewables "mega-buyers" emerge in European heavy industry' (2021), https://ec.europa.eu/eurostat/web/products-eurostat-news/w/ddn-20230314-1.
37. It needs however to be recognised that too many long-term contracts and/or contracts with inefficient design could distort short-term price signals as explained above.
38. ACER, 'ACER's Final Assessment of the EU Wholesale Electricity Market Design' (2022), https://www.acer.europa.eu/sites/default/files/documents/Publications/Final_Assessment_EU_Wholesale_Electricity_Market_Design.pdf.
39. Lion Hirth & Jan Christoph Steckel, 'The Role of Capital Costs in Decarbonizing the Electricity Sector' (2016), DOI: 10.1088/1748-9326/11/11/114010.

other low carbon technologies that are extremely capital-intensive but have near-zero marginal costs, this model leads to substantial uncertainty and volatility over the revenue that these technologies can expect in the future. Long-term contracts could provide the required certainty to ensure investments in the efficient production mix.

- *The EU decarbonisation ambition requires a step up in power sector investments, which in turn requires a predictable stream of revenues.*[40] Investments of EUR 800 bn are needed in power generation in the next decade, a significant increase compared to the previous decades. Long-term contracts are necessary to support investments in capital-intensive clean technologies, i.e., attracting private investments in energy assets requires predictability of revenues to facilitate financing. In this respect, most of the existing renewable generation fleet in Europe has been, to date, supported by public or private long-term contracts.
- *The EU decarbonisation ambition requires a coordination of investments along the value chain, which in turn requires predictable long-term price signals.*[41] In addition to clean generation, there is a need for significant investment in the electricity grid as well as flexible resources such as storage or demand response (e.g. through electric vehicles and the associated smart charging infrastructure), to prepare the electricity system to address the new challenges caused by renewables.[42] Indeed, large shares of intermittent renewables provoke sudden and uncontrollable ramp-ups in supply that need to be addressed (delivered somewhere else, stored, or used), which requires investment in transmission systems and other forms of infrastructure. These new investments exhibit complementarity with other investments in adjacent industries (EVs, H_2) that can also be supported through long-term contracts.
- *Market prices also embed policy and regulatory uncertainties associated with the energy transition.*[43] Policy and regulatory interventions affect market risk and limit the ability of market participants to hedge merchant risks. Regulatory or policy decisions (e.g., forced exit/entry, decision on mix) influence the electricity price signal as well as other typical sources of market risks (e.g., commodity price, demand volatility). Notably, Member States have adopted a range of market interventions to mitigate the impact of the energy crisis that contributed to further distorting the choices made by generators in the market. These include caps on wholesale electricity prices, caps on fuel prices, and the

40. See for instance European Commission (2022), 'Implementing the REPowerEU action plan: investment needs, hydrogen accelerator and achieving the bio-methane targets.', https://eur-lex.europa.eu/legal-content/EN/TXT/PDF/?uri=CELEX:52022SC0230&from=EN or European Commission (2022), 'Opening speech by Commissioner Simson at the 15th European Nuclear Energy Forum.', https://ec.europa.eu/commission/presscorner/detail/en/SPEECH_22_6804.
41. Roques, F. and Finon, D. (2017), 'Adapting electricity markets to decarbonisation and security of supply objectives: Toward a hybrid regime?', https://doi.org/10.1016/j.enpol.2017.02.035
42. European Commission (2022), 'Digitalising the energy system – EU action plan', https://eur-lex.europa.eu/legal-content/EN/TXT/PDF/?uri=CELEX:52022DC0552.
43. *Ibid.*

introduction of bilaterally negotiated contracts for electricity supply or infra-marginal taxes introducing de facto a revenue cap for renewable generators, which reduces incentives to invest.[44] These mechanisms are meant to temporarily remedy the effects of the energy crisis but should be replaced by a long-term solution in the form of a modification of the market design. Contrary to other market risks, regulatory or policy decisions channelling through to power price risks cannot be efficiently managed or hedged by market parties due to lack of predictability and hedging possibilities. Long-term contracts backed by Member States could signal commitment toward decarbonisation and support investments, thereby reducing policy and regulatory uncertainties.

5 THE EVOLUTION OF THE EC APPROACH TOWARDS LONG-TERM CONTRACTS AND ELECTRICITY MARKET DESIGN

All in all, these changes in market structure, technology cost structure and policy priorities for the electricity industry have strong implications for market design and the wider competition policy framework, which have been discussed in recent years and partly accounted for in the recent European Commission proposals for reform:

- First, there is a need to decouple short- and long-term markets to allow (i) short-term allocative efficiency through an efficient market and system operation signals based on marginal costs as well as (ii) long-term dynamic efficiency through efficient investment and retirement of power plants, leveraging a range of de-risking and contracting mechanisms.[45]
- Second, there is a need to coordinate the deployment of infrastructures such as networks and storage with generation plants.[46] This implies a coordination of infrastructure build out and generation investments which will require some form of commitment mechanism from governments. Long-term contracts can help meet these objectives.

In this context, the European Commission proposed in March 2023 a new regulation on market design which supports a greater role for long-term contracts[47] in the energy transition. This regulation recognises the key role of long-term contracts to support decarbonisation and to shield suppliers and consumers from price volatility in light of the recent energy crisis that followed the Russian invasion of Ukraine.

44. ACER (2023), 'Assessment of emergency measures in electricity markets', https://acer.europa.eu/sites/default/files/documents/Publications/2023_MMR_EmergencyMeasures.pdf.
45. Roques, F. and Finon, D. (2017), 'Adapting electricity markets to decarbonisation and security of supply objectives: Toward a hybrid regime?', https://doi.org/10.1016/j.enpol.2017.02.035.
46. *Ibid.*
47. Regulation (EU) 2019/943 of the European Parliament and of the Council of 5 June 2019 on the internal market for electricity, https://eur-lex.europa.eu/legal-content/EN/TXT/PDF/?uri=CELEX:32019R0943&from=EN.

The benefits of long-term contracts have also been emphasised in recent publications from the European Commission related to its approach towards competition policy:

- The revised Guidelines on Vertical Restraints published in 2022[48] open the door to an evolution of the assessment of a long-term contract in the context of its potential contribution to sustainability objectives. The European Commission outlines a case in which a long-term contract might be appropriate and illustrates it with the example of a power generator that might not undertake a given investment without the predictability of revenues.
- The Guidelines on State Aid for climate, environmental protection and energy[49] published in 2022 outline that aid can be appropriate to ensure that an already existing economic activity is carried out in a sustainable manner. Following the COVID crisis and the passing of the Inflation Reduction Act in the United States, the European Commission released the Temporary Crisis and Transition State aid Framework (TCTF),[50] which further relaxes the State Aid rules and allows to fast-track the implementation of pre-approved State Aid schemes, in particular for certain long-term contracts. This is aimed at guaranteeing a favourable environment for the development of clean generation and fostering the transition to a low-carbon economy in the face of the increased attractivity of the United States and the challenged business environment after the COVID-19 pandemic and the ongoing cost of the energy crisis.

6 CONCLUSION

In this chapter, we argued that the evolution of the market and technology context as well as the EU energy policy objectives call for revisiting the overall assessment of long-term contracts from a competition policy point of view, given the likely titling of the balancing test toward the pro-competitive effects of these long-term contracts in many cases. Indeed, long-term contracts can generate efficiencies by fostering an efficient allocation of risks thereby supporting investments in capital-intensive clean technologies, electrification. Long-term contracts can also, in some cases, contribute to the coordination of different investments along the fragmented value chain, and, in the

48. Annex to the Communication from the Commission Approval of the content of a draft for a Communication from the Commission Guidelines on vertical restraints, https://competition-policy.ec.europa.eu/system/files/2022-05/20220510_guidelines_vertical_restraints_art101_TFEU_.pdf.
49. Communication from the Commission Guidelines on State aid for climate, environmental protection and energy 2022, https://eur-lex.europa.eu/legal-content/EN/TXT/PDF/?uri=CELEX:52022XC0218(03).
50. Communication from the Commission Temporary Crisis and Transition Framework for State Aid measures to support the economy following the aggression against Ukraine by Russia, https://eur-lex.europa.eu/legal-content/EN/TXT/PDF/?uri=CELEX:52023XC0317(01).

case where states are involved, can help ensure a credible long-term policy commitment to decarbonisation.

At the same time, long-term contracts are less likely to have material foreclosure effects of actual or potential rivals today compared to the initial stages of liberalisation, given the substantial development of upstream and downstream (regional) competition in many countries. Similarly, long-term contracts are less likely to dry up spot markets liquidity and to result in unfair terms for customers, which now have stronger buyer power with some large buyers and/or buying consortia of smaller consumers.

The Commission has recognised this new context and the importance of long-term contracts to achieve ambitious decarbonisation objectives in the recent new regulation on market design. The recent updates to the guidelines on vertical restraint and on state aid are also noticeable but fall short of providing specific guidance regarding the competition assessment of long-term contracts in this new context.

Whilst the existing framework and the balancing test of the pro- and anti-competitive effects of long-term contracts remain fit for purpose, we argue that the lack of specific guidance on the specific types of efficiencies in particular that may be taken into account may cause uncertainty for the market participants regarding the appreciation by competition authorities of the long-term contracts that are likely to multiply in future years. Further predictability in the outcome of the competitive assessment is required to support the development of long-term contracts and facilitate investment towards decarbonisation.

Indeed, the current safe harbour is narrow and insights from case law are not fully fit for purpose, although the general principles are appropriate. In particular, it would not cover long-term contracts with a duration above five years, which is a too-short horizon, or with incumbents, which may have an important role to play in the transition. This means that in most cases, the assessment of long-term contracts may need to be carried out on a case-by-case basis, weighing the pro- and anti-competitive effects. In this respect, we conclude that future guidance from the Commission on how different dimensions of long-term contracts are likely to affect the outcome of the balancing test is needed. As highlighted in this paper, assessing the effects on competition of a long-term contract in the current context requires a comprehensive assessment of different factors affecting both pro- and potential anti-competitive effects. This raises a number of new challenges for competition authorities, both with regard to the evolution of the current balancing text framework and with regard to the specific types of efficiencies that should be accounted for and the specific methodologies and tools to be used to do so.

CHAPTER 9

A Sharper Tool to Tackle Market Abuse: The Proposed Reinforcement of REMIT and Lessons Learnt from Competition Enforcement

*Peter Willis**

1 BACKGROUND TO REMIT

Regulation No. 1227/2011 on wholesale energy market integrity and transparency (REMIT) has been in force since 28 December 2011. It provides a harmonised sector-specific set of rules to enhance transparency in energy markets and in particular to tackle market abuse in the electricity and gas markets, which were not thought to be easily addressed by the competition rules or by existing market abuse laws.[1]

REMIT imposes both prohibitions and obligations applying mainly to *market participants*:[2]

- it prohibits insider trading, market manipulation and attempted market manipulation in respect of wholesale energy products;
- it requires market participants to publish inside information, to register with the relevant National Regulatory Authority (NRA), and to report trade data concerning wholesale energy market transactions.

* I am grateful to my colleague Clara Desprez for her assistance with the text of this chapter.

1. Market Abuse Directive (MAD) was already in force before REMIT was adopted - DIRECTIVE 2003/6/EC of the European Parliament and of the Council of 28 January 2003 on insider dealing and market manipulation (market abuse).
2. Article 2(7) of REMIT provides: 'market participant" means any person, including transmission system operators, who enters into transactions, including the placing of orders to trade, in one or more wholesale energy markets.

The EU legislators considered that sector-specific regulation was also necessary because wholesale energy markets are increasingly interlinked across the Union. It was necessary to provide an EU framework, involving coordination between NRAs and cooperation with the European Agency for the Cooperation of Energy Regulators (ACER), in particular, to carry out cross-border market monitoring tasks and to ensure that NRAs carry out their tasks in a coordinated and consistent way.[3]

Market monitoring is carried out by both NRAs and ACER, in particular by means of a continuous exchange of data. Where ACER identifies suspicious conduct, it may refer it to the competent NRA, which may commence an investigation and, if applicable, use its enforcement powers.[4]

There have been over one hundred individual infringement decisions to date – mostly imposing penalties of only a few thousand euros, but the largest penalty to date was around EUR 42.5 million.[5]

In reaction to the recent energy market crisis, price volatility and increase, as well as regulatory interventions, the European Commission President announced in the 2022 State of the Union 'the need for a fundamental reform of the electricity market design'.[6] The EU Commission stated that 'the energy crisis has highlighted a number of shortcomings relating to: (...) the need for robust monitoring of the energy market to better protect against market abuse'.[7]

On 14 March 2023, the Commission published its proposal for a Regulation of the European Parliament and of the Council amending Regulation (EU) No. 1227/2011 and Regulation (EU) 2019/942 to improve the EU's protection against market manipulation ('the Proposal'). One of the claimed objectives is '[t]o enhance the public's trust in functioning energy markets and to protect the EU effectively against attempts of market manipulation'. In this respect, the Proposal provides that REMIT should be amended 'to further increase transparency and monitoring capacities as well as to ensure more effective investigation and enforcement of potential cross-border market abuse cases'.[8]

On the latter, the Commission observes an increase in cross-border market abuse cases and provides that '[m]arket abuse cases involving multiple cross-border elements and market participants established outside the Union is especially challenging from an enforcement perspective. The current supervisory set-up is not appropriate for the desired level of market integration. A situation where there is no mechanism to

3. Recital 4 of REMIT: 'Wholesale energy markets are increasingly interlinked across the Union. Market abuse in one Member State often affects not only wholesale prices for electricity and natural gas across national borders, but also retail prices to consumers and micro-enterprises. Therefore the concern to ensure the integrity of markets cannot be a matter only for individual Member States. Strong cross-border market monitoring is essential for the completion of a fully functioning, interconnected and integrated internal energy market.'
4. *See* Arts 7, 13 and 16 of REMIT.
5. Ofgem requires InterGen to pay GBP 37 million over energy market abuse | Ofgem.
6. Explanatory memorandum of the Commission's proposal for a Regulation of the European Parliament and of the Council amending Regulation (EU) No. 1227/2011 and Regulation (EU) 2019/942 to improve the EU's protection against market manipulation.
7. *Ibid.*
8. Recital 10 of the Commission's proposal for a Regulation of the European Parliament and of the Council amending Regulation (EU) No. 1227/2011 and Regulation (EU) 2019/942 to improve the EU's protection against market manipulation.

ensure the best possible supervisory decisions for cross-border cases, joint action by national regulatory authorities and the Agency requires complicated arrangements and where there is a patchwork of supervisory regimes cannot remain. There is therefore a need to set up an efficient and effective supervisory and investigatory regime for this type of market abuse cases, which cannot, due to its Union wide features, be addressed by Member State action alone'. As further explained below, this challenge seems to be one of the Proposal's key areas of focus.

2 THE PROPOSED EXTENSION OF REMIT OBLIGATIONS AND PROHIBITIONS

First of all, the Proposal provides a wider scope for the definition of wholesale energy products by including 'contracts for the supply of electricity or natural gas *which may result* in delivery in the Union' and not only products where 'delivery *is* in the Union'. It is not very clear what kind of situations are targeted by this proposed amendment - although it is likely that it slightly extends the overall scope of REMIT obligations and prohibitions. Other specific proposed amendments are set out below in more detail.

2.1 The Prohibition of Insider Trading and the Obligation to Publish Inside Information

The Proposal provides a wider definition of inside information, which includes a new category of 'information conveyed by a client or by other persons acting on the client's behalf and relating to the client's pending orders in wholesale energy products, which is of a precise nature, relating directly or indirectly, to one or more wholesale energy products'.

In addition, the Proposal develops the concept of *precise nature* and the meaning of 'if [the information] were made public, would be likely to significantly affect the prices of those wholesale energy products' which are characteristics required to identify inside information. Regarding the latter, that information would be likely to significantly affect the prices of wholesale energy products if a reasonable investor would be likely to use it as part of the basis for investment decisions.

Regarding the obligation to publish inside information, the Proposal explicitly requires market participants to publish inside information through Inside Information Platforms (IIPs), for which a dedicated framework is provided in an additional article (Article 4a of the Proposal). This framework provides that IIPs must register with ACER and be authorised by the latter before operating. It also requires IIPs to disclose information 'as close to real time as is technically possible' and 'free of charge'.

2.2 The Prohibition of Market Manipulation

The Proposal extends the scope of acts that may amount to market manipulation: '"market manipulation" means: (a) entering into any transaction, ~~or~~ *issuing any order to trade or engaging in any other behaviour relating to* in wholesale energy products

(...)'. Although it is likely that most forms of conduct caught by this amended wording would previously also have been caught either by the concepts of 'order' and 'transaction' or by the concept of 'fictitious device' falling within Article 2(2)(a)(iii), this amendment clarifies the scope of manipulative conduct.

The Proposal also extends liability for market manipulation to include individuals as well as legal entities[9] (although individuals are already liable in some jurisdictions).

2.3 New Obligations with Regard to Algorithmic Trading

The Proposal provides additional rules specific to algorithmic trading[10] in a new Article 5a. This article requires a market participant engaging in algorithmic trading to have in place *effective systems* and *risk controls* to ensure resilience, sufficient capacity, appropriate trading thresholds and limits to prevent errors and abuse. This establishes as a legal obligation what is already best practice in the trading rules of a number of markets.

A market participant that engages in algorithmic trading must notify its home NRA and ACER. In addition, it may be required to provide the NRA with details about the algorithm (e.g., its nature, trading strategy, etc.) and about the related systems and controls put in place.

2.4 The Obligation to Report Trade Data

The Proposal provides enhanced rules on transparency and reporting. In addition to the proposed extension to the subject matter of Article 8, which includes the obligation for organised marketplaces (OMPs) to make available to ACER 'data relating to the order book', the proposed amendments relate primarily to the reporting procedure.

According to the Proposal, data reporting must be carried out through Registered Reporting Mechanisms (RRMs). Such reporting systems were already mentioned in the REMIT Implementing Regulation (Regulation 1348/2014) and in ACER's REMIT Guidance. However, the Commission now proposes to include a whole authorisation and supervision framework for RRMs in REMIT itself (*see* Article 9a of the Proposal). In a similar way to the proposals for IIPs, RRMs would need to be authorised by ACER and to comply with an extensive set of principles and rules set out in Article 9a and in an implementing act to be adopted by the Commission at a later date.

9. Proposed amendment of Art. 2(2) of REMIT provides: 'Market manipulation may designate the conduct of a legal person, but also, in accordance with European Union or national law, of the natural persons who participate in the decision to carry out activities for the account of the legal person concerned.'
10. Article 2(18) of the Proposal defined algorithmic trading as: 'trading in wholesale energy products where a computer algorithm automatically determines individual parameters of orders such as whether to initiate the order, the timing, price or quantity of the order or how to manage the order after its submission, with limited human intervention or no such intervention at all, not including any system that is only used for the purpose of routing orders to one or more organised market places or for the processing of orders involving no determination of any trading parameters or for the confirmation of orders or the post-trade processing of executed transactions'.

2.5 The Obligation to Report Suspicious Transactions

The proposed version of Article 15 of REMIT extends the obligation to report suspicious transactions to persons professionally 'executing', and not only 'arranging', transactions (PPAETs). In addition, it further extends their reporting obligation in respect of 'orders to trade' to include 'any cancellation or modification thereof' that the PPAET suspects to be a breach not only of Article 3 or 5 but also of Article 4 of REMIT (i.e., obligation to publish inside information).

The Proposal also requires suspicious transactions or orders to trade to be reported not only to NRAs but also to ACER.

These proposed amendments are likely to substantially increase PPAETs' surveillance duties. In this respect, the Proposal explicitly requires PPAETs to establish and maintain effective arrangements and procedures to 'guarantee that their employees carrying out surveillance activities for the purpose of this Article are preserved from any conflict of interest and act in an independent manner'.

3 NEW TASKS, STRONGER INVESTIGATION AND ENFORCEMENT POWERS

The Proposal provides new powers for ACER and NRAs to improve enforcement and information-sharing capabilities between ACER, NRAs, the Commission and other market authorities.

3.1 ACER's New Tasks and Powers

The Commission proposes to grant ACER new tasks and powers to carry out price assessments and benchmarks regarding LNG in accordance with a specific methodology (*see* Articles 7a and 7b of the Proposal).

As mentioned in sections 2.1 and 2.4 above, ACER would also have new tasks regarding the authorisation and supervision of IIPs and RRMs (Articles 4a and 9a of the Proposal).

More importantly, the Proposal intends to confer on ACER extensive investigative powers in cases where:

- involving wholesale energy products for delivery in at least three Member States, or in at least two Member States if at least one of the natural or legal persons who is carrying or has carried out these acts is resident or established in a third country; or
- in the event that the competent NRA fails to comply with a request from ACER; or
- the relevant inside information is likely to significantly affect the prices of wholesale energy products for delivery in at least three Member States.[11]

11. *See* the proposed amendments of Art. 13 of REMIT.

In these cases, and subject to a set of procedural guarantees (Article 13c of the Proposal), ACER may have the power to:

- carry out on-site inspections in cooperation with the NRA of the Member States concerned (Article 13a of the Proposal);
- request information (Article 13b of the Proposal);
- impose penalties for obstruction (Article 13a of the Proposal);
- request the support of the relevant NRAs (Article 13d of the Proposal).

At the end of its investigation, the Proposal provides that ACER would draw up a report to be made public. If ACER concludes that a breach REMIT has occurred, it cannot issue a penalty itself but must inform the NRA(s) of the Member State(s) concerned and '*require that the breach be dealt with in accordance with Articles 18*'. In other words, in such cases, only NRAs would be entitled to issue penalties, but they would be bound by ACER's findings.

3.2 NRAs' New Tasks and Powers

The Proposal intends to require NRAs (and not only ACER) to establish mechanisms to share the data they receive in accordance with Articles 7(2) and 8 with the competent financial market authorities, the national competition authorities, the national tax authorities and EUROFISC and other relevant authorities at the national level.[12]

The Commission also proposes that NRAs are given the power to enforce the prohibitions and obligations set out in Articles 8, 9 and 15, as well as those in Articles 3, 4 and 5 as at present. Not all NRAs currently have the power to impose penalties for infringement of Articles 8, 9 and 15. The Proposal further specifies that NRAs must be competent to investigate all acts carried out on their national wholesale energy markets and to enforce REMIT, irrespective of where the registered market participant carrying out those acts is resident or established. This suggests that NRAs would be able to use their investigatory powers beyond their national borders.

In the event of a breach of the prohibitions and obligations mentioned in the above paragraph, the Proposal provides that NRAs should have the power to issue penalties and other types of administrative measures, which is not currently the case for all of the obligations. Regarding legal persons, the Commission proposes the following maximum financial penalties:[13]

- for breaches of Articles 3 and 5, 15% of the total turnover in the preceding business year;
- for breaches of Articles 4 and 15, 2% of the total turnover in the preceding business year; and
- for breaches of Articles 8 and 9, 1% of the total turnover in the preceding business year.

12. Provided that these NRAs meet the requirements of confidentiality, integrity and protection of the information received (Art. 12(1) of REMIT).
13. Subject to a total cap of 20% of the annual turnover in the preceding business year.

In contrast to the investigative powers conferred on ACER in cross-border cases, the Proposal does not guarantee the same powers for NRAs.

4 CONCLUSION

The Commission's Proposal has now gone to the Council and Parliament for the Trilogue procedure. The institutions have proposed various amendments, in particular around the circumstances in which ACER can investigate and the safeguards in the context of ACER investigations. The expectation is that REMIT II, as it is becoming known, is likely to be adopted towards the end of 2023 or early 2024.

So what difference will it make? In terms of the scope of the substantive obligations (e.g., the definition of market manipulation), not necessarily very much. The new obligations in respect of IIPs, RRMs, PPAETs and algorithmic trading will impose additional costs on market participants, and the operators of these various platforms. However, it is in the area of the new powers for ACER that we see the most significant likely change. Clearly inspired by the Commission's powers to conduct on-site investigations in competition cases, the proposed powers for ACER would see ACER carrying out high-profile investigations at the premises of market participants around Europe. ACER has a high level of REMIT expertise and will inevitably take an EU-wide view. However, it is perhaps less likely to have the local market expertise that the NRAs have, that is so critical to REMIT investigations.

However, although ACER's new investigative powers may be triggered by cases involving third countries, ACER will be limited to carrying out on-site investigations on the territories of EU Member States. On this point, it will be interesting to see to what extent ACER and NRAs are able to investigate and enforce REMIT against market participants established/resident in a third country but involved in a breach committed within the EU, where they will be able to investigate only by means of requests for information.

Finally, giving ACER more effective investigative powers but passing the enforcement on to the NRAs is a creative solution to ACER's agency status, but will it be workable in practice? It proposes important procedural changes that may disrupt Member States' administrative penalty procedures and may require amendments to national law. The proposed requirement that NRAs should enforce the findings set out in ACER reports without the market participant having any opportunity to challenge the findings now appears likely to be amended before the Proposal is adopted. Clearly, the original proposal was unsustainable in not securing the MP's rights to defend itself.

So the next steps in the evolution of REMIT are keenly awaited.

CHAPTER 10

The Potential for Using EU Competition Tools and Regulation to Tackle the Energy Crisis

Ulrich Scholz & Pascal Schönemann

1 INTRODUCTION

Competition is the central principle of our market economy, which efficiently distributes limited goods and ultimately maximises consumer welfare. However, the energy crisis has led to a disruption of competition, which is threatening energy security and leading to high energy prices then burdening energy-intensive industries and private households. Defining the role, the potential, but also the limits of competition tools in relation to market regulation becomes particularly relevant in situations where crisis scenarios add additional challenges to markets in transition, which, by their very nature, are in a more fragile state and not sufficiently resilient to overcome the crisis without regulatory intervention. The unprovoked attack on Ukraine in February 2022 serves as an undisputed example of this, albeit not the only conceivable one.

This chapter focuses on the potential for using EU competition law tools and regulation to tackle the challenges of the current energy crisis.

2 DEFINITION OF THE 'ENERGY CRISIS'

In order to analyse the potential for using EU competition law tools and regulation to address the energy crisis, it is first necessary to define what the term 'energy crisis' refers to and what problems it entails. The term 'energy crisis' is usually used to refer to the distortions that occurred in the natural gas, electricity and heat markets in Europe in 2022. The elements of this crisis are threefold:

First, it entails a scarcity of supply. Until the second half of 2021, the EU had covered about 40% of its demand for natural gas by using Russian imports.[1] As an immediate and direct response to the Russian aggression, the European Union and its Member States agreed on a comprehensive package of sanctions, including the reduction of imports from Russia in the energy sector,[2] which in turn led to counter-reactions by the Russian Government, including a drastic reduction in gas supplies to the European market.

Second, it resulted in excessive energy price increases. The significant shortage of natural gas in some European countries caused gas prices to soar during the summer of 2022. While gas prices over the previous decade were between EUR 5 per MWh and EUR 35 per MWh, the Title Transfer Facility (TTF) day-ahead price rose significantly to an all-time high of EUR 320 per MWh in August 2022.[3] The same occurred with heating prices, as they are largely based on the price of natural gas. In addition, the price of heating was also increased by the rise in the price of oil, which was also due to the reduction in the supply of Russian oil and the resulting shortage. Ultimately, electricity prices rose as a result of the merit order whenever natural gas was needed to meet electricity demand. This was quite often the case, not least due to the reduction of nuclear generation in France, the phase-out of nuclear power in Germany, and reduced hydro generation due to drought and low water levels, which meant less coal could be transported on rivers such as the Rhine.

Third, and unlike other scenarios, such as the oil crises of the 1970s and 1980s, the current energy crisis is occurring in parallel with the long-term goal of transforming energy markets into carbon-neutral markets. While the transition to renewables, along with the diversification of supply sources, may help to overcome the energy crisis and strengthen the resilience of the market, there is certainly a risk that the necessary implementation of first-aid measures may distract from such long-term goals. This is even more true as the energy crisis has now become a buzzword for a multiple supply crisis having both a short-term and a long-term dimension. In the short term, Russian gas must be replaced by other sources, including gas from floating and fixed liquefied natural gas (LNG) terminals already completed or under development. However, even if these short-term challenges are met, the risk of supply shortages leading to rising prices cannot be excluded. If demand for LNG increases in world markets, LNG prices are likely to rise again. At the same time, in pursuing long-term goals, sector coupling and the decarbonisation of markets are driving up demand for electricity, while conventional generation capacity is declining.

1. Commission, Quarterly report on European gas markets, Volume 15, issue 4, p. 8.
2. For an overview of the sanctions imposed, see European Parliamentary Research Service, Briefing – EU sanctions on Russia: Overview, impact, challenges, March 2023 (available at https://www.europarl.europa.eu/RegData/etudes/BRIE/2023/739366/EPRS_BRI(2023)739366_EN.pdf).
3. Commission, Quarterly report on European gas markets, Volume 15, issue 4, p. 21.

3 REGULATORY TOOLS TO ADDRESS THE ENERGY CRISIS

This raises the question of what regulatory tools exist to address the energy crisis. It follows from the above that, broadly speaking, regulation serves two objectives in the present energy crisis scenario.

3.1 Objectives of Regulatory Tools

On the one hand, short-term measures are necessary to provide immediate relief in emergency situations, acknowledging that market forces, as such, cannot sufficiently mitigate the market disruption caused by the energy crisis. In particular, regulatory measures must be implemented wherever immediate and controllable effects are needed and where incentivising market participants is not sufficient as it would take too long to influence their behaviour before the desired effects become apparent. Likewise, the simple prohibition of market behaviour clearly does not serve its purpose. Rather, immediate action is required, which can only be brought about by regulatory mechanisms. In this vein, the Commission determined back in 1983 that market forces regularly fail to ensure stable supplies in emergency situations and that short-term interventions in the markets are therefore necessary.[4]

On the other hand, regulation serves the function of providing for a legislative framework to pursue long-term energy policy goals, such as decarbonisation, increased energy efficiency and decreased energy dependence. Such measures are not primarily designed to address the immediate crisis; they may, however, strengthen the transition to a more resilient market overall and thus prevent a recurrence of the energy crisis.

3.2 Regulatory Tools Used in the Energy Crisis

Looking at the recent regulatory measures adopted in the context of the current crisis, one can see both short-term measures to prevent supply bottlenecks and medium- or long-term measures. However, these medium- or long-term measures were in fact implemented to address perceived or actual distributional injustice resulting from the energy crisis.

3.2.1 Short-Term Regulatory Measures to Safeguard Security of Supply

Achieving security of supply is a macroeconomic objective aimed at protecting against worst-case scenarios.[5] In times of crisis, a lack of energy security can lead to negative externalities in the form of either partial or total supply disruption or abrupt price

4. Commission, Case IV/30.525, decision 83/671/EWG of 12 December 1983, para. 29 – *International Energy Agency I.*
5. Commission, Green Paper 'For a European Union energy policy', COM(94)659, paras 27 et seqq.

increases with severe macroeconomic consequences.[6] However, the resulting costs are not internalised by consumers and investors in their decisions.[7] From an economic point of view, markets are not efficient if external costs are not internalised and consequently market players do not take them into account.[8] In other words, the public interest in ensuring security of supply is often not aligned with the individual companies' interests. Companies oriented towards shareholder value typically have no intrinsic interest in taking on the risks necessary to ensure security of supply, such as stranded investments. In general, companies do not take into account the external costs that their decisions impose on other consumers.[9] Rather, they merely have the incentive to maximise shareholder value and thereby risk damaging the general public as a result of supply bottlenecks in crisis scenarios. In addition, ensuring energy security creates incentives for free-riding, i.e., for consumers having the ability to benefit from security of supply without contributing sufficiently to its availability.[10] Therefore, addressing security of energy supply as a problem of negative externalities requires state intervention to correct these market failures and to guide the decisions of market participants.[11] Accordingly, in the current energy crisis, regulatory measures have been adopted to provide sufficient incentives for the market to work towards ensuring security of supply.

With regard to natural gas, Regulation (EU) 2017/1938[12] provides for filing targets and filing trajectories and requires all Member States to have a three-level energy plan to respond to a gas supply crisis. These three levels include early warning, alert and emergency state. While the first two levels comprise market-based tools, the third level provides for non-market-based measures such as rationing and central allocation of natural gas.

In reaction to Russia's unprovoked attack on Ukraine, Regulation (EU) 2022/1369[13] was then adopted to ensure that voluntary and mandatory demand reduction measures in the gas sector be implemented by Member States for the period from 1 August 2022 to 31 March 2023.

Furthermore, Regulation (EU) 2022/1854[14] provides for similar measures aimed at the overall reduction of electricity consumption. Member States shall, among other things, seek to reduce overall electricity consumption by at least 10% compared to the average gross electricity consumption in corresponding months of the reference period.

6. *Paoli/Sacco/Pochettino*, Evaluating Security of Energy Supply in the EU: Implications for project appraisal, pp. 4 and 22 (available at https://institute.eib.org/wp-content/uploads/2016/04/2010BocconiStarebei.pdf); *Muder/Cate/Zwart*, The economics of promoting security of energy supply, EIB papers, Volume 12 No. 2, p. 41.
7. *Paoli/Sacco/Pochettino, ibid.*, pp. 4 and 22.
8. *Ibid.*, p. 23.
9. *Ibid.*, p. 22.
10. *Ibid.*, p. 23.
11. *Ibid.*
12. Regulation (EU) 2017/1938 of 25 October 2017 concerning measures to safeguard the security of gas supply and repealing Regulation (EU) No. 994/2010, OJ L 280/1, 28.10.2017.
13. Council Regulation (EU) 2022/1369 of 5 August 2022 on coordinated demand-reduction measures for gas, OJ L 206/1, 8.8.2022.
14. Council Regulation (EU) 2022/1854 of 6 October 2022 on an emergency intervention to address high energy prices, OJ LI 261/1, 7.10.2022.

In June 2023, the Commission submitted its report on the review of emergency interventions to address high energy prices in accordance with Regulation (EU) 2022/1854, concluding that the measures have contributed to stabilising the energy markets overall and that there is no need to prolong emergency measures.[15]

3.2.2 Long-Term Regulatory Measures to Redistribute Welfare

Moreover, the energy crisis had and still has a social dimension. Higher and more volatile energy prices contribute to inflation and hurt energy-intensive industries and private households. At the same time, existing market and pricing mechanisms allowed some energy companies to generate substantial profit margins from higher energy prices without a corresponding increase in costs. This, in turn, has led to public and media expectations of redistributive measures. Policymakers then instrumentalised regulatory law to satisfy this demand for redistribution.

In response to massive price increases, regulations have been adopted to address high energy prices in the electricity[16] and gas sectors.[17] Mechanisms to limit profits and overall prices are a key aspect of these regulations. For example, Regulation (EU) 2022/1854 introduces a temporary *ex post* cap of EUR 180 per MWh on the revenues of inframarginal producers, allowing direct intervention by Member States in the setting of electricity prices, and introduces a temporary solidarity contribution on excess profits from fossil fuel activities. In contrast, Regulation (EU) 2022/2578 takes a different approach to gas supply, linking the price cap to a dynamic reference price.

In order to protect consumers from price increases, national legislators have introduced electricity and natural gas price subsidies to final consumers, e.g., the German Electricity Price Brake Act and the German Natural Gas and Heat Price Brake Act.

The Commission's proposal to reshape the European electricity market design,[18] presented on 14 March 2023, aims, among other things, to lower the barriers to entry for long-term PPAs in favour of market participants with higher credit risks. Member States will have to define categories of eligible electricity consumers and provide financial support for PPAs concluded with such market participants. In other words, this scheme may be seen as suppressing the reactions of the competitive process to

15. Commission, Report on the review of emergency interventions to address high energy prices in accordance with Council Regulation (EU) 2022/1854, COM(2023)302, pp. 6 et seq. and 16 (available at https://energy.ec.europa.eu/system/files/2023-06/COM_2023_302_1_EN_ACT_part1_v2.pdf).
16. Council Regulation (EU) 2022/1854 of 6 October 2022 on an emergency intervention to address high energy prices, OJ LI 261/1, 7.10.2022.
17. Council Regulation (EU) 2022/2578 of 22 December 2022 establishing a market correction mechanism to protect Union citizens and the economy against excessively high prices, OJ L 335/45, 29.12.2022.
18. Commission, Proposal of 14 March 2023 on amending Regulations (EU) 2019/943 and (EU) 2019/942 as well as Directives (EU) 2018/2001 and (EU) 2019/944 to improve the Union's electricity market design, SWD(2023)58 (available at https://eur-lex.europa.eu/legal-content/EN/TXT/PDF/?uri=CELEX:52023PC0148).

typical market risks, such as the creditworthiness and reliability of a market participant.

In conclusion, the general observation is that the use of regulatory instruments in energy markets has increased. Traditionally, regulation has only been used to target essential facilities in order to liberalise downstream supply markets. However, in crisis scenarios, regulation is generally required to restore market functionality, ideally recognising the primacy of market self-healing forces. Now, in the current crisis, regulatory law is also being used as an instrument to redistribute economic welfare, largely replacing the results of market-based allocation. In pursuing this path, attention must be paid to the risk that regulatory redistribution measures may undermine security of supply measures, for example, by limiting incentives to expand generation capacity or reducing incentives to use energy efficiently.

4 THE FUNCTION OF COMPETITION LAW IN THE ENERGY CRISIS

In light of the increasing role of regulatory tools in crisis scenarios, the question remains as to the role of competition law, acknowledging that competition law can neither guarantee energy security nor are competition tools suitable instruments to generally reduce energy prices. In its note to the OECD of November 2022, the Commission considered the role of competition law to be twofold.[19] One obvious function of competition law and competition enforcement is to prevent and sanction anti-competitive behaviour that contributes to the energy crisis, and in particular to high prices. Second, the Commission considers providing informal guidance on how companies can cooperate in order to overcome or at least mitigate the effects of the crisis for the ultimate benefit of citizens.[20] In this section, we will discuss how these two functions are reflected in the application of Articles 101 and 102 TFEU.

4.1 The Role of Article 102 TFEU in a Crisis Scenario

Particularly in situations where security of supply is at stake, where markets are faced with important restrictions and with a lack of relevant infrastructure, the control of unilateral conduct and the prevention of market abuse are likely to become more important. In these scenarios, pivotal market players may withhold capacities. Article 102 TFEU and its national equivalents will continue to serve as a legal basis for sanctioning such behaviours, in particular in situations of scarcity, when this leads to higher prices.

As investment in new infrastructure will be one of several key factors to overcome the energy crisis and to ensure the long-term resilience of the market, the question arises as to whether companies can also be obliged to undertake such necessary investments under Article 102 TFEU. One might be tempted to point to the

19. OECD, Competition in Energy Markets – Note by the European Union of 28 November 2022, p. 2 (available at https://one.oecd.org/document/DAF/COMP/WP2/WD(2022)28/en/pdf).
20. OECD, Competition in Energy Markets – Note by the European Union of 28 November 2022, pp. 2 et seq.

investigations against ENI back in 2010, where the Commission found that ENI had abused its dominant position as a transmission operator by limiting its investments in transport capacities and thereby strategically ignoring the demand of its competitors on the downstream wholesale market.[21] However, it should be kept in mind that, by its very nature, the scope of application of competition law may force dominant market players to grant access to existing infrastructure; however, this does not entail investment obligations. Moreover, sector-specific regulation, at least de facto, limits the scope of ex-post control by Article 102 TFEU. More specifically, the relevance of Article 102 TFEU will decrease to the extent that the terms and conditions for offering goods and services (in particular in relation to the use of infrastructure such as networks, LNG terminals and storage facilities) are subject to sector-specific ex-ante control. Due to this interplay of ex-post control by competition law and ex-ante regulation, Article 102 TFEU does not qualify as an appropriate enforcement tool to order companies to invest in new infrastructure. It is not the task of competition law, but rather of regulation, to provide incentives for investments and, if necessary, to sanction underinvestment that may contribute to the crisis.

4.2 The Role of Article 101 TFEU in a Crisis Scenario

The twofold nature of competition law, i.e., sanctioning of anti-competitive behaviour, on the one hand, and establishing a reliable framework for cooperation where necessary to overcome the crisis, on the other hand, particularly comes into play in the context of Article 101 TFEU.

4.2.1 Enforcement Policy

Strict enforcement of competition law to prevent anti-competitive behaviour remains crucial in crisis situations. This applies, in particular, to anti-competitive behaviour that contributes to or takes advantage of the energy crisis, in particular high prices. Consequently, the European Competition Network (ECN) announced in its joint statement on the application of competition law in the context of the war in Ukraine that 'it will therefore not hesitate to take action against companies taking advantage of the current situation by entering into cartels or abusing their dominant position'.[22] In this context, one might recall the investigations initiated by the Commission in the gas sector in March 2022, followed by inspections at the premises of several market players.[23] Another example at the national level is the ad hoc sector enquiry of the German Federal Cartel Office (FCO) in the fuel sector in April 2022, which was

21. Commission, Case COMP/39.315, decision of 29 September 2010 – *ENI*.
22. ECN, Joint statement by the ECN of 21 March 2022 on the application of competition law in the context of the war in Ukraine (available at: https://competition-policy.ec.europa.eu/system/files/2022-03/202203_joint-statement_ecn_ukraine-war.pdf).
23. Commission, Press release of 31 March 2022 – Commission confirms unannounced inspections in the natural gas sector in Germany (available at https://ec.europa.eu/commission/presscorner/detail/en/IP_22_2202).

triggered by extremely high price increases and the decoupling of retail prices from crude oil.[24]

4.2.2 *Allowing for Cooperation and Collaboration to Mitigate the Effects of the Crisis*

However, cooperation between market players, whether they be energy suppliers or (mostly industrial) consumers, will be necessary to mitigate the damage caused by the crisis.[25] As described above, the crisis is particularly evident in the scarcity of supply, which leads to high energy prices. Consequently, the ECN acknowledged the need for cooperation in order to ensure the purchase, supply and fair distribution of scarce products and inputs to overcome the disruption caused by the crisis.[26] Possible forms of cooperation to address supply shortages include purchasing agreements, production agreements, trade supply agreements and cooperation to invest in infrastructure. The Commission has therefore proposed an emergency regulation to mitigate the impact of high gas prices by establishing a joint purchasing mechanism to help gas companies and gas consumers negotiate better prices and thereby ensure security of supply.[27] Joint purchasing arrangements are typically designed to create some buying power vis-à-vis suppliers.[28] Therefore, such joint purchasing mechanisms can countervail the increasing market power of suppliers due to supply shortages and may lead to lower prices.

The challenge will thus be to draw a clear line between practices violating Article 101 TFEU that contribute to the energy crisis and cooperation measures that merely mitigate the effects of severe disruption brought about by the current crisis. As the ECN notes, the latter 'would likely not amount to a restriction of competition under Article 101 TFEU or generate efficiencies that would most likely outweigh any such restriction'.[29] The test applied by the ECN is whether measures are (i) strictly necessary, (ii) of a temporary nature, and (iii) targeted at avoiding severe disruptions caused by the impact of the war and/or of sanctions in the Internal Market.[30] When assessing

24. FCO, Ad hoc sector enquiry focusing on refineries and fuel wholesalers – Executive summary of the interim report 28 November 2022 (available at https://www.bundeskartellamt.de/SharedDocs/Publikation/EN/Sector%20Inquiries/Sektoruntersuchung_Raffinerien_Zwischenbericht.pdf?__blob=publicationFile&v=2).
25. OECD, Competition in Energy Markets – Note by the European Union of 28 November 2022, p. 2; ECN, Joint statement by the ECN of 21 March 2022 on the application of competition law in the context of the war in Ukraine.
26. ECN, Joint statement by the ECN of 21 March 2022 on the application of competition law in the context of the war in Ukraine.
27. Commission, Proposal for a Council Regulation Enhancing solidarity through better coordination of gas purchases, exchange of gas across borders and reliable price benchmarks of 18 October 2022, COM(2022)549 (available at https://eur-lex.europa.eu/resource.html?uri=cellar:6104f668-4f01-11ed-92ed-01aa75ed71a1.0001.02/DOC_1&format=PDF).
28. Commission, Guidelines on the applicability of Article 101 TFEU to horizontal co-operation agreements, OJ C 259/1, 21.07.2023, para. 275.
29. ECN, Joint statement by the ECN of 21 March 2022 on the application of competition law in the context of the war in Ukraine.
30. *Ibid.*

whether a given form of cooperation is compatible with competition law, it is necessary to distinguish between the question of whether (i) the cooperation infringes Article 101(1) TFEU and the question of whether (ii) the cooperation creates efficiencies that justify an infringement pursuant to Article 101(3) TFEU.

4.2.2.1 *Infringement of Article 101(1) TFEU*

There is no need to redefine what is classed as a restriction of competition under Article 101(1) TFEU in the light of a crisis scenario. According to general rules, measures which are necessary and targeted at avoiding or overcoming disruption caused by the war or by sanctions in the Internal Market are not classed as restrictions of competition by object and are thus subject to an assessment of anti-competitive effects. The concept of restrictions by object is interpreted very narrowly in practice and covers only those agreements that, on the basis of sufficiently reliable and robust experience, are, by their very nature, harmful to the proper functioning of competition or, on the basis of the specific characteristics of the agreement, from which it can be inferred that they are particularly harmful to competition.[31] In contrast, agreements that are necessary to avoid or to overcome disruptions are not harmful to the proper functioning of competition by their very nature. Rather, they may even have pro-competitive effects. The crisis can be seen as an external shock that threatens the structure of the market and thus competition. In a counterfactual scenario without such agreements, certain market players with high energy demand might disappear and the market would become even more concentrated.

4.2.2.2 *Justification Pursuant to Article 101(3) TFEU*

Regarding justifications under Article 101(3) TFEU, the ECN stated that cooperation measures that mitigate the effects of disruption brought about by the energy crisis generate efficiencies that would most likely outweigh any such restrictions.[32] Article 101(3) TFEU requires that consumers receive a fair share of the benefits claimed. According to the Commission, this is the case 'when the benefits deriving from the agreement outweigh the harm caused by the agreement. So that the overall effect on consumers in the relevant market is at least neutral'.[33] In this context, the question arises as to which benefits can be taken into account within the framework of the balancing test pursuant to Article 101(3) TFEU. In general, a pass-on to consumers is possible for both individual and collective benefits.[34] As regards collective benefits, it should be noted that merely out-of-market benefits (i.e., benefits that do not accrue to

31. Commission, Guidelines on the applicability of Article 101 TFEU to horizontal co-operation agreements, OJ C 259/1, 21.7.2023, paras 23 and 25 with further evidence.
32. ECN, Joint statement by the ECN of 21 March 2022 on the application of competition law in the context of the war in Ukraine.
33. Commission, Guidelines on the applicability of Article 101 TFEU to horizontal co-operation agreements, OJ C 259/1, 21.7.2023, para. 569.
34. *Ibid.*, paras 571 et seqq.

consumers in the relevant market) cannot outweigh the harm caused by the agreement.[35] In view of this, cooperation to mitigate the effects of the energy crisis creates benefits not only in terms of security of supply but also in terms of sustainability, which may outweigh any harm caused by such agreements.

First, the cooperation may lead to efficiency gains in terms of security of supply, which in turn may also lead to reducing or at least stabilising energy prices by reducing supply shortages. In the past, the Commission has positively assessed purchase agreements under Article 101(3) TFEU in the light of their contribution to ensuring security of supply in times of crisis.[36] The mitigating effect on energy prices can also be taken into account, as it not only qualifies as an indirect but also as a direct advantage of cooperation.

Second, cooperation may lead to efficiency gains in terms of sustainability benefits. In its new Horizontal Guidelines, the Commission also considers sustainability benefits in the form of collective benefits to be efficiency gains within the meaning of Article 101(3) TFEU if consumers in the relevant market substantially overlap with (or are part of) the beneficiaries outside the relevant market.[37] The Commission provides the example that drivers purchasing less polluting fuel are also citizens who would benefit from cleaner air if less polluting fuel were used.[38] The sustainability benefits of cleaner air can be taken into account to the extent that a substantial overlap can be identified between the consumers (here: the drivers) and the wider beneficiaries (here: the citizens).[39] The idea behind this is that there is a market failure if positive externalities (here: cleaner air) are not fully taken into account by consumers.[40] This is the case when these consumers do not substantially overlap with the beneficiaries. As a result, such sustainable products would be under-provided by the market.[41] If applied to the cooperation discussed in the context of the energy crisis, the sustainability benefits associated with decarbonisation can be taken into account within the framework of the balancing test pursuant to Article 101(3) TFEU. Measures aimed at avoiding disruption caused by the war or by sanctions in the Internal Market may also contribute to progress on decarbonisation targets. Cooperation targeted at substituting natural gas with hydrogen or hydrogen derivatives may serve as an example. Here, end-customers affected by the cooperation also benefit from reduced CO_2 emissions. Therefore, positive externalities in the form of CO_2 reduction are internalised, as consumers affected by the cooperation also benefit from CO_2 reduction and thus take these benefits into account in their decision-making.

35. *Ibid.*, paras 583 et seqq.
36. Commission, Case IV/33.151, decision 93/126/EEC of 22 December 1992, para. 32 – *Jahrhundertvertrag*; Commission, Case IV/33.473, decision 91/329/EWG of 30 April 1991, paras 33 et seqq. – *Scottish Nuclear*.
37. Commission Guidelines on the applicability of Article 101 TFEU to horizontal co-operation agreements, OJ C 259/1, 21.7.2023, paras 582 et seqq.
38. *Ibid.*, para. 585.
39. *Ibid.*
40. *Ibid.*, fn. 404.
41. *Ibid.*

4.2.2.3 *Decision-Making Practice in the Energy Crisis*

The application of the ECN test and the possibility of competition authorities making use of their discretionary powers when evaluating cooperation in crisis scenarios can be illustrated by two cases in particular. The first good example is the case regarding the cooperation of four German sugar producers.[42] In this case, the FCO allowed a one-time temporary cooperation project between sugar producers to mitigate the effects of possible gas shortages. The FCO argued that a shortage of gas would lead to production shortages, which would ultimately affect consumers by causing excessive peaks in prices for the base product sugar, thus affecting the entire value chain. It also emphasised that the flow of information would be limited to what was necessary and that the cooperation would be temporary.

A second example concerns the cooperation regarding the investment in LNG terminals.[43] In this case, the FCO agreed that the major German gas importers and wholesalers could cooperate in the construction and operation of floating LNG terminals. Also, the FCO did not object to the companies using the terminal capacities exclusively. It concluded that the benefits to consumers due to the LNG terminals creating urgently needed and price-reducing import capacities for gas in a relatively short period of time outweighed any negative effects on competition. Further, the FCO again emphasised the temporary nature of the exclusive use of import capacities at the terminals.

However, it appears questionable whether such emphasis on the temporary nature of cooperation qualifies as a feasible parameter when it comes to assessing its compatibility with the prerequisites set forth in Article 101(3) TFEU. Agreements for the purchase of fuels, such as LNG or hydrogen derivatives, may only secure reliable supply under appropriate market conditions if they are concluded on a long-term basis. This is particularly true given the lack of any indications as to how long the crisis will last. Furthermore, joint ventures for investment in new technologies and joint utilisation may in many circumstances only be feasible under a long-term perspective.

4.2.3 *How to Give Guidance to Market Participants*

Measures targeted at avoiding or overcoming disruption caused by the crisis may raise doubts as to their compatibility with competition law. At the same time, such measures may often be inherent in heavy investments and long-term commitments, which cannot easily be dissolved. Further, it is generally up to the companies to assess, by way of a self-assessment, whether a cooperation falls under Article 101(1) TFEU and is

42. FCO, Press release of 6 September 2022: Mitigation the effects of possible gas shortages – Bundeskartellamt allows one-time temporary cooperation project between sugar producers (available at https://www.bundeskartellamt.de/SharedDocs/Publikation/EN/Pressemitteilungen/2022/06_09_2022_Zucker.pdf?__blob=publicationFile&v=4).
43. FCO, Press release of 15 September 2022: LNG terminals – no competition concerns about planned cooperation between Uniper, RWE and EnBW/VNG (available at https://www.bundeskartellamt.de/SharedDocs/Publikation/EN/Pressemitteilungen/2022/15_09_2022_LNG_Terminals.pdf?__blob=publicationFile&v=2).

exempt under Article 101(3) TFEU. In this context, the Commission has also clarified that companies participating in the joint purchasing of gas must self-assess whether the participation is compliant with EU competition rules.[44] Also, companies claiming the benefits of Article 101(3) TFEU bear the burden of proof.[45] In light of this uncertainty, market participants will, in some cases, need a sufficient degree of investment security before undertaking measures that will eventually contribute to restoring the functioning of the market. In particular, legal certainty can be achieved through general guidelines, block exemptions and guidance from competition authorities in individual cases.

Since the challenges of the crisis may be complex and manifold, as are the measures to be implemented to meet these challenges, general guidelines that go substantially beyond what has been set out in the joint ECN statement do not appear feasible. This is equally the case for even more far-reaching block exemptions.

Ensuring legal certainty can thus be achieved at an individual case level. To this extent, the need for market participants to have legal certainty for investments is currently reflected in two mechanisms: First, declarations of inapplicability under Article 10 of Regulation 1/2003 allow for the Commission to find by decision, on its own initiative, that Article 101 TFEU or 102 TFEU is not applicable to an agreement. However, this should only be limited to exceptional cases in order to promote the clarification of the law and to ensure consistent application.[46] Since the decision is only taken ex officio and has been applied restrictively, this option has not gained much practical significance.[47]

Another option at the individual case level is to seek informal guidance from the Commission or, where appropriate, from national competition authorities.[48] The ECN's invitation to market participants to seek informal guidance is certainly welcome. In October 2022, the Commission adopted a revised Informal Guidance Notice,[49] which outlines the circumstances under which the Commission will consider providing informal guidance. The Commission acknowledged that the tool of informal guidance was never used in practice, as its 2004 Notice[50] set out strict criteria for issuing guidance letters.[51] In contrast, the revised Informal Guidance Notice is intended to provide for more flexible conditions.[52] Thereafter, the Commission considers issuing a

44. OECD, Competition in Energy Markets – Note by the European Union of 28 November 2022, p. 7.
45. Article 2 of Council Regulation (EC) No. 1/2003 of 16 December 2002 on the implementation of the rules on competition laid down in Articles 81 and 82 of the Treaty, OJ L 1/1, 4.1.2003.
46. Recital 14 of Council Regulation (EC) No. 1/2003 of 16 December 2002 on the implementation of the rules on competition laid down in Articles 81 and 82 of the Treaty, OJ L 1/1, 4.1.2003.
47. *Ritter/Wirtz* in: Immenga/Mestmäcker, Wettbewerbsrecht Band 1, Art. 10 VO 1/2003 para. 3.
48. Recital 38 of Council Regulation (EC) No. 1/2003 of 16 December 2002 on the implementation of the rules on competition laid down in Articles 81 and 82 of the Treaty, OJ L 1/1, 4.1.2003.
49. Commission Notice on informal guidance relating to novel or unresolved questions concerning Articles 101 and 102 TFEU that arise in individual cases, OJ C 381/9, 4.10.2022.
50. Commission Notice on informal guidance relating to novel questions concerning Articles 81 and 82 of the EC Treaty that arise in individual cases, OJ C 101/78, 27.4.2004.
51. Commission, Press release of 3 October 2022, Commission adopts a more flexible antitrust Informal Guidance Notice (available at: https://ec.europa.eu/commission/presscorner/detail/en/ip_22_5887).
52. *Ibid.*

guidance letter if the substantive assessment of the agreement (i) raises novel or unresolved questions and (ii) there is an interest in providing guidance due to the added value in terms of legal certainty.[53] In order to ensure legal certainty, it will be crucial for market participants that they can make use of the ECN invitation to ask for swift and clear guidance in individual cases. This implies that the Commission will apply a less restrictive practice with regard to informal guidance and is committed to reviewing the intended measures within a given timeframe.

An additional option that would provide companies with more legal certainty in the context of their self-assessment would be a presumption that measures that are necessary and targeted at avoiding or overcoming disruption caused by the war or the sanctions in the Internal Market are presumed to give consumers a fair share of the efficiencies within the meaning of Article 101(3) TFEU.

5 CONCLUSION

The ongoing energy crisis is a complex multi-supply crisis with both short-term and long-term dimensions. Such complex crises can only be addressed through a combination of both regulation and competition law.

The role of regulation is to implement short-term regulatory measures that ensure security of energy supply and long-term regulatory measures that provide for a legislative framework to pursue long-term energy policies such as decarbonisation, increased energy efficiency and decreased energy dependence.

Competition law, on the other hand, can prevent companies from contributing to the crisis by strictly enforcing its rules. It can also help to mitigate the effects of the crisis by allowing a certain level of cooperation and collaboration between companies. However, as sanctions can be severe, legal certainty must be provided to companies willing to cooperate to mitigate the effects of the crisis. For this purpose, competition authorities should adopt a less restrictive approach with regard to informational guidance and provide such guidance in a swift and clear manner. In addition, Article 101(3) TFEU should be applied in such a way as to provide companies with a presumption that measures that are necessary and targeted at avoiding or overcoming disruption caused by the war or the sanctions in the Internal Market are presumed to give consumers a fair share of the efficiencies.

53. Commission Notice on informal guidance relating to novel or unresolved questions concerning Articles 101 and 102 TFEU that arise in individual cases, OJ C 381/9, 4.10.2022, para. 7.

CHAPTER 11

Should 'Green' Merger Control Be Allowed to Shift the Burden of the Energy Transition?

Carsten Grave & Maximilian Weber

Just a few years back, the idea of including non-competition policy objectives in competition law, as well as the question of whether competition law could help in pursuing such objectives, would have been met with disbelief. Since then, however, a lively debate has developed around sustainability[1] in competition law. Although most contributions so far have focused on horizontal cooperation,[2] merger control is increasingly coming into the spotlight.[3] At first glance, competition law might not

1. The concept of "sustainability" in this chapter is mainly used with regard to environmental efficiencies, hence, disregarding social or governance aspects; this also corresponds to the focus of the current academic debate. Note that European Commission, Guidelines on Horizontal Cooperation, OJ EU 2023/C 259, p. 1, para. 516, define sustainability in accordance with the United Nations' sustainable development goals, thus, including human rights, animal welfare and other objectives beyond environmental considerations.
2. *Inter alia*, European Commission, Expert Advice (by Roman Inderst), 'Incorporating Sustainability into an Effects-Analysis of Horizontal Agreements', 2022; Martin Gassler, 'Sustainability, the Green Deal and Art. 101 TFEU: Where We Are and Where We Could Go', JECL, Vol. 12, No. 6, 2021, pp. 430-442 DOI: 10.1093/jeclap/lpab001; Daniel Higer, 'Nachhaltigkeitsvereinbarungen im Lichte jüngster Entwicklungen – endlich Rechtssicherheit?', NZKart 2022, pp. 547-555; Giorgio Monti, 'Four Options for a Greener Competition Law', JECL, Vol. 11, No. 3-4, 2020, pp. 124-132 DOI: 10.1093/jeclap/lpaa007; Eva van der Zee, 'Quantifying Benefits of Sustainability Agreements under Article 101 TFEU in Terms of Human Well-Being', ILE Working Paper Series, No. 31; Simon Holmes, 'Climate Change, Sustainability, and Competition Law', JAE, Vol. 8, 2020, pp. 354-405 DOI: 10.1093/jaenfo/jnaa006; Justus Haucap, Rupprecht Podszun *et al.*, 'Wettbewerb und Nachhaltigkeit in Deutschland und der EU', 2023; Edith Loozen, 'Strict Competition Enforcement and Welfare: A Constitutional Perspective Based in Article 101 TFEU and Sustainability', Common Market Law Review, Vol. 56, pp. 1265-1302, 2019 DOI: 10.54648/cola2019102.
3. Cf., *inter alia, Fila*, 'Fusionskontrolle und Nachhaltigkeit – (noch) nicht alles im grünen Bereich', NZKart 2023, 65; *Kar/Cochrane/Spring*, 'Environmental Sustainability and EU Merger Control: EU Competition Policy's Dark Horse to Support Green Investment', in Competition Law, Climate

necessarily seem to be the most suitable starting point for transforming the economy. Based on the general assumption, however, that markets are especially in need of governmental intervention when they fail,[4] it is an obvious suggestion that competition law might serve as an additional instrument in the fight against climate change.[5] In this context, the so-called first-mover disadvantage is regularly brought forward of standing in the way of the economy transforming itself through market mechanisms alone. Although some voices are critical of a 'greening' or generally of considering (non-economic) efficiencies in antitrust,[6] both practice and academic scholars seem to have increasingly adopted a 'green course' in recent years.[7]

Regardless of the regulatory starting point in competition law – i.e., regardless of whether we talk about 'green' cooperation agreements, abuse of dominance or merger control – the central element, in any case, is and remains a balancing of effective competition and the public interest of environmental protection.[8] Depending on the specific legislative or executive implementation of this balancing process, the burden of the fight against climate change might, however, shift considerably.

In the context of merger control, the consideration of environmental efficiencies – i.e., the balancing of the protection of the environment and preservation of competition – presents itself as potentially problematic in only two scenarios: (i) an anti-competitive merger has a positive impact on the environment, e.g., when there is a choice between higher prices and lower emissions, and (ii) a merger that is at least neutral on competition has a predictably negative impact on the environment, e.g.,

Change & Environmental Sustainability, by Simon Holmes, pp. 117 et seqq.; Emanuela Lecchi, 'Sustainability and EU Merger Control', ECLR, Vol. 44, pp. 70 et seqq.

4. Strictly speaking, market failure does not only occur when a market completely collapses, but also when a market does not lead to the best possible outcome with regard to public welfare.
5. Already in 2006, the economist Sir Nicholas Stern called climate change the 'greatest market failure the world has ever seen', cf. Stern, 'Stern Review: The Economics of Climate Change', 2006, p. viii.
6. Thomas, 'Normative Goals in Merger Control', 2021; Rhiel, Schlüter, 'Less Competition for More Sustainability?' in Kartellrecht in der Zeitenwende, 1. Ed. 2023, pp. 313 et seqq.; Böge, Jakobi, 'Die Berücksichtigung von Effizienzen in der Fusionskontrolle', Betriebs-Berater 2005, 3, 113 (117 et seq.); Inderst/Thomas, 'Der Freiheit und dem Wettbewerb drohen Gefahren', Frankfurter Allgemeine Zeitung, 7 July 2023.
7. European Commission, Guidelines on the applicability of Article 101 of the Treaty on the Functioning of the European Union to horizontal co-operation agreements, [Question to publisher: replace reference? OJEU C 259 of 21 July 2023, pp. 1-125] 1 June 2023 (C(2023) 3445 final); Competition and Markets Authority ('CMA'), 'Draft guidance on the application of the Chapter I prohibition in the Competition Act 1998 to environmental sustainability agreements', 28 February 2023; Autoriteit Consument & Markt, 'Guidelines on Sustainability Agreements', 2021; Haucap/Podszun et al., Wettbewerb und Nachhaltigkeit in Deutschland und der EU, 2023; note also the European Commission's statement to potentially include sustainability considerations in its new exclusionary abuse guidelines which are planned to be adopted by the end of 2025: https://globalcompetitionreview.com/article/sustainability-will-be-included-in-exclusionary-abuse-guidelines-dg-comp-official-says (last accessed: 20 August 2023).
8. On approaches beyond balancing, *see*: Nowag/Teorell. 'Beyond Balancing: Sustainability and Competition Law', Concurrences On-Topic No. 4-2020, pp. 34-39.

lower prices but an increase in emissions.[9] This chapter will focus on the first scenario.[10]

What, at first glance, may appear as an ordinary legal balancing exercise known from other areas of law can become a process of considerable complexity due to two distinct factors: environmental efficiencies, in particular a reduction of greenhouse gas emissions, constitute by their very nature positive externalities, and (ii) usually do not only occur locally or regionally but also have a national or even global geographic dimension, i.e., they might not only affect a (portion of a) specific economy but also – especially with regard to emissions – the world's population in its entirety. In other words, the predominant weight of the benefit, which is already difficult to quantify and hence to monetise, lies outside the market primarily affected by the concentration, and regularly does not even stop at national borders. It is the consideration of precisely these out-of-market efficiencies – i.e., the discrepancy between consumers negatively affected by a merger and the general public being its beneficiaries – that leads to the "shift of burden" mentioned above. The key question is how wide the scope is to be drawn when looking at those consumers (or citizens) whose benefits are to compensate for the merger-specific competitive harm. It is here where the question of the shift of the burden of the energy transition is decided. Should a relatively small group of consumers bear the burden of benefits occurring for the general public?

While this chapter will not be able to answer these questions definitively, it shall contribute to the discussion and will focus on three points: There will first be a brief introduction to the current merger control system (section 1). The main part of the chapter will then discuss how out-of-market efficiencies could be dealt with in the future, with particular reference to current approaches by the European Commission ("**Commission**"), the Dutch Autoriteit Consument & Markt ("**ACM**") and the UK Competition and Markets Authority (CMA), as well as describe two instruments in German competition law (section 2). Finally, we draw some conclusions (section 4).

1 CURRENT MERGER CONTROL SYSTEM

The current merger control system follows a relatively simple decision-marking rule: while mergers with anti-competitive effects are prohibited, mergers that have no negative effects on competition are cleared. In simple terms, the objective of merger control is to avert merger-related harm from competition in order to protect consumers

9. That is, using competition law as 'sword and shield', meaning that competition law may serve as a 'sword' to prohibit harmful measures to achieve sustainability as in scenario (ii) or as 'shield' to allow sustainability measures counteract any anticompetitive effects (ii), cf., *inter alia*, Holmes, JAE, Vol. 8, 2020 354 (384, 388).

10. There is no competition policy problem the remaining two scenarios, where (i) a merger is anti-competitive and expected to increase damage to the environment (e.g., higher prices and higher emissions), and where (ii) a merger does not harm competition and does not harm the environment either (e.g., lower prices and lower emissions).

in the markets affected by the concentration. Consumers are, thus, protected by effective competition, not from it.[11]

Merger-specific anti-competitive effects must, however, not necessarily result in the prohibition of a merger. Via the so-called efficiency defence – showing certain similarities to Article 101(3) TFEU –, anti-competitive effects may be compensated by demonstrating merger-specific efficiencies.[12] Companies shall be allowed to achieve rationalisation effects based on economies of scale, i.e., cost savings, which in turn will benefit consumers in the form of lower prices or innovation.[13] Its basic concept is that harm to competition can be compensated by efficiencies if these cumulatively benefit the affected consumers and are merger-specific and verifiable.[14] Although these requirements might at first sight include environmental efficiencies, since the Commission has been considering efficiencies in its assessments of mergers (at least 1991),[15] there has been no decision which explicitly takes environmental benefits into account. This can essentially be attributed to three factors: First, the burden of proof for any efficiencies – particularly their quantification and monetisation – lies with the undertakings concerned.[16] Second, the Commission handles the efficiency defence – in accordance with its character of an exemption – restrictively. Third, the consideration of out-of-market efficiencies – as is oftentimes the case with environmental efficiencies – is difficult to reconcile with the Commission's focus on consumer welfare.[17] Overall, today's merger control system hence does not seem equipped for the Commission to adopt a 'green' approach to merger control.

2 APPROACHING OUT-OF-MARKET EFFICIENCIES

But how best to deal with green out-of-market efficiencies if we wanted to consider them in the future? In view of the above, a review of the current merger control system seems necessary, i.e., at least explicit political, if not legislative changes such as revised guidelines or a revised EU Merger Regulation.[18] In the remainder of this section, we will provide an overview of (i) approaches adopted so far by certain competition authorities and (ii) certain instruments in German law which offer interesting concepts for including non-competition interests in merger control assessments.

11. Velianovski, 'The Case Against Green Antitrust', 2021; Luc Peeperkorn, Competition and Sustainability: What Can Competition Policy Do?', Concurrences On-Topic No. 4-2020, p. 40; Immenga/Mestmäcker/Körber, 6th edn, Art. 2 FKVO, para. 353.
12. EC Merger Regulation, OJ L 24/1, recital 29.
13. Oliver Williamson, 'Economies as an Antitrust Defense: The Welfare Tradeoffs', AER Vol. 58 (1968), 18 et seqq. DOI: 10.1007/978-1-4613-4231-1_12. Williamson was one of the first to ask whether any increase in market power, however small, should trump any cost saving; his model is, however, limited to considering the price effect of a merger, but not the effect on quality etc., let alone on public interests like sustainability.
14. European Commission, Horizontal Merger Guidelines, OJ C 31/5, para. 78.
15. COMP/M.050 AT&T/NCR of 18 January 1991, paras 807 et seqq.
16. European Commission, Horizontal Merger Guidelines, OJ C 31/5, paras 86 et seqq.
17. Haucap/Podszun/Rösner/Rohner/Offergeld, 'Wettbewerb und Nachhaltigkeit: Reformoptionen für ein nachhaltiges Kartellrecht', Wirtschaft und Wettbewerb 2023, 303, 305.
18. For this, *see* '3. The Issue of Democratic Legitimacy'.

2.1 RECENT POLICY INITIATIVES BY THE COMMISSION AND EUROPEAN NATIONAL COMPETITION AUTHORITIES

2.1.1 European Commission: Draft Horizontal Guidelines

It is not only since the introduction of the so-called European Green Deal that a debate on greener competition law has gained momentum at the EU level. The discussion focuses on restrictive agreements and concerted practices. By referring to the European Union's primary law objective of a sustainable development of both the EU and the Earth as well as a high level of environmental protection, as set out in Article 3(3) and (5) Treaty on European Union (TEU) as well as Article 11 TEU, it is argued that sustainability considerations can already today be considered, at least within the exemption of Article 101(3) TFEU. Indeed, the Commission has recently taken cautious steps towards 'greening' European competition policy. In addition to its draft revised Block Exemption Regulation for Research and Development Agreements,[19] the Commission published its draft revised Guidelines on Horizontal Cooperation in June 2023.[20] The latter include guidance on so-called sustainability agreements,[21] i.e., 'horizontal cooperation agreements that pursue a sustainability objective, irrespective of the form of the cooperation'.[22]

Although the Commission acknowledges that consumption decisions regularly lead to market failure, as negative externalities are usually not reflected in a product's price, it also expressly points to the strength of effective competition to contribute to consumer welfare and states that public policies and regulation remain the primary instrument towards a greener economy.[23] This suggests that the revised Guidelines will bring about a revolutionary approach to sustainability considerations in competition policy. A closer look confirmed this first impression.

The most notable changes to the guidelines were made in relation to the exemption of Article 101(3) TFEU, as the Commission expressly states that it will consider sustainability benefits as 'efficiencies' in the future. Such efficiencies include polluting production or distribution technologies.[24]

As was to be expected, the new guidelines focus on whether consumers receive a fair share of the efficiencies from a sustainability agreement. It is still required to fully compensate consumers in the markets affected by the cooperation for the harm suffered, i.e., the overall effect of the agreement must still have to be at least neutral.[25]

19. Commission, Revised Horizontal Block Exemption Regulations on Research and Development ('R&D') and Specialisation agreements of 1 June 2023 (C(2023) 3448 final).
20. Commission, Draft Revised Guidelines on Horizontal Cooperation, 1 June 2023 (C(2023) 3445 final).
21. The Commission points out, however, that sustainability agreements must not be understood as a distinct category of horizontal cooperation agreements, cf. *ibid.*, para. 523.
22. cf. *ibid.*, para. 521.
23. Commission, Draft Revised Guidelines on Horizontal Cooperation, 1 June 2023 (C(2023) 3445 final), paras 518, 519.
24. *Ibid.*, para. 558.
25. EU Commission, Draft Revised Guidelines on Horizontal Cooperation, 1 June 2023 (C(2023) 3445 final), para. 569.

The Commission is willing to take three different types of benefits into account, namely: (i) individual use value benefits (as is already the case today), i.e., benefits that derive directly from the consumption or use of a product covered by the agreement (e.g., a price decrease, as a result of cost efficiencies), (ii) individual non-use value benefits, i.e., indirect benefits resulting from the consumers' (altruistic) appreciation of the impact of their sustainable consumption on others. In these cases, consumers may not directly benefit from an improvement of the product itself but are willing to pay more because of a product is environmentally friendly (and consumers consider this a quality improvement).[26] (iii) Finally, and at first glance revolutionary appears the Commission's willingness to consider collective benefits. These can be defined as potential benefits in the form of positive externalities from which the individual consumer neither benefits directly through consumption nor does the sustainable improvement result in an increased willingness-to-pay. In short, the respective benefits accrue to (parts of) the society outside the market affected by the cooperation. The Guidelines are, however, not entirely clear on these 'collective benefits'. Although out-of-market efficiencies seem to be included, the Commission still requires a substantial overlap of consumer groups and beneficiaries and calls for such benefits to be significant enough to compensate for the harm suffered by the consumers in the affected market.[27] Consequently, 'in cases where collective benefits are dispersed among a large section of society, it is less likely that the overlap with the consumers in the relevant market will be substantial'[28] - which calls into question the concept of 'collective benefits' for sustainability agreements.

The Guidelines unfortunately do not offer any insight into the question of quantifying collective benefits, and it remains unclear which methodology and degree of accuracy will be expected by the Commission. The Guidelines rather state that quantifying these benefits remains an issue and that the Commission will provide further guidance after accumulating experience in dealing with specific cases.[29] The Commission, thus, shifts the risk of applying suitable methods to the enterprises, which raises the overall question of whether businesses will go to the expense and trouble of claiming them at all.

Overall, the draft revised Guidelines show a relatively conservative approach by the Commission.

2.1.2 UK: Draft Guidance on Chapter 1

Early in 2023, the CMA published its Draft Guidance on Chapter 1,[30] in which it dealt in detail for the first time with environmental efficiencies in the context of horizontal

26. Considering the consumers increased WTP the question remains, however, whether agreements resulting in non-use value benefits can regularly be considered 'indispensable' within the meaning of Art. 101(3) TFEU.
27. EU Commission, Draft Revised Guidelines on Horizontal Cooperation, 1 June 2023 (C(2023) 3445 final), paras 584 et seq.
28. *Ibid.*, para. 587, fn. 410.
29. *Ibid.*, para. 589.
30. CMA, 'Draft guidance on the application of the Chapter I prohibition in the Competition Act 1998 to environmental sustainability agreements', 28 February 2023.

cooperation. In the future, the CMA would like to grant companies significantly more leeway if the agreements or concerted practices in question are so-called environmental sustainability agreements.[31] For an exemption of such restrictive but environmentally friendly agreements, four conditions are to be fulfilled cumulatively (which are similar to Article 101(3) TFEU): (i) the agreement must contribute to certain environmental benefits, (ii) both the agreement and its restricting effects must be indispensable, (iii) consumers must receive a fair share of the benefits, (iv) the agreement must not eliminate competition.
Of particular importance for our considerations is a sub-category of these agreements, the so-called climate change agreements. These are agreements that contribute towards the UK's climate change targets binding under domestic or international law, i.e., agreements that focus on reducing negative externalities from greenhouse gases.[32] Climate change agreements are in principle also to be assessed against the above requirements for all environmental sustainability agreements. However, due to their role for combating climate change, the requirement of a 'fair share to the consumer' is handled more generously. The CMA also wants to take into account out-of-market efficiencies. However, the circle of beneficiaries to be included is national, i.e., only the benefits accruing to UK consumers are taken into account when balancing against the harm from restricting competition. The requirement of 'fair share' is therefore also satisfied if the benefits accruing to consumers in the affected market are not sufficient to outweigh the anti-competitive effects, but a compensation can be assumed by including all UK consumers.[33]

The CMA also addresses the quantification in its guidelines. First, it clarifies that quantifying environmental benefits in climate change agreements is not necessary when it is obvious that they fully compensate for the competitive disadvantages. It also discusses - however, without getting specific - methodologies that can be used to quantify environmental benefits.[34]

2.1.3 The Netherlands: Draft Sustainability Guidance

The ACM, too, has published Draft Sustainability Guidelines as early as 2021.[35] The ACM guidelines also provide for a sub-category of 'sustainability agreements', the so-called environmental damage agreements, i.e., agreements between undertakings which aim to reduce negative externalities in the form of environmental damages and,

31. These are 'agreements or concerted practices between competitors and potential competitors which are aimed at preventing, reducing or mitigating the adverse impact that economic activities have on environmental sustainability or assessing the impact of their activities on environmental sustainability', CMA Draft Guidance on Chapter I, para. 2.1.
32. Cf. *ibid.*, para. 2.4.
33. *Ibid.*, paras 6.1 et seqq.
34. *Ibid.*, paras 5.23 et seqq.
35. In contrast to the CMA Guidance, however, these do not only refer to sustainability in relation to the environment but also oriented towards the UN's concept of sustainability, cf. ACM Draft Guidelines on Sustainability Agreements, para. 7; in this respect, sustainability agreements also include agreements that refer, for example, to higher standards in animal welfare, human rights or working conditions.

thereby, aim for a more efficient use of natural resources.[36] As these agreements aim to reduce negative externalities, i.e., social costs of consumption, they shall be much more likely to qualify for an exemption.

Following Article 101(3) TFEU, an exemption requires the cumulative compliance with almost the same four conditions as according to the CMA, i.e., (i) agreement-specific sustainability benefits, (ii) indispensability, (iii) fair share to consumers and (iv) no elimination of competition.[37] The most interesting criterion is again the 'fair share to consumers'. For the standard sustainability agreement, the ACM provides that consumers in the affected markets are to be fully compensated for the competitive harm suffered; out-of-market efficiencies are thus not relevant. However, this is different for 'environmental-damage agreements', insofar as these help in an efficient manner to comply with an (inter)national environmental standard or help to realise an environmental policy goal.[38] In this case, and only in this case, consumers in the relevant market need not be fully compensated for the harm suffered. The ACM justifies this with the fact that the social costs, which should at least be mitigated by the 'environmental-damage agreement', only arise as a result of consumer demand in the relevant market. Since negative externalities are not part of the market price of a product, the consumption-related shift of costs from consumers to the general public should be reversed. The ACM sees the consideration of out-of-market efficiencies thus rather as a correction of the preceding shift of costs than as an original agreement-specific shift that is simply accepted for the sake of combating climate change.[39]

2.1.4 Interim Conclusions

It is thus evident that reforming competition policy towards more sustainability is possible. Both the CMA and ACM expressly point to their open-door policy, but that, ultimately, already today it is to the respective undertakings to provide proof for the merger-specific efficiencies. Still, the authorities should bear in mind that, in order for green antitrust to have the desired effect, a reliable, cost-efficient and uniform methodology for quantification is necessary. To retreat entirely, as the Commission does,[40] to the fact that first sufficient case practice is needed in order to provide guidance for the quantification of 'collective benefits' could end in a vicious cycle in which neither corporations nor authorities dare to take the first step.

2.2 EXISTING INSTRUMENTS UNDER GERMAN COMPETITION LAW

The German national competition authority (*Bundeskartellamt* – Federal Cartel Office, hereinafter "FCO") follows a very conservative course in relation to sustainability

36. ACM Draft Guidelines on Sustainability Agreements, paras 8, 36, 46.
37. *Ibid.*, para. 30.
38. *Ibid.*, para. 45.
39. *Ibid.*, para. 60.
40. EU Commission, Draft Revised Guidelines on Horizontal Cooperation, 1 June 2023 (C(2023) 3445 final), para. 589.

efficiencies. So far, it has neither published draft guidelines nor otherwise attempted to take a progressive course in its practice. While there have been recent decisions[41] with a sustainability dimension, the FCO has not taken a revolutionary new approach but has applied standard competition policy thinking to the agreements in question. Although in its last annual report, the FCO published a concise overview of its approach to cases with a sustainability dimension, its approach is still markedly different from how the CMA and the ACM have tackled the issue.[42] The FCO states, and arguably not without reason, that it does not see itself in a position to carry out such a revision of competition policy by means of a change of guidelines (or other "soft-law" issued by the FCO) or a simply change of case-law. Rather, this would be the task of the legislator, which is – unlike companies and authorities – the only actor to have sufficient democratic legitimacy such an important change. The German legislator will most likely take a position in the context of the planned 12th amendment to the German competition act (*Gesetz gegen Wettbewerbsbeschränkungen* – Act against Restraints of Competition or "**ARC**").[43]

The German merger control regime, however, already provides for two legal instruments which reach beyond traditional analysis of competitive harm, and require a more detailed discussion as to whether they are suitable for considering sustainability benefits: the balancing clause and the Ministerial Authorisation (*Ministererlaubnis*).

2.2.1 Balancing Clause

The so-called balancing clause (section 36(1) no. 1 ARC) allows a merger which is expected to lead to a significant impediment to effective competition ("**SIEC**") not to be prohibited if the merger also leads to improvements in the conditions of competition. These improvements must (i) materialise in markets other than the market negatively affected by the SIEC, (ii) outweigh[44] the SIEC and, (iii) the improvements must occur in (or partially in) Germany.[45] The provision's purpose is to avoid the prohibition of mergers which, after balancing the positive and negative effects still have an overall positive effect on competition.[46] It appears, however, as a far stretch for sustainability efficiencies as such to be considered improvements of conditions of competition. As for

41. FCO case summary, 8 March 2022, B2-72/14; FCO case summary, 10 January 2022, B2-87/21.
42. Also the Hellenic Competition Commission has tackled the issue recently.
43. Federal Ministry for Economic Affairs and Climate Action, 'The Competition Policy Agenda of the Federal Ministry for Economic Affairs and Climate Action up to 2025', 21 February 2022; Haucap, Podszun et al., Wettbewerb und Nachhaltigkeit in Deutschland und der EU, 2023.
44. The literal translation and also the FCO's approach is 'outweigh'. However, especially in consideration of constitutional arguments (proportionality), it is argued that the improvements do not have to outweigh but only compensate for the harm suffered, cf. Ulrich Klump, 'Die "Efficiency Defense" in der Fusionskontrolle', in Wirtschaftsrecht und Wirtschaftspolitik Bd. 204, 1. Ed. 2006, pp. 140 et seqq.; Immenga/Mestmäcker/Thomas, 6. Ed. 2020, GWB § 36, para. 645.
45. *See* FCO's Merger Control Guidelines ('Leitfaden zur Marktbeherrschung in der Fusionskontrolle'), 2012, para. 193.
46. Josef L. Schulte, Handbuch Fusionskontrolle, 3. Ed. 2020, III. Abwägungsklausel, Rn. 640.

improvements to be relevant, they must be of a structural nature, i.e., any improvements to the economy as a whole or non-competition policy public interests[47] are irrelevant. Structural improvements within this meaning can, in particular, be maintaining a large number of competitors in a given market, the continued existence of a brand and thus of competing products or the reduction of barriers to market entry. The realisation of such improvements must be highly likely, substantiated and there must not be a less competitively harmful way to secure the same improvements. Pure sustainability benefits, e.g., cleaner air or a decrease in emissions, could as such not be considered relevant.

The balancing clause, thus, goes further than the efficiency defence in European merger control, where only efficiencies are considered that arise to consumers in the affected market, but not in other markets. However, the balancing clause is interpreted narrowly and very strict requirements are set for proving the claimed improvements.[48] Considering the aforementioned difficulties with quantifying environmental benefits, it, therefore, does not surprise that there is no decisional practice with regard to green efficiencies.

2.2.2 Ministerial Authorisation

The Ministerial Authorisation pursuant to section 42 ARC allows a merger that has initially been prohibited by the FCO to be cleared by the Federal Minister of Economic Affairs and Climate Protection (*Bundeminister für Wirtschaft und Klimaschutz* – hereinafter "Minister"). Again different public interests must be balanced; this time, however, it is (i) a restriction of competition and (ii) macroeconomic benefits or overriding public interests. The ministerial authorisation, by its very conception, is not simple execution of the law (although, pursuant to section 48(1) ARC, the Minister acts as competition authority), the political dimension of the decision is apparent, particularly in view of the vagueness of the statutory provision. While macroeconomic benefits cover aspects like price stability, employment or general economic growth, overriding public interests can be of a social, cultural, ecological or military nature.[49] Lastly, the authorisation may only be granted if the restriction of competition to be authorised by the Minister does not generally jeopardise the market economy.

Contrary to how a court, the Minister does not review the FCO's prohibition decision. He does not (re-)examine whether the concentration leads to a SIEC. In fact, the Minister is bound by the FCO's prohibition decision in two ways: by the FCO's

47. These, however, may be considered in a ministerial authorisation, see below.
48. In *Miba/Zollern* the FCO summarised its approach to assessing the balancing test as follows: 'If a merger leads to the creation or strengthening of a dominant position, an improvement in the conditions of competition can, according to the Bundeskartellamt's constant practice, only outweigh this impediment to competition on the dominated market if it is suitable for reducing or at least mitigating a dominant position on another market. If a merger leads to a significant impediment of effective competition on one market, it must reduce a corresponding impediment of competition on the other market.', cf. FCO B5-29/18, para. 420.
49. Ulrich Klumpp, ,'Die "Efficiency Defense" in der Fusionskontrolle', Wirtschaftsrecht und Wirtschaftspolitik Bd. 204, 1. Ed. 2006, pp. 152 et seqq.

statement of facts (although the Minister may add to those facts through his or her own investigation) and by the FCO's finding of a SIEC.

Interesting from a sustainability point of view was the ministerial authorisation in the *Miba/Zollern* case: Austrian Miba AG and German Zollern GmbH & Co. KG had planned to merge their hydrodynamic plain bearing production activities in a joint venture. The FCO prohibited the concentration in January 2019.[50] It took the view that both companies had a very strong position in the supply of bearings for large bore engines used in ships, locomotives or power generators leading to a combined market share between 60% and 80%. It stressed that customers would lose an important alternative supplier in a market with considerable barriers to entry. The efficiencies and synergies brought forward by the parties were considered under the efficiency defence and – after finding a SIEC – also under the balancing clause of section 36(1) no. 1 ARC.[51] In its assessment of the efficiency defence, the FCO considered sustainability benefits but concluded that the parties' submissions did not meet the relevant requirements. It stated that although some of the synergies claimed by the merging parties appeared plausible, no detailed documents had been submitted to verify them and despite naming specific synergies, the descriptions had remained general and abstract. The FCO, thus, concluded that it had neither been possible to verify the claimed overall potential of the merger nor to critically assess the efficiencies in detail. In addition, the parties had not substantiated that consumers would benefit from these efficiencies in a timely manner. Ultimately, the FCO left it open whether it would have taken these efficiencies into account in its competitive assessment.

In the following decision,[52] the Minister set out that Miba's and Zollern's know-how and innovation potential would have a positive impact on the energy transition and thus on climate protection, which both constituted paramount public interests. Only through joint research the merging parties would be able to make decisive technological progress in slide bearings for wind turbines, for example, increasing their efficiency and reducing noise reduction. However, the Minister found that the concentration nevertheless needed commitments of the parties to outweigh the restrictions of competition. Therefore, Miba and Zollern had to commit to maintain the intended joint venture for at least five years and to invest a minimum of EUR 50 million in Germany during this period.

The decision by the Minister was criticised heavily by legal scholars and the public.[53] Still, it showed that German antitrust law, although (and righteously so) seen as very conservative, has the necessary flexibility to consider public interests that go beyond competition policy. It did, however, also shed light on the deficiencies of the

50. FCO Decision of 17 Jan 2019, B 5-29/18.
51. Cf. *ibid.*, paras 372 et seqq. regarding the 'efficiency defence' and paras 413 et seqq. regarding the 'balancing clause'.
52. German Federal Ministry of Economic Affairs, Reference-No. I B 2 – 20302/14–02, available at: https://www.bmwk.de/Redaktion/DE/Downloads/V/verfuegung-verwaltungsverfahren-miba-zollern.pdf?__blob=publicationFile&v=4 (last accessed: 20 August 2023).
53. Hans Jürgen Meyer-Lindemann, 'Das Ministererlaubnisverfahren: "Wichtiges Element" im "Zentrum der Wirtschaftspolitik"' in Kartellrecht in der Zeitenwende, 1. Ed. 2023, pg. 275 et seqq.; Stöhr/Budzinski, WuW 2019, 508 et seqq.

instrument: Although the decision is evidently highly political, there is no direct parliamentary control over the decision. Democratic legitimation entirely rests with the appointment of the government, which implies that the decision is entirely dependent on the ruling coalition's or party's political agenda.[54]

The key advantage of the current institutional design is a clear delimitation of competences: the assessment of competition is left to the FCO, while the Minister identifies and balances any conflicting public interests. This avoids the issue of an authority dealing with a matter (such as environmental affairs) that it is generally unfamiliar with.

3 CONCLUSIONS

In summary, not even the most progressive European jurisdictions seem to envisage changes towards a green merger control in the near future. The approaches discussed in this section all provide food for thought. However, their common issues remains the quantifying of environmental benefits as well as the reluctance to look beyond the national horizon. With regard to cooperation between undertakings, this may be less harmful. After all, competition authorities can correct a possible exemption decision at any time if the benefits do not materialise to a sufficient extent. With regard to merger control, however, this poses a major problem, as such flexibility simply does not exist. Irrespective of merger control specifically, a general consensus seems to be forming on prospectively (and gradually) taking out-of-market efficiencies into account and on accepting the shift of burden this entails. When considering these efficiencies, however, the scope should not remain purely national. In view of the global crisis that is climate change and in view of the fact that our globalised economy is accelerating this crisis day by day, limiting oneself to the efficiencies that occur solely on a national scale simply does not seem bold enough.

So, should a green merger control be allowed to shift the burden of the energy transition? There seems to be no simple answer. There is no question that competition law could make a contribution to the fight against climate change. Then, the answer to the follow-up question, i.e., the permissibility of a shift of burden by taking out-of-market efficiencies into account, seems obvious: A green merger control would be considerably deprived of its effectiveness if out-of-market efficiencies were not to be taken into account.

54. Arguably, a stronger democratic legitimation is desirable. In fact, the Federal Ministry for Economic Affairs and Climate Action at the beginning of 2022 published a competition policy agenda where it plans to reform the Ministererlaubnis. Specifically, it plans introduce appropriate legal remedies against these decisions and to democratise the procedure by at least partly including the German Parliament in the decision-making process. As of May 2023, there are, however, no indications regarding the specific substance of the reform yet, cf. Federal Ministry for Economic Affairs and Climate Action, 'The Competition Policy Agenda of the Federal Ministry for Economic Affairs and Climate Action up to 2025', 21 February 2022.

Part V EU State Aid Tools: A Fitness Check of Their Appropriateness to Solve the EU Energy Dilemma

CHAPTER 12

The Implications of the Proposed Electricity Market Design Reform on Competition Policy and Notably State Aid Control

Guillaume Gonzalez & Nicola Pesaresi[*]

1 CONTEXT AND PURPOSE OF THE ELECTRICITY MARKET DESIGN REFORM

The past year was marked by a significant gas price surge that spread to electricity prices all over the European Union. Indeed, the European electricity system is dependent on gas import, as gas turbines still represent the main technology to produce electricity when renewable and nuclear outputs are not sufficient to meet the electricity demand. The reductions in gas supply, particularly after the Russian invasion of Ukraine and the weaponization of gas exports, led to an increase in gas prices with a significant impact on electricity prices - especially when gas was the marginal technology of the power system. In addition, as the availability of nuclear and hydropower assets reached record low levels over 2022-2023 (respectively because of delayed maintenance programmes and of the draught endured over 2022), operating costs of gas turbines set the electricity price during most hours ('paid-as-cleared') thus multiplying the impact of this gas crisis on final electricity prices.

As these price rises were rapidly felt by households, industry and businesses across the European Union, the European Commission introduced short-term measures to mitigate the impact of this energy crisis:

* European Commission DG Competition. The views expressed represent the opinions of the authors and should not be taken as the official position of the institution.

- four emergency Regulations were adopted over 2022 to enhance gas storage,[1] coordinate gas demand reduction[2], mitigate the impact of high electricity prices on consumers[3] and implement joint gas purchasing;[4]
- a temporary State Aid framework to allow Member States to intervene in a coordinated manner to provide a rapid emergency response ('Temporary Crisis Framework' (TCF)) was adopted in March 2022. The TCF was then amended twice and then enlarged to enable Member States to benefit from a simplified framework to accelerate the deployment of renewables and industrial decarbonization schemes ('Temporary Crisis and Transition Framework' (TCTF)).[5]

In addition to these short-term measures, the European Commission has prepared structural proposals to better face the possibility of a future fossil fuel crisis. From a State Aid control perspective, an amended General Block Exemption Regulation was endorsed on 9 March 2023 in view to further facilitate and speed up the deployment of standardized support schemes for renewable energy sources (RES) – as accelerating the deployment of RES remains the most efficient way out of fossil fuel dependency.

From a regulatory perspective, the electricity market design (EMD) proposal discussed in this paper represents an important structural development, which aims at: (i) preserving short-term markets, (ii) enhancing the development of longer-term instruments towards better price hedging, and (iii) protecting consumers against future fossil fuel crisis. The proposal follows a public consultation that took place from 23 January 2023 to 13 February 2023 and is also the result of a collaborative dialogue within the European Commission to ensure a consistent approach between market design legislation and State Aid control, building upon the experience that DG Competition developed in case investigations regarding the design of long-term contracts.

2 EFFICIENT SHORT-TERM MARKETS SHOULD BE SAFEGUARDED

The development of European energy markets is a crucial achievement of the EU process of liberalization and integration of national energy markets, carried out through a few EMD packages, in particular the third energy package (Clean Energy Package adopted in 2019) and the subsequent network codes. The development of short-term electricity markets in Member States where they did not exist, the market coupling of day-ahead and intraday markets and the creation of a system for evaluating

1. Regulation 2022/1032.
2. Regulation 2022/1369.
3. Regulation 2022/1854.
4. Regulation 2022/2576.
5. Communication from the Commission on the Temporary Crisis and Transition Framework for State Aid measures to support the economy following the aggression against Ukraine by Russia (C(2023) 1711 final, 9 March 2023), available at: https://competition-policy.ec.europa.eu/state-aid/temporary-crisis-and-transition-framework_en.

and addressing daily needs for balancing reserves at the European level have significantly reduced market failures within the internal market and allowed Europeans to make optimal use of infrastructure and generation resources. This therefore has reduced bills and freed up money to develop relevant electricity projects. The benefits of the integration of short-term markets were extensively documented in the Final Assessment on EU Wholesale Electricity Market Design published in April 2022 by the Agency for the Cooperation of Energy Regulators (ACER).[6]

Short-term markets have also played a key role in managing the energy crisis thereby avoiding major security of supply issues, as they enabled significant energy savings when the system needed it the most and allowed efficient exchange of electricity within the European Union.[7] It is thanks to the European Energy Union and the functioning of integrated short-term markets that electricity kept on flowing throughout Europe and the crisis did not lead to consumers' curtailments and black-outs. Clearly, very high prices have been reached at the peak of the crisis, with serious consequences for all households and industrial consumers. Nevertheless, these price spikes represented more a problem of effective or expected resource scarcity than inefficient or distorted market functioning. It is why the serious consequences induced by such price levels were better addressed through temporary emergency measures, including the use of extraordinary State aid tools, rather than by amending the functioning of short-term markets.

While the objective of the EMD reform is to develop long-term tools to better protect electricity customers against future fossil fuel crises, the European Commission has been very careful to ensure that the design of these long-term contracts preserves incentives from short-term markets for efficient behaviour of both generators and consumers, all of which are crucial to limit market failures and the public support needed to address them.

3 THE MARKET DESIGN PROPOSAL INTRODUCES NEW ELEMENTS TO BETTER PROTECT CUSTOMERS AGAINST VOLATILITY AND TO MANAGE PEAK DEMAND SITUATIONS

The EMD reform proposal introduces provisions aimed at supporting the development of several market-based energy-related products. The EMD proposes, *inter alia*:

- to develop forward market hubs and to allocate long-term cross-border capacity to increase the liquidity of long-term markets (i.e., several years in advance);

6. According to ACER, the benefits of cross-border electricity trading amounted to around EUR 34 billion in 2021 alone. Cf. https://www.acer.europa.eu/events-and-engagement/news/press-release-acer-publishes-its-final-assessment-eu-wholesale.
7. ACER's Final Assessment on EU Wholesale Electricity Market Design notably shows that the benefits of efficient cross-border exchanges significantly increased during the crisis compared to normal market conditions and that the internal market contributed to significantly reduce price volatility during this crisis.

- to facilitate the uptake of market-based Power Purchase Agreements on market terms as a complementary tool to provide revenue visibility and predictability to investors in renewable energy sources and customers based on their lower and decreasing operating costs of renewables;
- to allow the Transmission System Operator to contract peak shaving products (i.e., reduction of power demand in times of peak net demand). National Regulatory Authorities would remain competent to ensure the efficiency of this market measure *('limited to ensure that the expected benefits of the product do not exceed the forecasted costs')*.

What are the implications of these proposals for State aid control? In so far as these instruments are market-based and/or procured independently from the State and without State resources, they may not fall within the scope of State Aid control.

The market transformation that these provisions may trigger will, however, be relevant for the State Aid practice, as any additional revenues arising from the development of these products will need to be taken into account when assessing the necessity and the proportionality of aid (for example, to calculate a project's *'funding gap'*). For example, flexible resources should increasingly be able to stack revenues from different ancillary services, and these various revenues should be taken into account to determine if there is still a need for additional aid to support required projects.

4 ACCELERATING THE DEPLOYMENT OF INFRA-MARGINAL TECHNOLOGIES WHILE HEDGING CUSTOMERS AGAINST FUTURE PRICE VOLATILITY

The EMD reform also deals with instruments that have proven to be useful in the crisis to hedge customers against price volatility, i.e., two-way contracts for difference. These contracts have been developed by Member States to support the electricity production of renewables and low carbon technologies (e.g., solar, wind, nuclear), that are often infra-marginal in the market clearing mechanism, as they don't set the price of equilibrium that clears demand and supply and therefore may profit of an infra-marginal rent corresponding to the difference between the clearing price and their production costs. Two-way contracts for differences allow for limiting the risk associated with market revenues when investing in these technologies and contribute to protecting national customers against high prices, by recouping possible infra-marginal rents. While the proposed definition of these contracts is deliberately rather broad to allow contractual innovation, it entails both protection on the likely minimum remuneration for the generator and a limit to excess remuneration (i.e., clawback mechanism).

The Guidelines on State aid for climate, environmental protection and energy adopted in 2022 already acknowledged that *'where there is significant uncertainty concerning future market developments related to a large part of the business case [...], limits to profitability and/or clawbacks [...] may be required to ensure proportionality'*.[8] As this energy crisis confirmed that high-price periods – and price regulation in times of energy crisis – are not always predictable, the market design proposal requires public authorities to use two-way contracts for difference as a mandatory financing instrument for direct price support schemes[9] for the development of mature low-carbon technologies.[10] Subsequently, the award of new support under one-way contract for differences (i.e., sliding feed-in premium without clawbacks) would, for these technologies, be incompatible with the proposed sectoral law if this provision enters into force.

The proposal for the reform of the EMD contains another important innovation, as it mandates the uniform allocation of the excess revenues from two-way contracts for differences to all consumers on the basis of their electricity consumption. Funding the aid and redistributing the proceeds of contracts for differences to consumers on a pro rata basis – as opposed to the use of budgetary tools – constitutes an important attempt to provide more coherence in the approach to hedging customers against future high prices across the energy Union and to promote a better level playing field among Member States and between competitors. Mandatory, harmonized rules on the redistribution of the proceeds of these contracts to all consumers may not be subject to State aid control. This might also lead to a lower need for ad hoc aid schemes for energy-intensive users, thereby enhancing a level-playing field between European industrial consumers ('avoidance of undue negative effects on competition and trade').

5 INTRODUCING THE OPTION FOR A SUPPORT SCHEME FOR NON-FOSSIL FLEXIBILITIES

The Regulation introduces provisions for flexibility measures to make sure that the European power system disposes of sufficient low-carbon flexibility to integrate further intermittent energy sources. Indeed, maintaining the stability of the power system (in particular, maintaining the electricity frequency at its harmonized level of 50 Hz) requires matching power supply and demand at any point in time. In the context of the accelerated deployment of intermittent RES, developing flexible assets will be crucial to match sudden drop or rise in power generation (hourly flexibility), to supply daily

8. CEEAG 2022/C 80/01 available at https://competition-policy.ec.europa.eu/sectors/energy-environment/legislation_en.
9. Article 2 of the Directive (EU) 2018/2001 of the European Parliament and of the Council of 11 December 2018 on the promotion of the use of energy from renewable sources: '"support scheme" means any instrument, scheme or mechanism applied by a Member State, or a group of Member States, that promotes the use of energy from renewable sources by reducing the cost of that energy, increasing the price at which it can be sold, or increasing, by means of a renewable energy obligation or otherwise, the volume of such energy purchased, including but not restricted to, investment aid, tax exemptions or reductions, tax refunds, renewable energy obligation support schemes including those using green certificates, and direct price support schemes including feed-in tariffs and sliding or fixed premium payments'.
10. The list of these technologies deemed sufficiently mature is detailed in Art. 19b(2) of the draft Electricity Regulation and includes: wind energy, solar energy, geothermal energy, hydropower without reservoir and nuclear energy.

consumption peak when low-carbon generation is not sufficient (daily flexibility) or even to store energy to manage long periods when RES output remains lower than demand (seasonal flexibility). As most flexible units are currently fossil-based, State support may be required in some situations to ensure adequate development of low-carbon flexibilities.

The EMD proposal states that Member States should assess every two years the need for flexibility in the electricity system for a period covering at least the next five years. Such a calculation should be based on a European framework – harmonizing the data inputs and the methodology – proposed by the European federations of European Transmission System Operators (ENTSO-E) and European Distribution System Operators (EDSO) and approved by the ACER.

Article 19f of the draft electricity Regulation introduces a new support scheme for non-fossil flexibilities – with a broader definition than the current scheme for capacity mechanism – to support the development of flexibility in order to: (i) cost-effectively address security of supply issues which are not related to adequacy, and/or (ii) remunerate flexibility activation as opposed to capacity mechanisms that remunerate the availability to produce. Overall, the aim of such measures remains the achievement of security of supply (at least cost and with a mix that respects environmental objectives).

The proposal requires several steps to follow for the introduction of such flexibility schemes. As a first step, Member States shall calculate their flexibility needs based on a cost-benefit analysis based on the afore-mentioned methodology (Article 19c of the Electricity Regulation). To ensure the proportionality of support schemes for flexibility, in situations where market revenues are not sufficient to reach the level of flexibility needs calculated in each Member State, Member States shall investigate the least distortive solutions (e.g., removing entry barriers of existing capacity mechanism) before introducing a separate dedicated support scheme (Article 19e of the Electricity Regulation). While Member States may introduce objective technical criteria to make sure that the laureate capacities can address the security of supply problem identified (e.g., several weeks without wind) and environmental criteria are encouraged, these flexibility auctions should be open to all non-fossil technologies that can comply with these criteria (Article 19f of the Electricity Regulation). The draft Regulation introduces several mandatory design features for these flexibility support schemes which are fully consistent with the approach in force for capacity mechanisms (e.g., no distortion of short-term markets, cross-border participation), thus supporting coherence between support schemes financing flexible resources and other schemes for security of supply.

From a state aid point of view, any such measure for flexibility under these provisions is likely to involve State aid and will need to be assessed under State Aid rules. Flexibility schemes may therefore be assessed under the Guidelines on State aid for climate, environmental protection and energy, which already make it possible to introduce non-discriminatory support measures for flexibility, either as measures for security of supply or as decarbonization measures, depending on their design and effects.

6 PROTECTING EUROPEAN CUSTOMERS AGAINST FUTURE PRICE CRISIS

Article 66a of the draft regulation allows Member States to introduce regulated tariffs below costs for households, microenterprises and small and medium-sized enterprises in price crisis situations – triggered by the European Commission based on objective criteria detailed in the Regulation. Regulated tariffs below costs are an extreme emergency remedy whose availability may provide predictability with respect to the protection of the consumers most in need in case of an established price crisis. Such support schemes would remain under State Aid control to maintain a level playing field and avoid subsidy races – which is even more important in crisis situations.

As examples, the Temporary Crisis and Transition Framework and the General Block Exemption Rules (GBER) both provide a harmonized framework to mitigate the impact of the current energy crisis on consumers – including households, microenterprises and small- and medium-sized enterprises (SMEs). On the one hand, the TCTF allows Member States to provide a limited amount of aid to undertakings affected by the crisis (section 2.1) or a higher amount of aid to compensate for part of the increase in energy bills compared to the reference year 2021 (section 2.4). On the other hand, the GBER sets up a framework to temporarily adopt regulated prices below costs in accordance with the Emergency Regulation to protect against high prices.[11] State support allowed by both frameworks should not remove incentives to reduce consumption in high-price situations, in line with the proposed Electricity Regulation.

7 ENHANCING TRANSPARENCY IN THE INTERNAL MARKET FOR ELECTRICITY

Finally, to ensure competitive markets and transparent price-setting, ACER and national regulators will have an enhanced ability to monitor energy market integrity and transparency. In particular, the updated European Regulation on Wholesale Energy Market Integrity and Transparency(REMIT) will ensure better data quality as well as strengthen ACER's role in investigations of potential market abuse cases of cross-border nature. Overall, this will contribute to the competition in the internal market for electricity by stepping up the protection of EU consumers and industry against market abuse.

8 CONCLUSION

To ensure the development of efficient and non-distortive long-term contracts while protecting European customers against future fossil-fuel crises, the energy market design proposal builds on recent State Aid experience, such as the design of two-way contracts for differences, the deployment of adequate security of supply measures or

11. Regulation 2022/1854.

even time-limited grants as an answer to price shocks. As such, this draft sectorial legislation provides a structural framework for an accelerated and cost-efficient energy transition while maintaining a high-standard security of supply.

CHAPTER 13

The Revised State Aid Toolkit: Fit to Address the Energy Dilemma?

Giorgio Motta[*]

1 INTRODUCTION

The European Green Deal, adopted by the European Commission (Commission) in 2019, sets the goal to achieve climate neutrality in Europe by 2050, in accordance with the Paris Agreement. Only four months after the Commission took office, the outbreak of the COVID-19 pandemic caused an economic crisis as a result of large-scale lockdowns. As the European Union (EU) started to recover from the economic crisis, the Commission directed further investment towards the objectives of the European Green Deal, and in 2021, an intermediate target of reducing net greenhouse gas emissions by at least 55% by 2030 was set.[1]

In late 2021, the EU started to face an energy crisis caused by limited global energy supplies during the economic recovery from the COVID-19 pandemic, lower domestic energy production and reduced natural gas supplies from Russia which was, until recently, the EU's main oil, gas and coal supplier. Russia's invasion of Ukraine in February 2022 and its use of energy as a political weapon led to energy prices reaching record highs. This accelerated the EU's need to transition away from its dependence on Russian fossil fuels and highlighted a broader need to reduce dependence on third countries to ensure the security of supply of energy.

* The opinions expressed in this article are those of the author and do not reflect the views of Skadden Arps or its clients. The author wishes to thank Niels Baeten and Elizabeth Malik for their contributions to this chapter.

1. The EU's targets of achieving climate neutrality in Europe by 2050 and reducing net greenhouse gas emissions by at least 55% by 2030 have been written into legislation by the European Climate Law (Regulation (EU) 2021/1119 of 30 June 2021 establishing the framework for achieving climate neutrality and amending Regulations (EC) No. 401/2009 and (EU) 2018/1999).

By late 2022, it also became clear that the EU was facing competitive pressures for attracting investment in green technologies, in particular from the United States (US) and China. In light of this geopolitical context, together with the effect of high energy prices within the EU, there were calls for the EU to react to prevent clean energy firms from shifting their manufacturing facilities outside of the European Economic Area (EEA) and accelerate Europe's goal of becoming the first climate-neutral continent by 2050.

The Commission took action. In February 2023, it proposed the Green Deal Industrial Plan for the Net-Zero Age (Green Deal Industrial Plan). The Green Deal Industrial Plan was designed to enhance the competitiveness of Europe's net-zero industry and accelerate the transition to climate neutrality by creating a more supportive environment for scaling up the EU's manufacturing capacity for the net-zero technologies and products required to meet Europe's climate targets.

The Commission recognised that reaching the EU's ambitious climate targets, as well as the goal of ensuring the EU's competitiveness in the international context, requires significant private and public funding. The EU's State aid regime, which governs the ability of EU Member States to provide state subsidies to national businesses, therefore plays an important role. The Green Deal Industrial Plan in particular built predominantly on relaxing the State aid rules by facilitating the provision of aid to low-carbon manufacturing in order to retain green technologies within Europe, as well as offering broader categories of compatible aid to allow for public funding of energy projects and sustainable investments to meet the objectives of the European Green Deal.

This chapter sets out the background to the revision of the State aid toolbox for the green transition, examines how those tools have been used since their introduction, and considers whether they are suitable to address the EU's energy challenge.

2 THE STATE AID REGIME AND CRISIS MANAGEMENT

2.1 The State Aid Regime

The main function of the State aid regime is to underpin the single market of the EU, which ensures the freedom of movement of goods, capital and services. The regime was designed to prevent the distortion of competition within the European market that may arise as a result of preferential treatment given by Member States, which each have different budgets, to firms and industries located on their territory.

State aid refers to selective financial support (subsidies in the form of grants, tax reductions, interest-free loans, etc.) granted by Member States to undertakings within the EU/EEA. The EU's State aid rules are contained in Articles 107 to 109 of the Treaty on the Functioning of the European Union (TFEU), which prohibit all State aid by Member States unless it is deemed 'compatible' with the single market for reasons of general economic development. Compatibility assessments are based on Article 107(2) of the TFEU when an intervention *shall* be compatible with the internal market, and Article 107(3) of the TFEU when a measure *may* be considered as compatible with the internal market. The main rationale is that there needs to be some sort of market failure that requires public funding to help support, and not distort, the normal forces of competition on the market.

The objective of State aid control is to ensure that, when needed to achieve the objective pursued, such aid does not unduly distort competition and trade between Member States. State aid control is the exclusive competence of the Commission. As a result, the Commission defines the conditions under which it will consider State aid to be compatible with the single market in soft law instruments, such as guidelines or temporary frameworks.

For large amounts of aid or more complex measures, Member States are required to notify planned aid to the Commission, which is then responsible for assessing and issuing a decision on whether the aid meets the compatibility conditions. Member States may notify aid schemes (on the basis of which individual aid awards may be made to undertakings without needing to notify individually to the Commission), or ad hoc aid to individual companies (which must be approved on a case-by-case basis).

To minimise the burden of notification, a General Block Exemption Regulation (GBER) was adopted in 2008, which declares certain categories of aid as compatible with the single market where they meet certain conditions. Accordingly, individual aid measures or an aid scheme falling within the scope of the block exemption do not require prior notification to or approval of, the Commission. The scope of the GBER has been expanded since its introduction in 2008, and the current version[2] applies across a range of sectors and numerous types of aid measures such as aid for environmental protection and energy, aid for local infrastructures and aid to support small- and medium-sized enterprises (SMEs).

The Commission has also issued guidance and adopted additional Regulations with the aim of further simplifying the process of State aid notification and approval. These include, for example, the *de minimis* Regulation, which exempts small aid amounts from the scope of EU State aid control because they are deemed to have no impact on competition and trade in the internal market.[3]

2.2 Temporary State Aid Frameworks

Over time, there have been challenges to the State aid regime which demanded rapid action, such as the financial and economic crisis of 2008-2009, the coronavirus pandemic, Russia's war on Ukraine and most recently the increasingly urgent need for a green economic transition. In these exceptional circumstances, the Commission has introduced temporary frameworks which allow Member States to support their economies by means of more direct intervention through the adoption of temporary measures derogating from State aid rules for a limited period.

2. Regulation (EC) 651/2014 of 17 June 2014 declaring certain categories of aid compatible with the internal market in application of Articles 107 and 108 or the Treaty, (OJ L 187, 26 June 2014), as amended.
3. Commission Regulation (EU) 2023/2831 of 13 December 2023 on the application of Articles 107 and 108 of the Treaty on the Functioning of the European Union to *de minimis* aid.

In a temporary framework, the Commission sets out the criteria it will use to assess various typical aid measures required in the specific context under Article 107(2) and/or Article 107(3) of the TFEU. Measures that meet the conditions set out in the temporary framework must still be notified to the Commission, but the Commission will approve the aid as compatible. Often, this significantly accelerates the notification and approval procedure. Temporary frameworks therefore provide clarity to Member States that measures designed to address the challenge in question will be compatible where they fall within the boundaries specified in the framework.

3 BACKGROUND TO THE REVISED STATE AID TOOLKIT

3.1 The European Green Deal and the Initial State Aid Toolbox

The European Green Deal is the EU's main growth strategy to transition the EU economy to a sustainable economic model. Presented in December 2019, it involves a broad roadmap to make the EU economy and society carbon neutral by 2050.[4]

The implementation of the European Green Deal depends in part on large-scale mobilisation of public and private funding, and State aid plays an important role in this. The Commission therefore started to adjust its State aid toolbox to allow for public funding to meaningfully contribute to the achievement of the Green Deal.

In 2019, the Commission carried out a 'Fitness check' of a number of State aid rules and guidelines to evaluate whether they were still necessary and fit for purpose. The Commission published the results of its fitness test in October 2020.[5] The package broadly passed the test, but the Commission deemed some changes necessary, in particular, in light of the challenges ahead in the form of the EU Green Deal. This led to the revision of a number of existing State aid instruments.

The Guidelines on State Aid for Climate, Environmental Protection, and Energy 2022[6] (CEEAG) were a central part of this initial State aid reform. The CEEAG were adopted by the Commission on 27 January 2022 and, although they do not have an end date, will be evaluated as of 31 December 2027. They replaced the Guidelines on State Aid for Environmental Protection and Energy 2014-2020[7] (EEAG) which were extended by one year in 2020.

The CEEAG provide the conditions that an individual aid measure or an aid scheme for climate, environmental protection and energy must fulfil in order to be authorised in the context of a notification to the Commission under Article 107(3)(c) of the TFEU. The CEEAG have a broader scope than the EEAG, with new categories including (amongst others) aid for the reduction and removal of greenhouse gas

4. Annex to the Communication from the Commission, 'The European Green Deal', COM (2019) 640 final.
5. Commission Staff Working Document, 'Fitness Check of the 2012 State aid modernisation package, railways guidelines and short-term export credit insurance', SWD (2020) 257 final.
6. Commission, 'Guidelines on State aid for climate, environmental protection and energy 2022', COM (2022) OJ C 80.
7. Commission, 'Guidelines on State aid for environmental protection and energy 2014-2020', COM (2014) OJ C 200.

emissions including support for renewable energy and energy efficiency. The CEEAG also include a wider variety of aid instruments, including decarbonisation aid in the form of contracts for difference.

Some categories of aid measures are explicitly excluded from the scope of the CEEAG, such as State aid for nuclear energy (which has to be evaluated under the Euratom Treaty and general State aid rules) and all aid measures falling under sector-specific rules that contain provisions on environmental protection and energy, such as State aid for research, development and innovation (which is dealt with under the framework for Research, Development and Innovation[8] (RDI framework), discussed below).

The Regional Aid Guidelines[9] were also updated following the announcement of the Green Deal. The revised Regional Aid Guidelines, which came into force on 1 January 2022, allow: (i) additional support for less developed areas, (ii) increased aid intensities for projects supporting the Green Deal, and (iii) the possibility of combining regional aid and aid under the CEEAG.

From 1 January 2022, the revised Important Project of Common European Interest (IPCEI) framework[10] also started to apply. The IPCEI framework applies to projects of strategic significance for the EU involving cross-border collaboration between Member States and industry and is designed to facilitate the growth of new technologies and production processes in line with Green Deal objectives. The revised IPCEI Communication sets out the criteria under which Member States may support such cross-border projects under Article 107(3)(b) of the TFEU. The potential IPCEI project must, in particular, contribute to a common objective by supporting a key value chain for the future of Europe and aim to develop technologies and processes that go beyond what the market currently offers. IPCEIs must be notified to, and approved by, the Commission. Approved IPCEIs include a project to support the development of innovative and sustainable technologies for lithium-ion batteries; a project to contribute to the development of significant new technological breakthroughs in the battery value chain; and projects designed to boost the supply of renewable and low-carbon hydrogen.

Finally, the Commission adopted a revised RDI framework in October 2022. The revised framework aimed to simplify the rules on State support for research, development and innovation and align them with the Green Deal by facilitating aid for investments in green technology. Amongst other things, it introduced the possibility of granting aid to support the construction and upgrade of testing and experimentation infrastructures (also known as technology infrastructures) which are expected to play a role in contributing to the green transition.

8. Commission, 'Framework for State aid for research and development and innovation', COM (2022) OJ C 414.
9. Commission, 'Guidelines on regional State aid', COM (2021) OJ C 153/01.
10. Commission, 'Criteria for the analysis of the compatibility with the internal market of State aid to promote the execution of important projects of common European interest', COM (2021) OJ C 528.

3.2 Energy Prices: The Temporary Crisis Framework

In autumn 2021, gas and electricity prices rose to unprecedented highs. In October 2021, the Commission published a toolbox proposing several measures to address the high prices and secure energy supplies.[11] This set out the measures which Member States could take under the existing legislative and State aid frameworks.

Following the start of the Russian invasion of Ukraine in February 2022, the prices for gas and electricity increased substantially. The dependency on Russian fossil fuels refocused attention on one of the cornerstones of the European Green Deal: increasing energy autonomy and supply from renewable energy sources.

The Commission took several measures with the goal of mitigating the negative effects of the energy price volatility on the economies of the Member States. As part of this action, on 23 March 2022, the Commission adopted a Temporary Crisis Framework,[12] which enabled Member States to act quickly and effectively in adopting aid measures in favour of companies affected by the considerable economic uncertainties while facilitating the transition to clean energy, the disruption to trade flows and supply chains, and the exceptionally sharp and unexpected price rises. It was due to run until 31 December 2022. It provided for limited amounts of aid for undertakings affected by the crisis (section 2.1), liquidity support in the form of guarantees (section 2.2) and subsidised loans (section 2.3) and aid for additional costs due to exceptionally severe increases in natural gas and electricity prices (section 2.4).

The Commission extended the scope of application of the Temporary Crisis Framework as it became clear that the effects of the war were going to continue for some time, and in order to implement RepowerEU.[13] The first amendment, made on 20 July 2022,[14] addressed the need to become less dependent on fossil fuels through the inclusion of provisions on aid for the rollout of renewable energy, storage and renewable heat (new section 2.5) and aid for the decarbonisation of industrial production processes (section 2.6). On 28 October 2022, the Commission prolonged and amended the Temporary Crisis Framework once again.[15] Most notably, the Commission included a new section (section 2.7), which addressed aid for additional reduction of electricity consumption.

3.3 Global Competition for Green Technologies: The EU Green Deal Industrial Plan

The recent geopolitical and economic events (most notably the COVID crisis and Russia's invasion of Ukraine) are effectively global in scope and have had global

11. Commission, 'Tackling rising energy prices: a toolbox for action and support', COM (2021) 660 final.
12. Commission, 'Temporary Crisis Framework for State Aid measures to support the economy following the aggression against Ukraine by Russia', COM (2022) OJ CI 131/1.
13. Commission, 'REPowerEU Plan', COM (2022) 230 final.
14. Commission, 'Amendment to the Temporary Crisis Framework for State Aid measures to support the economy following the aggression against Ukraine by Russia', COM (2022) OJ C 280/01.
15. Commission, 'Temporary Crisis Framework for State Aid measures to support the economy following the aggression against Ukraine by Russia', COM (2022) OJ C 426/1.

implications. As a result, these events have triggered a global race to the adoption and expansion of investments in green technologies.

The US adopted the Inflation Reduction Act (IRA) on 16 August 2022, a legislative package which includes (amongst other things) an estimated USD 369 billion in tax credits and direct subsidies to promote the adoption of clean energy in the US over ten years.

The IRA includes: (i) subsidies for vehicle purchases, including tax credits for electric cars and or companies that buy clean vehicles; (ii) production and investment subsidies for manufacturers of clean-tech products such as batteries; and (iii) subsidies for producers of carbon-neutral electricity as well as hydrogen and other clean fuels. Several of these subsidies are conditional on content being 'made in America', which discriminates against foreign producers.

These local content requirements sparked concerns within the EU that the IRA could result in the relocation of European businesses' production facilities to the US to benefit from large subsidies and cheaper energy. In parallel, China has been investing heavily in green technologies such as wind power generation, batteries and electrolysers. This reinvigorated a discussion on how to foster fair competition not only inside the EU but also on how to make its industries competitive globally through targeted state subsidies.[16] Member States were divided on whether a revision of the State aid rules was a suitable response to increasing global competition. The Member States with the most spending power - Germany and France - urged the Commission to loosen State aid restrictions, whereas other Member States considered that it would risk fragmenting the single market further, particularly in light of the temporary relaxation of the regime that was already in place.[17]

In early 2023, largely in response to rising global competition in the context of the limited supply of raw materials and products necessary for the transition to a net-zero economy, the EU announced the Green Deal Industrial Plan.[18] The Green Deal Industrial Plan complemented progress under the Green Deal; it was designed to make Europe the home of clean tech and industrial innovation and to promote the clean tech manufacturing capacity required to meet Europe's ambitious green targets. It is based on four complementary pillars: (i) a predictable and simplified regulatory environment; (ii) speeding up access to finance; (iii) enhancing skills; and (iv) open trade for resilient supply chains. EU State aid law was pinpointed as a key implementation tool for the second pillar, accelerating investment and financing for clean tech production

16. On 15 December 2022, President von der Leyen acknowledged that the global competition was rising and explicitly mentioned the IRA: Ursula von der Leyen, 'Speech by President von der Leyen at the European Parliament Plenary on the preparation of the European Council meeting of 15 December 2022' (European Parliament Plenary, Strasbourg, 14 December 2022).
17. For example, eleven Member States urged the Commission to exercise great caution in relaxing the State aid rules in a document dated 10 February 2023 (Denmark, Finland, Ireland, Poland, Sweden, the Netherlands, Hungary, Latvia, the Czech Republic, Slovakia and Belgium); Valdis Dombrovskis, Frans Timmermans and Margrethe Vestager also wrote an op-ed in the Financial Times on 26 January 2023 warning that 'a tit-for-tat reaction risks significant economic self-harm'; available here: https://www.ft.com/content/0bf3708d-20fe-4700-8702-bd0f6ef55 91e.
18. Commission, 'A Green Deal Industrial Plan, for the Net-Zero Age', COM (2023) 62 final.

in the EU. To this end, the Commission introduced a package of reforms to EU State aid law to encourage Member State support measures in sectors essential to the transition to a net-zero-emissions economy.

4 STATE AID REFORMS TO ACCELERATE THE GREEN TRANSITION

On 9 March 2023, following the announcement of the EU Green Deal Industrial Plan, the Commission adopted new State aid rules to accelerate the energy transition. The package comprised a revised and rebranded temporary framework together with an amended GBER. Ad-hoc environmental aid measures not subject to the temporary framework or exempt from notification under the GBER could still be approved, for example, on the basis of Article 107(3)(c) of the TFEU together with the CEEAG or the RDI framework.

4.1 Temporary Crisis and Transition Framework

The centrepiece of the Commission's green State aid package was the new Temporary Crisis and Transition Framework (TCTF).[19] The TCTF built on, and prolonged, the Commission's Temporary Crisis Framework. While the Temporary Crisis Framework focused on reducing fossil fuel use, the TCTF (and the Green Deal Industrial Plan more broadly) also looked at enhancing low-carbon manufacturing and retaining green technologies within Europe.

4.1.1 Extension of Aid Linked to the Effects of War in Ukraine

In relation to the pre-existing categories of aid schemes more directly linked to crisis consequent to the war in Ukraine (sections 2.1-2.4 and 2.7), the Commission amended the Temporary Crisis Framework by prolonging those measures from 30 June 2023 until 31 December 2023 and relaxing the application of those provisions in certain respects, such as by allowing the calculation of maximum aid ceiling on a per Member State basis for limited amounts of aid (section 2.1, which is aimed at relatively low and simple aid grants to businesses affected by the crisis). These aid categories continued to be based on Article 107(3)(b) of the TFEU, which allows aid to be granted in order to remedy a serious disturbance in the economy of a Member State.

The evolving geopolitical context necessitated a further extension of some of these provisions. Shortly before the end of 2023, the temporal scope of section 2.1 (limited amounts of aid) and section 2.4 (aid for additional costs due to exceptionally severe increases in natural gas and electricity prices) were extended from 31 December

19. Commission, 'Temporary Crisis and Transition Framework for State aid measures to support the economy following the aggression against Ukraine by Russia', COM (2023) OJ C 101/3.

2023 until 30 June 2024.[20] At the same time, the ceilings for limited amounts of State aid (section 2.1), which includes aid in the form of direct grants, tax and payment advantages or other forms such as repayable advances, guarantees loans and equity, were raised slightly. The provisions in sections 2.2 (liquidity support in the form of guarantees), 2.3 (liquidity support in the form of subsidised loans) and 2.7 (aid for additional reduction of electricity consumption) expired on 31 December 2023.

4.1.2 Simplification of Aid for Renewable Energy and Storage

The TCTF prolonged, from 31 December 2023 until 31 December 2025, the existing possibility for Member States to grant aid on the basis of approved aid schemes to support renewable energy production as well as energy storage (section 2.5) on the basis of Article 107(3)(c) of the TFEU, which allows aid to be granted to facilitate the development of certain economic activities or certain economic areas. No cap on the aid is set, but the aid must be awarded on the basis of a scheme with an estimated capacity volume and budget.

The amendments broadened the scope of section 2.5. The provisions were extended to include all renewable energy sources (as defined in the Renewable Energy Directive), including renewable hydrogen and hydrogen-derived fuels (but exclude electricity production from renewable hydrogen). The framework continued to cater for the increasingly crucial role of storage for the integration of renewable energy in the electricity system. The provisions were also clarified to include aid granted not only to newly installed capacities but also to repowered capacities. The amendments also simplified the application of section 2.5. For example, the aid calculation no longer requires a competitive bidding process for less mature clean tech, for which tenders may work less well.

The TCTF permitted aid not only for investment (i.e., aid to companies to support investments in new production facilities, such as land, buildings, plant, machinery, and intellectual property) but also for operation (i.e., aid for the normal costs of running a business, such as salary costs, rents and utility bills). Both types of aid therefore contribute to the economic feasibility of environmental protection measures, but in different ways.

Investment aid may be granted for: (i) the production of energy from renewable sources; (ii) electricity storage and thermal storage; and (iii) investments in storage for renewable hydrogen, biofuels, bioliquids, biogas and biomass fuels. Unusually, the maximum aid intensity for this aid (expressed as a percentage relative to the 'eligible costs', in this case, investment costs) was increased to 100% of the total investment cost if the aid is granted in a competitive bidding process; otherwise, it remains at 45% of the total investment. Investment aid may take the form of direct grants, repayable advances, loans, guarantees or tax advantages, and notably tax credits (this amendment in the

20. Commission, 'Amendment to the Temporary Crisis and Transition Framework for State Aid measures to support the economy following the aggression against Ukraine by Russia', COM (2023) OJ C/2023/118.

TCTF was motivated by the investment tax credits that are the basic aid vehicle in the US IRA).

The addition of operating aid is also unusual, as aid for the normal costs of running a business is seen by the Commission as more likely to cause market distortions by directly supporting variable production costs and is only allowed in exceptional circumstances. Moreover, the Commission expressly permitted investment aid to be cumulated with operating aid for the same projects under section 2.5, provided that the notified aid scheme foresees that possibility at the time of its initial notification. To prevent overcompensation, the Commission specified that operating aid must only be granted in the form of two-way contracts for difference, which is notably more limited than other aid categories under the TCTF. The aid amount is determined either through a competitive bidding process or with a strike price set by the relevant energy regulator to cover expected net costs.

4.1.3 Simplification of Aid for Decarbonisation

To encourage a reduction in the dependency on imported fossil fuels, the TCTF prolonged from 31 December 2023 until 31 December 2025 and made minor amendments to the possibility of Member States setting up aid schemes aimed at the decarbonisation of industrial production (section 2.6) on the basis of Article 107(3)(c) of the TFEU.

Aid for the decarbonisation of industrial processes must reduce greenhouse gas emissions via a switch to the electrification of the production process or to the use of renewable or low-carbon electrolytic hydrogen. Again, the investment aid may be granted in the form of direct grants, repayable advances, loans, guarantees, or tax advantages. The TCTF clarified that tax credits were a permitted form of aid.

The TCTF did not amend the requirement that the investment must lead to at least a 40% reduction of greenhouse gas emissions from industrial activities currently relying on fossil fuels by means of electrification of the production processes or a 20% reduction of energy consumption in industrial activities and processes. The TCTF continues to offer the possibility for the aid to cover 100% of the difference between the costs of the project and the cost savings or additional revenues, compared to the situation in the absence of the aid, over the lifetime of the investment (the eligible costs) where the aid amount is determined through a competitive bidding process. Otherwise, the aid intensity for projects remains at a maximum of 40% of the difference between the costs of the eligible costs. The intensity may be increased by 10% to 20% for SMEs and by an additional 15% for investments delivering higher reductions of greenhouse gas emissions or energy consumption. The TCTF introduces a higher maximum aid intensity of 60% of the eligible costs linked to investment costs such as the costs of equipment, machinery or installations other than for electrification projects, for which the aid intensity is set at 30%.

The maximum individual aid amount per undertaking is generally limited to 10% of the overall State aid scheme budget for decarbonisation, and the TCTF capped the allowable individual aid at EUR 200 million per undertaking. The TCTF also clarified that the aid may be cumulated with other aid. Finally, the TCTF extended the completion periods for the installation or equipment to be financed by the investment.

4.1.4 New Aid for Industrial Production in Strategic Net-Zero Sectors

The TCTF introduced a new possibility for Member States to support investments in sectors with 'strategic importance for the transition towards a net-zero economy' to ensure that they do not relocate outside the EU/EEA because of better subsidies elsewhere (section 2.8). These measures would be approved on the basis of Article 107(3)(c) of the TFEU. Section 2.8 was primarily an attempt to remain competitive compared with third non-EU countries such as the US and represents one of the most radical changes ever made to the EU State aid regime.

The Commission's position under the general State aid rules was, in principle, not to approve aid facilitating industrial production except for initial investments in less economically advantaged areas ('assisted areas') and under specific conditions. Section 2.8 now enables Member States to grant aid for investments in the production of the following strategic net-zero equipment: batteries, solar panels, wind turbines, heat pumps, electrolysers, equipment for carbon capture usage and storage (CCUS), as well as key components designed and primarily used as direct input for the production of this equipment. This list of equipment closely follows the scope of the IRA.

The aid must be granted by 31 December 2025, and the investment must be maintained in the area concerned for at least five years (or three years for SMEs) after completion of the investment. The risk that the investment would not take place in the EEA without the aid must be demonstrated, as well as the absence of relocation of the investment within the EEA. The Member State concerned will also have to provide detailed information on the investment, including its expected positive effects for the area concerned in terms of job creation, R&D activities, etc. The aid may be granted in the form of direct grants, or other forms such as tax advantages, subsidised interest rates on new loans or guarantees on new loans.

Section 2.8 provides for the possibility of establishing an aid scheme or granting individual aid. In the case of an aid scheme, the maximum aid intensity may vary from 15% to 60% of the investment costs incurred depending on the size of the beneficiary, the location of the investment as well as the form of the aid. For large companies, the aid intensity may not exceed 15% of the investment costs, with a maximum aid amount of EUR 150 million per undertaking per Member State where the aid is directed at non-assisted areas. The aid intensity increases to 20% of investment costs (capped at EUR 200 million per undertaking per Member State) for investments directed at sparsely populated areas ('c'-assisted areas); and increases to 35% of investment costs (capped at EUR 350 million per undertaking per Member State) for investments directed at areas with low economic growth ('a'-assisted areas). These aid intensities may be further increased by 5% when the aid is granted in the form of tax advantages, loans or guarantees; and increased by a further 10% to 20% for investments made by SMEs.

The TCTF introduces a major novelty: on the basis of individual notification, the Commission may exceptionally approve the grant of aid to a company to match the level of subsidy that would be available outside of the EU (so-called *matching aid*) or the amount needed to incentivise the company to locate the investment in the EEA (the '*funding gap*'), whichever is lower. Given the exceptional nature of this aid, a number of conditions apply to qualify for matching aid. For example, the Commission prescribes that the investment must take place in assisted areas of the EU or – in cases of cross-border investments – if the investment includes at least three Member States, with a significant part of the overall investment taking place in at least two assisted areas. The beneficiary must also commit to using state-of-the-art production technology from an environmental-emissions perspective and show that the aid does not create counter-cohesion effects, for instance, because the project could have been located in an even poorer area of the EEA.

In attaching these conditions to the grant of individual aid, the Commission aims to incentivise businesses to invest in areas where there is still potential for economic development, and thereby strengthen the EU's cohesion policy.

4.2 GBER Amendment

The TCTF was accompanied by an amendment to the GBER.[21] These amendments were introduced to align the GBER with the revised State aid guidelines and frameworks, such as the CEEAG and the RDI framework, and to bring the GBER in line with the EU policy priorities as expressed in the European Green Deal (as well as the Industrial and Digital Strategy). The GBER amendment was endorsed on 9 March 2023, after a long period of revision that started in 2019 with an evaluation of the State aid rules, a targeted revision of the GBER in July 2021,[22] and a public consultation launched in October 2021.[23] The amended GBER entered into force on 30 June 2023 and has been extended until the end of 2026.

The revised GBER incorporated changes to various different categories of aid, including RDI aid, training aid, regional aid and training aid. In line with the Commission's objectives, the most extensive amendments were made to aid in environmental protection and energy. The amendments provided for broader aid categories for green projects, together with increased notification thresholds and maximum aid intensities for several categories of aid. This widened the scope of application of the GBER and is expected to result in even fewer formal notifications to the Commission.

21. Commission, 'Approval of the content of a draft for a Commission Regulation amending Regulation (EU) No. 651/2014 declaring certain categories of aid compatible with the internal market in application of Articles 107 and 108 of the Treaty and Regulation (EU) 2022/2473 declaring certain categories of aid to undertakings active in the production, processing and marketing of fishery and aquaculture products compatible with the internal market in application of Articles 107 and 108 of the Treaty', COM (2023) 1712 final.
22. Commission, 'State aid: Commission simplifies rules for aid combined with EU support and introduces new possibilities to implement aid measures supporting the twin transition and the recovery from coronavirus pandemic that was not subject to a public consultation', press release, 23 July 2021. This revision was not subject to consultation.
23. Commission, 'State aid: Commission invites comments on draft proposal to further facilitate implementation of aid measures promoting the green and digital transition', press release, 6 October 2021.

The thresholds for environmental aid as well as aid for RDI projects increased significantly. For example, the thresholds for operating aid for renewable energy and aid for recharging infrastructure both doubled from EUR 15 million to EUR 30 million (per undertaking, per project), and the threshold for energy infrastructure increased from EUR 50 million to EUR 70 million. Moreover, for many types of aid, the maximum aid intensity rates were raised. Where the aid is granted through competitive procedures or on the basis of the funding gap methodology, the aid intensity can be up to 100%.

Certain provisions were made simpler for Member States to apply. For example, instead of stipulating that the 'aid shall not exceed the difference between eligible costs and the operating profit of the investment' with respect to support of energy infrastructure, the new text simply says that the 'aid intensity may reach up to 100 percent of the funding gap.'[24]

There was also an extension and facilitation of the possibilities for aid in the area of environmental protection and energy, such as to support the rollout of renewable energy, facilitate investments in green hydrogen, support decarbonisation projects, increase energy efficiency or support green mobility. The amendments also facilitated the implementation of certain IPCEI-related projects by means of higher aid intensities and notification thresholds.

4.3 EU Funding to Support the Green Transition

Contrary to other jurisdictions, the TCTF does not create any common fund to strategically invest in Green Deal technologies, which means that each individual member State must provide the required public funding. Not all Member States are, however, in a position to support the green transition to the extent proposed by the Commission. EU funding therefore remains critical to the success of the revised State aid package.

The Green Deal Industrial Plan envisaged increasing EU funding by redirecting financial resources already available under REPowerEU (a plan to reduce energy use, increase clean energy production and diversify energy supplies), the InvestEU Programme (which provides a budget guarantee for public and private investments in sustainable infrastructure and R&D) and the Innovation Fund (which supports the development of new technological solutions that decarbonise energy-intensive industry), as well as by increasing financing volumes generally. A pilot auction was also launched under the Innovation Fund in November 2023 to award up to EUR 800 million to renewable hydrogen producers in the EEA, in the form of a fixed premium in EUR/kg of renewable hydrogen over ten years.[25] The Green Deal Industrial Plan explained that the competitive bidding process was designed to have a similar impact as the production tax credit in the US IRA.

24. Article 48 GBER. The 'funding gap' is the net extra cost determined by the difference between (i) the economic revenues and costs of the aided project and (ii) those of the alternative project which the aid beneficiary would carry out in the absence of aid; *see* Art. 2, para. 118 GBER.
25. Commission, 'Commission launches first European Hydrogen Bank auction with €800 million of subsidies for renewable hydrogen production', press release, 28 November 2023.

Also announced was a new European Sovereignty Fund with, crucially, new funding to support critical and emerging technologies relevant to the green (and digital) transitions, and to enhance all Member States' access to such projects. While details of the proposed Sovereignty Fund were not fully set out, the Green Deal Industrial Plan recognised that it would '[safeguard] cohesion and the Single Market against risks caused by unequal availability of state aids.'[26] However, due to the failure to establish the Sovereignty Fund, the Commission announced in June 2023 the Strategic Technologies for Europe Platform (STEP) initiative to replace it. STEP included a proposal for existing funding to be directed towards areas of technological development that are crucial for Europe's leadership and only an extra EUR 10 billion for existing programmes in an effort to mobilise investment in critical technologies. The scope of the fund was also narrowed to three sectors deemed critical: deep tech, clean tech and biotech. On 17 October 2023, the relevant European Parliament committees endorsed the STEP proposal and adopted amendments to broaden its scope to allow for a Sovereignty Fund. It remains under discussion in the Council, which is seeking to reduce the EUR 10 billion in new funding to EUR 1.5 billion.

5 IS THE REVISED TOOLKIT FIT TO ADDRESS THE ENERGY DILEMMA?

5.1 Accelerating the Green Transition

Switching the EU's reliance on fossil fuels to renewable energy sources is critically important in tackling the energy crisis. The simplification and broadening of the possibilities to establish aid schemes to support renewable energy production as well as, crucially, storage, has boosted the ability of Member States to invoke this part of the TCTF. Five schemes have already been approved under the revised section 2.5, whereas none of the measures under the Temporary Crisis Framework was based on this provision.[27]

The new possibility to provide investment aid of up to 100% of the total investment cost has already been taken up by Italy in a scheme to provide EUR 450 million of aid for developing renewable hydrogen production capacities in brownfield industrial areas.[28] This amendment was important, as investment aid under the previous framework may have failed to cover the increased costs of investment because of the lower maximum aid intensities. The new possibility to provide

26. Commission, 'A Green Deal Industrial Plan, for the Net-Zero Age', COM (2023) 62 final, p. 13.
27. Overview of the list of Member State measures approved as of 24 March 2023, available here: https://emeca.eu/public/2023-05/EEIA_European_State_Aid_Temporary%20Crisis%20Framework%20Ukraine_12_05_2023.pdf. The majority of the aid approved under the TCTF to date has concerned the pre-existing categories of aid more directly linked to crisis consequent to the war in Ukraine (sections 2.1-2.4 in particular), in particular through the provision of direct grants to support sectors affected by the crisis. There has not yet been any cases approved under section 2.7, which allows aid for additional reduction of electricity consumption.
28. State Aid SA.106007 (2023/N) – Italy TCTF: RRF – Italy: Support for the development of hydrogen valleys.

operating aid has also been taken up by Lithuania, in a scheme to provide up to EUR 192 million of both investment and operating aid for the construction and operation of an offshore wind farm as well as (importantly) its connection to the grid.[29] The novel ability to offer both investment and operating aid to the same project is also significant and is likely to encourage further environmental aid projects, as they are often capital-intensive and require various combinations of aid.

The decarbonisation of existing industrial processes will also play a central role in achieving the EU's green targets. However, the Commission's revisions to the TCTF in this regard (section 2.6) are less expansive than those for renewable energy production and storage, which may hold back Member States from pursuing such activities. Section 2.6 only provides for investment, and not operating, aid, whereas industrial decarbonisation projects require both high investment costs and high operating costs for their implementation. Notably, only one scheme has been approved under the revised section 2.6 in the first ten months of the framework (and none of the measures under the Temporary Crisis Framework were based on this provision): a Czech scheme to provide over EUR 2 billion of aid to support the electrification of production processes, use of renewable hydrogen, or use of renewable hydrogen-derived fuels.[30]

The amended GBER also contains several positive developments. The GBER enables Member States to support their economies using a wider range of measures and to grant larger amounts of aid, without the administrative burden of notification. The importance of the GBER should not be underestimated: more than 90% of State aid measures are implemented without prior notification to the Commission under this tool.[31]

The broader package of EU measures, of which the revised State aid rules form only a part, will also play an important role in accelerating the EU's transition to net zero. As just one example, the use of the TCTF by EU countries may be incentivised by coming legislation, such as the Net-Zero Industry Act[32] which sets a benchmark of 40% of EU deployment needs for the green transition to be covered by manufacturing capacity of strategic net-zero technologies located in the EU.

5.2 Ensuring Global Competitiveness for Green Technologies

The adjusted State aid rules will provide a level of flexibility that should, in principle, enable Member States to compete with the aid available in foreign jurisdictions, most notably the US and China. Member States now have the ability to give sector-specific tax breaks (which the Commission has taken a very restrictive approach to in the past) and use the new category of matching aid. Nevertheless, the EU measures are structured

29. State Aid SA.102871 (2023/N) – Lithuania TCTF: Offshore wind support scheme.
30. State Aid SA.109055 (2023/N) – Czechia TCTF: Modernisation Fund – Programme ENERG ETS.
31. Letter from Executive Vice-President Vestager to national ministers, 13 January 2022, available here: https://www.politico.eu/wp-content/uploads/2023/01/16/Letter_EVP_Vestager_to_Ministers__Economic_and_Financial_Affairs_Council__Competitiveness_Council_aressv398731.pdf.
32. Commission, 'Proposal for a regulation of the European Parliament and of the Council on establishing a framework of measures for strengthening Europe's net-zero technology products manufacturing ecosystem (Net Zero Industry Act)' COM (2023) 161, SWD (2023) 68.

quite differently from the US ones, and some argue that the IRA framework is wider and easier to access and navigate. In particular, the TCTF requires the individual notification and approval of schemes and ad hoc aid projects, which can take several months. Nonetheless, the Commission is acutely aware of the need to speed up its process, and some approvals, including under the new section 2.8 for strategic sectors, have been obtained by Member States in less than a month.

The strategic equipment which falls within the scope of section 2.8 reflects the scope of the IRA, despite calls from some Member States to adopt a more tailored position. For example, the Netherlands submitted that the EU should only target investments in sectors specifically needed for the green transition to prevent strategic dependencies instead of matching the aid granted by third countries in a knee-jerk reaction to rising global competition.[33] Time will tell how the Commission's strategy plays out.

The Commission has already approved ten instances of State aid on the basis of section 2.8, which enables aid for investments in sectors strategic for the green transition where investments are at risk of being diverted away from the EEA. These schemes have been put forward by various Member States so far: Austria, Belgium, France, Germany, Hungary, Italy, Slovakia and Spain. Some of these schemes support the production of all strategic technologies available under the TCTF,[34] whereas others target only a selection of the in-scope technologies[35] or specific technologies such as batteries for use in electric vehicles[36] or electrolysers.[37]

The first (and currently, the only) individual aid under section 2.8 was approved in January 2024. The measure concerned EUR 902 million of German aid to Swedish battery manufacturer Northvolt to support the construction of a production plant for

33. HT. 6323 Response of the Netherlands to the consultation on a draft proposal to amend the State aid Temporary Crisis Framework to support the EU economy in the context of Russia's invasion of Ukraine.
34. State Aid SA.109989 (2023/N) – Slovakia TCTF: State aid scheme for providing Extraordinary Investment Aid in sectors strategic for the transition to a net-zero economy in accordance with section 2.8 of the Temporary Crisis and Transition Framework; State Aid SA.108068 (2023/N) – Germany TCTF: Aid to support the transition to a net-zero economy; and State Aid SA.107689 (2023/N) – Hungary TCTF: scheme for accelerated investments in sectors strategic for the transition towards a net-zero economy (although Hungary envisioned that the scheme would mainly be used by the electric vehicle battery industry.
35. State Aid SA.109334 (2023/N) – France TCTF: Tax credit for investments in green industries (aid for solar panels, wind turbines, batteries and heat pumps); State Aid SA.109169 (2023/N) – Belgium RRF-TCTF: Decarbonisation of Walloon companies – Enhancing investments in value chains linked to the energy transition (aid for batteries and electrolysers); State Aid SA.108653 (2023/N) – Spain RRF – TCTF: scheme for projects of equipment necessary for the transition towards a net-zero economy (batteries, solar panels, wind turbines, heat-pumps and electrolysers); and State Aid SA.109170 (2023/N) – Austria TCTF – Scheme for accelerated investments in sectors strategic for the transition towards a net-zero economy (batteries, solar panels, wind turbines, heat-pumps and electrolysers).
36. State Aid SA.107094 (2023/N) – Spain RRF – TCTF: Integrated action line on the industrial value chain – Batteries.
37. State Aid SA.108953 (2023/N) – Italy TCTF: RRF – Investment aid scheme for the production of electrolysers.

electric vehicle batteries in the North German town of Heide.[38] The Commission confirmed that, without the aid, Northvolt would have established the plant in the US where support was offered under the IRA. Germany's economy minister, Robert Habeck, noted that Northvolt chose the region because of the windy conditions and high renewable energy output. Heide was also an assisted area, which made it possible for the measure to meet the conditions attached to the grant of individual aid under section 2.8. It remains to be seen whether these conditions might similarly be met for projects which rely more on direct access to economic hubs, such as CCUS which must be installed on existing power plants.

Overall, it is clear that section 2.8 is starting to meet its objective of ensuring that green value chains in manufacturing stay within the EU, at least with the backing of less fiscally restrained Member States. This is important because the EU does not have sufficient industrial production capacity to meet the rapidly growing demand for technologies necessary for the transition towards a net-zero economy, especially from domestic production. For example, there are major dependencies in the photovoltaic industry, where almost 90% of photovoltaic cells are produced in Asia. The battery and wind power value chains are also highly dependent on and economically vulnerable to third countries. Therefore, the risks of not having such value chains develop in the EU seem to outweigh the costs of industrial policy support.

5.3 Maintaining the Single Market

The Commission's approach to the new State aid rules is mindful that the additional flexibility to compete globally entails significant risks for competition and cohesion in the internal market, which the State aid rules aim to prevent.[39] The TCTF therefore includes a number of safeguards to the new category of aid for strategic sectors, which, so far, appear to have avoided 'opening the floodgates.' For instance, SMEs, as well as businesses located in assisted areas, are eligible for higher amounts of support. Also, individual aid can only be granted where the investment is fully directed at an assisted area or, where it involves cooperation across at least three Member States (a requirement included to ensure that 'any public support granted to a rich region should pull other regions along'[40]), a significant part must take place in at least two assisted areas.

38. Commission, 'Commission approves €902 million German State aid measure to support Northvolt in the construction of an electric vehicle battery production plant to foster the transition to a net-zero economy', press release, 8 January 2024 (non-confidential decision has not yet been published). The Commission's Executive Vice-President Margrethe Vestager confirmed that Germany had not gone as far as matching the subsidies in offer in the US, but offered 'enough for the investment to take place in Europe.'
39. The Commission's Executive Vice-President Margrethe Vestager, while emphasising that any changes to State aid rules in response to the IRA 'must preserve the integrity of the single market', also admitted that 'European countries are not equal when it comes to State aid.' According to the statistics released by the Commission, since March 2022, Germany and France together account for 77% of the EUR 672 billion approved programmes under the Temporary Crisis Framework.
40. Remarks by Executive Vice-President Margrethe Vestager on the proposal for a State aid Temporary Crisis and Transition Framework, 1 February 2023.

While these safeguards duly take cohesion objectives into account, they cannot be expected to fully mitigate the risk of internal market fragmentation given the different fiscal power of each Member State. Notably, Germany is already in the lead with EUR 3.9 billion of approved aid under section 2.8, followed by France with EUR 2.9 billion and Spain with EUR 1.4 billion.

This fiscal inequality could be addressed, at least partially, through increased EU funding. However, there remains a lack of EU funding within the already complicated landscape of funds; the EUR 10 billion of new funding announced as part of the STEP fund is insufficient to tackle the crisis, and may even be reduced to a mere EUR 1.5 billion.

5.4 A Short-Term Tool for a Long-Term Crisis

The Commission has primarily chosen the instrument of a temporary State aid framework to encourage Member States to invest in green technologies, the same tool that was used to help address the financial crisis in 2008-2009, the COVID-19 pandemic in 2020 and the effects of the Russian aggression against Ukraine in 2022.

The Commission's strategy with the TCTF (and the Green Deal Industrial Plan more broadly) is to focus on the innovation and early-stage deployment of new low-carbon technologies, whereas the IRA focuses on reducing the running costs of production. The idea is that nascent technologies produced within the EU may become more efficient once a certain scale has been reached and require less public support. However, it remains to be seen whether the transitional framework will have served its purpose by 2026 and whether the Commission will be inclined to extend the TCTF even in the absence of a sufficient EU budget which puts the Member States on a more equal footing. Germany has already started campaigning for the extension of the TCTF and is likely to step up its campaign following the November 2023 ruling of the German Federal Constitutional Court[41] which effectively reduced Germany's Climate and Transformation Fund (from which many subsidies are being or are intended on being paid) by EUR 60 billion.

The climate crisis and EU competitiveness do not clearly represent a temporary challenge in the same way as, for example, a health pandemic – they are likely to remain a challenge for future generations. By choosing the temporary framework as a tool, the Commission potentially closes off the possibility for medium to long-term aid instruments. Its current end date of 31 December 2025 is also out of line with both the IRA (which extends under 2032) and the EU target of a reduction of at least 55% of greenhouse gas emissions by 2030.

5.5 Role of EU Industrial Policy

It is ultimately for Member States to consider whether and how to use the possibilities provided for in the State aid framework to offer financing incentives to companies

41. Judgment of 15 November 2023, case 2 BvF 1/22.

driving the EU's energy transition. This might lead to a patchwork of uncoordinated approaches within the EU, as well as multiple incentive systems at the EU and national levels, which prevents innovative European companies from reaching a scale that is sufficient to compete globally such as with counterparts in the US and China. There have therefore been increasing calls for the EU to develop a comprehensive and overarching green industrial policy at the EU level instead of expanding State aid at the national level,[42] something which to date has been resisted by Member States who see industrial policy as an issue of national sovereignty and competition.

6 CONCLUSION

In designing the scope of the Green Deal Industrial Plan, the Commission was faced with a dilemma: on the one hand, it did not want green industries to relocate production outside of the EEA yet; on the other hand, it had to protect the internal market, notably by applying the EU State aid rules and maintaining a level playing field between the Member States. For these reasons, the revised State aid package essentially represents a compromise with both benefits and drawbacks. This has led some commentators to argue that State aid is not the appropriate tool to facilitate the green transition. The debate on the need for greater industrial policy is likely to continue into the next political mandate, and it remains to be seen what impact the 2024 European elections will have on the EU's energy strategy.

Ultimately, reaching the EU's ambitious climate goals, as well as the goal of improving or at least maintaining the EU's competitiveness in the international context, cannot only depend on State aid law. The revised State aid tools are part of a larger initiative, and successful implementation of all elements of this strategy will be key to ensuring European competitiveness in the long term.

42. *See*, for example, 'A Green Industrial Policy for Europe', Brugel, December 2020.

CHAPTER 14

Emergency State Aid Rules in the Energy Sector: A Temporary Episode or a Long-Lasting Legacy?

Francesco Maria Salerno

1 INTRODUCTION

The EU emergency law is a subset of rules within the EU legal structure that, in parallel with the constitutional traditions of EU Member States, enables 'urgent exceptional and consequently temporary actions ... not permissible when ordinary conditions exist'.[1] The TFEU provisions on State aid are part of this subset of rules.

Building on this legal basis, in March 2022 the European Commission ('Commission') adopted the 'Temporary Crisis Framework to enable Member States to support the economy in the context of Russia's invasion of Ukraine'. This Framework was prolonged and modified until March 2023, when the Commission adopted the 'Temporary Crisis and Transition Framework for State Aid measures to support the economy following the aggression against Ukraine by Russia'.

The Framework is an emanation of these EU emergency rules with a significant impact on the energy sector. This chapter tries to assess such impact. In particular, the chapter investigates the deviation from the normal State aid rules and whether such deviation is a purely temporary episode.

1. Greene, *Emergency Powers in a Time of Pandemic* (Bristol University Press, 2020), p. 12. For the notion of EU emergency law, *see* De Witte, Guest Editorial, 59 *Common Market Law Review* (2022), 3-18 DOI: 10.54648/cola2022002.

2 EU EMERGENCY LAW AND STATE AID

In many States, there is an 'emergency constitutional law', granting designated authorities the power to suspend temporarily the normal constitutional rules to tackle 'urgent threats to core community values and structures'.[2]

By contrast, according to de Witte, 'the European Union does have its own body of law that can be described as emergency law. This is not a coherent body of law found in one place of the legal system, but rather a complex and disparate set of rules found in many different parts of primary and secondary law, supplemented by institutional practice and judicial interpretations'.[3] Among this 'disparate set of rules' forming the *corpus* of EU emergency law, one can find two provisions dealing with State aid:

- Article 107(2)(b) TFEU, stipulating that 'aid to make good the damage caused by natural disasters or exceptional occurrences', shall be treated as compatible aid by the Commission. This provision has been used extensively during the COVID period.
- Article 107(3)(b) TFEU – the second part, according to which 'aid ... to remedy a serious disturbance in the economy of a Member State' may be declared compatible with the internal market.

As the Court of Justice held,[4] these two provisions can apply concurrently, insofar as an event – in casu, the COVID-19 pandemic – may be classified both as an 'exceptional occurrence' within the meaning of Article 107(2)(b) TFEU and as an event giving rise to a 'serious disturbance in the economy' within the meaning of Article 107(3)(b) TFEU.

Nevertheless, when describing the State aid components of the EU emergency law, de Witte only refers to Article 107(3)(b) TFEU. One reason for excluding Article 107(2)(b) is that, while connected with urgent threats and potentially sharing with Article 107(3)(b) TFEU the same triggering event, compensation for damages is a backwards-looking measure, in the sense that it only seeks to remedy a prejudice that occurred in the past.

By contrast, Article 107(3)(b) TFEU has wider implications, since it allows Member States to grant, and the Commission to authorise, wider categories of aid measures.

In addition, the Court of Justice also clarified that Article 107(3)(b) TFEU differs from Article 107(3)(c) TFEU – the legal basis to authorise aid in 'normal times', due to the 'particular nature' of the aid measures referred therein.[5] More specifically, according to the Court of Justice, Article 107(3)(b) TFEU is limited to aid measures contributing to specific objectives outlined in such provision (either the execution of an

2. *See* Boin, 't Hart and McConnell, 'Crisis Exploitation: Political and Policy Impacts of Framing Contests', 16 *Journal of European Public Policy* (2008), 81-106, 83 DOI: 10.1080/13501760802453221.
3. De Witte, Guest Editorial, *Common Market Law Review*, cit., p. 5.
4. Judgment of 28 September 2023, Ryanair/Commission (C-320/21 P) ECLI:EU:C:2023:712, point 51.
5. Judgment of 23 November 2023, Ryanair/Commission (C-209/21 P) ECLI:EU:C:2023:905.

important project of common European interest or remedying a serious disturbance in the economy of a Member State): once an aid measure is found to contribute to one of these objectives 'of an exceptional nature',[6] then 'the Commission is not required to carry out a new balancing of those effects when it examines the compatibility of aid which is envisaged to be granted on the basis of that provision'.

Article 107(3)(b) TFEU was relied upon in March 2020 to adopt the Temporary Framework for State aid measures to support the economy in the current COVID-19 outbreak (the 'Covid TF').[7] Through a series of six amendments, the Covid TF remained in force until 30 June 2022, with investment support expiring on 31 December 2022 and solvency support on 31 December 2023.

In March 2022, Article 107(3)(b) TFEU was again relied upon to adopt the Temporary Crisis Framework for State Aid measures to support the economy following the aggression against Ukraine by Russia (Temporary Crisis Framework (TCF)).[8] There have been several amendments to the TCF;[9] in March 2023, the Commission adopted a significant amendment of the TCF, renaming it the Temporary Crisis and Transition Framework (TCTF).[10] The TCTF was further amended on 20 November 2023.[11] This amendment extends the TCTF until June 2024.

Under the TCTF, Member States have several possibilities to grant aid in the energy sector to remedy the serious disturbance stemming from the aggression of Ukraine. Point 75 of the TCTF states that these measures are expressly designed to go beyond the 'existing possibilities available in accordance with Article 107(3)(c) TFEU', thus underscoring the difference between (i) emergency State aid rules for the energy sector and (ii) 'normal' State aid rules for the energy sector, where the reference must be to the rules in the 2022 Guidelines on State aid for climate, environmental protection and energy (the '2022 Guidelines').[12]

The remainder of this chapter tries to assess the difference between such emergency rules and the 'normal' rules, with a view to 'measuring' the distance between the two and, in so doing, gauging the extent to which the emergency rules are a significant departure from normal rules. In turn, these findings provide a basis to address the research question underlying this paper as to the impact of the emergency rules for the direction of travel of State aid in the energy sector, i.e., whether the emergency rules are a purely temporary episode or whether their impact may go beyond the emergency.

3 THE EMERGENCY STATE AID RULES IN THE ENERGY SECTOR

The paragraphs below describe the TCTF's sections with implications for the energy sector. In particular, the section discusses first the general provision enshrined in

6. Judgment of 23 November 2023, Ryanair/Commission, cit., point 87.
7. OJ [2020] C91 I/1.
8. OJ [2022] 131 I/1.
9. 20 July 2022, 28 October 2022.
10. OJ [2023] C101/1.
11. OJ C, C/2023/1188.
12. OJ [2022] C 80/1.

section 2.1 because it has a direct link with the increase in energy costs. Then, there is a description of two sections addressing energy consumers and energy projects. Lastly, there is a description of the provisions for the transition to the Net-Zero economy.

Section 2.1

Section 2.1 of the TCTF allows the granting of limited amounts of aid to undertakings affected by the crisis, including, where applicable, for rising energy costs. Such measures are limited to EUR 2.25 million per undertaking (or EUR 280,000 for undertakings active in the primary production of agricultural products, and EUR 335,000 for undertakings active in the fishery and aquaculture sectors) per Member State.

In terms of beneficiaries, this measure is not specific to energy operators. However, it remains a measure of State aid in the energy sector, since the primary reason justifying the aid is the increase in such energy costs. Thus, it can be considered essentially a measure to alleviate energy costs. Case SA.107640 (2023/N) – Italy TCTF: Sicilian Energy Bonus is a good illustration:[13]

- The Sicilian Energy Bonus consists of direct grants handed out to undertakings in Sicily active in all sectors, save for a few exceptions (among which, notably, agriculture, fishery, and banking).
- The objective of the scheme is to alleviate part of the financial burden caused by the cost increase of gas and electricity in 2022, compared to 2021 prices and, thereby, to help overcome financial difficulties caused by the energy crisis.
- The scheme entails a maximum nominal amount of aid of EUR 200,000 per undertaking and an aid intensity of up to 30% for an estimated budget of EUR 150 million.
- The Commission concluded that the scheme is necessary, appropriate and proportionate to remedy a severe disturbance in the economy of Italy and, thus, approved the scheme under Article 107(3)(b) TFEU and under section 2.1 of the TCTF.

Section 2.4

Section 2.4 allows the granting of aid to alleviate the consequences of exceptionally severe increases in natural gas and electricity prices. The rules set out a methodology for calculating eligible costs, which consist of the difference between the energy price paid in the eligible period (1 February 2022 and 30 June 2024) and 1.5 times the energy price paid in the reference period (1 January 2021 to 31 December 202), further multiplied by a discount factor where the aid is referred to eligible periods after September 2022.

13. OJ C/2023/91. Decision in case State Aid SA.107640 (2023/N) – Italy TCTF: Sicilian Energy Bonus – C(2023) 5507 final of 9 August 2023.

The structure of the formula was specifically studied to achieve multiple objectives at the same time.

On the one hand, the formula allows Member States to shoulder an important share of the extra costs incurred by the aided companies to help them weather the crisis. On the other hand, two provisions ensure that market mechanisms are not overrun by the aid: (i) the fact that the price in the reference period must be multiplied by 1.5 provides an adjustment of 2021 prices (which were abnormally low in historical terms), and (ii) the discount factor seeks to ensure that affected companies retain incentives to lower their energy consumption and, at the same time, that the production prices partly reflect increased energy prices.

Also, the discount factor bridges the gap between the aided period and the foreseeable non-aided future, allowing market prices to start to reflect the increased costs and thereby, *inter alia*: (a) reducing the consumption of aided goods, and (b) increasing companies' willingness to invest in energy efficiency.

While the general aid cap is set at EUR 4 million per undertaking with a maximum aid intensity of 70%, in specific instances, the overall aid can reach EUR 50, EUR 100 or EUR 150 million per beneficiary undertaking.

Undertakings that qualify as 'energy intensive businesses'[14] must prove that they suffered a reduction in EBITDA (excluding aid) of at least 40% in the eligible period compared to the reference period or a negative EBITDA (excluding aid). In such cases:

(a) if they are active in one (or more) of the sectors or sub-sectors listed in Annex I,[15] the overall aid per beneficiary may be increased to a maximum of 80 % of the eligible costs and the overall aid per undertaking per Member State may not exceed EUR 150 million at any point in time;
(b) if they are not active in sectors or sub-sectors listed in Annex I, the overall aid per beneficiary may reach a maximum of 65% of eligible costs, and the overall aid may not exceed EUR 50 million per undertaking per Member State.

Undertakings that are not energy intensive are not subject to specific EBITDA requirements. The aid can reach EUR 100 million and must not exceed 40% of the eligible costs.

A good example of the application of section 2.4 of the TCTF is case State Aid SA.104385 (2022/N) – Hungary TCTF: Aid for additional costs due to exceptionally severe increases in natural gas and electricity prices.[16]

14. The TCTF defines 'energy intensive businesses' as those legal entities in which the purchases of energy products (including energy products other than natural gas and electricity) amount to at least 3.0% of the production value or turnover, based on data from the financial accounting reports for the calendar year 2021. In the alternative, the TCTF allows data for the first semester of 2022 to be used, in which case the beneficiary may qualify as 'energy-intensive business' if the purchases of energy products (including energy products other than natural gas and electricity) amount to at least 6.0% of the production value or turnover.
15. Annex I to the TCTF, reading 'Particularly affected sectors and sub-sectors'.
16. OJ [2023] C276/1. Decision in case State Aid SA.104385 (2022/N) – Hungary TCTF: Aid for additional costs due to exceptionally severe increases in natural gas and electricity prices – C(2023) 2583 final of 13 April 2023.

The measure consists of an aid scheme in the form of guarantees and loans, with a maximum of: (i) EUR 4 million per undertaking and an aid intensity of up to 50 % for all undertakings, or (ii) the maximum aid intensities set out above. The estimated total budget of the measure is a nominal amount of EUR 1 billion, directed towards companies which suffered extraordinary energy price increases.

Originally foreseen to expire on 31 December 2023, the measure was later prolonged until 30 June 2024.[17] The Commission concluded that the scheme is necessary, appropriate, and proportionate to remedy a severe disturbance in the economy of Hungary and, thus, approved the scheme under Article 107(3)(b) TFEU and under section 2.4 of the TCTF.

Section 2.5

Section 2.5 allows the granting of aid to accelerate the rollout of renewable energy and energy storage for a wide range of renewable energy sources and for hydrogen. The admissible aid includes investment aid and operating aid, and the timeframe for aided projects is significantly longer than that foreseen for sections 2.1 and 2.4, i.e., 31 December 2025. This is because, while the aid under sections 2.1 and 2.4 aims to alleviate temporary high energy costs, section 2.5 designs a proactive approach aiming to shape medium-term energy policy.

Investment aid can take any form, including grants and subsidised loans, and is subject to several conditions listed under letters from a. to q., point 77 of section 2.5.1 of the TCTF.

In particular, the investment aid amount can be determined either via a competitive bidding process or administratively by the Member State concerned. The main difference between the two hypotheses resides in the fact that aid granted following competitive bidding processes can reach 100 % of the investment, whereas aid based on costs administratively set can reach 45 % of the investment (which can be increased by 10 percentage points in case the beneficiary is a medium-sized undertaking or by 20 percentage points if the beneficiary is a small-sized undertaking).

Operating aid is granted in the form of two-way contracts for differences in relation to the energy output of the installation, with a maximum duration of contract set at twenty years after the installations start operation and is subject to several conditions listed under letters from a. to p., point 78 of section 2.5.2.

In particular, the operating aid amount can be determined either through a competitive bidding process or with the strike price administratively set by the energy regulatory authority. However, aid for the production of electricity via solar photovoltaic, onshore and offshore wind, and hydropower must be only granted via a competitive bidding process.

17. State Aid SA.110218 (2023/N) – Hungary TCTF: Prolongation of and amendments to the schemes SA.104385 and SA.103089 (amended by SA.104009, SA.104850, SA.106542, SA.107379). Decision C(2023) 8609 final of 6 December 2023.

A good example of aid granted under section 2.5 is case State Aid SA.106613 (2023/N) – Slovenia TCTF: Investment aid for accelerating the introduction of energy from renewable sources, storage and heat from renewable sources.[18]

The measure consists of an aid scheme in the form of direct grants, with a maximum of EUR 25 million per undertaking per project. Slovenian authorities opted to administratively set the costs of the measure, resulting in an aid intensity of up to 45% of the total investment cost which may be increased by a further 20% for SMEs or 10% for Mid-caps. The aim of the scheme is to accelerate the rollout of renewable energy (with a total of 600 MW) and energy storage (up to 550 MWh). The estimated total budget of the measure amounts to EUR 150 million. The Commission concluded that the scheme is compatible with the internal market and, thus, approved the scheme under Article 107(3)(c) TFEU and under section 2.5.1 of the TCTF.

Section 2.8

Section 2.8 allows the granting of aid in manufacturing sectors that are deemed 'strategic' for the transition towards a net-zero economy. Aid can be granted to incentivise the production of renewable energy equipment (solar panels, batteries, wind turbines, heat pumps, electrolysers, and equipment for carbon capture usage and storage), the production of components used as direct input for the production of said equipment, and the production or recovery of related critical raw materials.

The admissible aid can take any form, including direct grants and subsidised loans, and the timeframe for aided projects is significantly longer than that foreseen for sections 2.1 and 2.4, i.e., 31 December 2025.

Aid intensity may reach 15% of eligible costs, with a maximum of EUR 150 million per undertaking per Member State, which can be increased up to 20% (and EUR 200 million) in 'c' areas or to 35% (and EUR 350 million) in 'a' areas.[19]

A good example of aid granted under section 2.8 is case State Aid SA.108953 (2023/N) – Italy TCTF: RRF-Investment aid scheme for the production of electrolysers.[20] The measure consists of an aid scheme in the form of direct grants (with a maximum of EUR 150 million per undertaking), an aid intensity of up to 15% of the eligible costs, and an estimated budget of EUR 100 million. The aided project will concern the production of electrolysers. The Commission concluded that the scheme is compatible with the internal market and, thus, approved the scheme under Article 107(3)(c) TFEU and under section 2.8 of the TCTF.

In terms of permissible aid amount, section 2.8 includes a 'matching clause', allowing the Member State to match the aid amount that the beneficiary was offered in

18. OJ [2023] C231/11. Decision in case State Aid SA.106613 (2023/N) – Slovenia TCTF: Investment aid for accelerating the introduction of energy from renewable sources, storage and heat from renewable sources. Decision C(2023) 3855 final, of 9 June 2023.
19. Please note that 'c' areas are defined as assisted areas designated in the applicable regional aid map for the Member State concerned in accordance with Art. 107(3)(c) TFEU, whereas 'a' areas are defined as assisted areas designated in the applicable regional aid map for the Member State concerned in accordance with Art. 107(3)(a) TFEU.
20. OJ [2023] C258/1. Decision State Aid SA.108953 (2023/N) – Italy TCTF: RRF-Investment aid scheme for the production of electrolysers – C(2023) 6798 final of 9 October 2023.

a jurisdiction outside the EU. A good illustration is the decision to authorise a German measure worth EUR 902 million to support Northvolt in the construction of a production plant for advanced and high-efficiency electric vehicle batteries in the city of Heide, a city in a disadvantaged area as defined under the German regional aid map.

Under the measure, the aid will take the form of a EUR 700 million direct grant and a EUR 202 million guarantee. According to the Commission press release,[21] without the aid, Northvolt would establish the plant in the United States, where the same amount of support was offered in particular under the Inflation Reduction Act.

In addition, the project was eligible because Northvolt committed to 'building the world's most environmentally-friendly battery, which produces significantly less CO_2 emissions than other companies when measured on produced level including recycling at the end of life', including through the use of fossil-free energy in the production and a circular design of the production process, including recycling of battery cell materials.

4 COMPARING THE EMERGENCY STATE AID RULES IN THE ENERGY SECTOR WITH THE NORMAL RULES

The paragraphs below follow a benchmark-comparison methodology, assessing the provisions in the TCTF against corresponding provisions in the 2022 Guidelines. Then, there is an attempt to measure the distance between emergency and normal rules using a scale from 1 to 3 (where 3 is the highest level of deviation).

4.1 Section 2.1: The General Provision to Alleviate Increase in Energy Costs Compared with the Normal State Aid Rules in the 2022 Guidelines

The 2022 Guidelines do not have a provision that is comparable to section 2.1 of the TCTF.

More specifically, the 2022 Guidelines do grant the possibility to cover operating costs. For instance, point 48 of the 2022 Guidelines sets out the general principle that the funding gap analysis to determine proportionality includes the investment and operation of the aided project.

However, aid is connected to an investment project, falling into one of the categories in the 2022 Guidelines. Thus, the aid to cover operating costs is connected to, e.g., the production of electricity from renewable energy sources or the separate collection and sorting of waste in relation to specific waste streams or types of waste.

By contrast, section 2.1 of the TCTF allows Member States the possibility to grant aid in the face of higher energy costs, but without any connection to any investment or commitment on the part of the beneficiary. Thus, the aid under section 2.1 of the TCTF stands out as a measure of pure alleviation of certain (increased) operating costs, departing from the 'normal' aid measures to a very significant extent.

21. The press release is available at: https://ec.europa.eu/commission/presscorner/detail/en/ip_23_6823.

In sum, the distance is very significant, given that the normal rules do not foresee anything comparable and, even more, it would be hard to conceive as compatible aid in normal times an aid measure that essentially does nothing to change the behaviour of consumers in the energy sector and, in fact, simply metes out money to lessen the costs of consuming energy.

4.2 Section 2.4: The Provision for Energy-Intensive Users Compared with the Normal State Aid Rules in the 2022 Guidelines

Points 399-419 of the 2022 Guidelines cover State aid in the form of reductions from electricity levies for energy-intensive users. The only levies concerned are those that have, as their objective, the financing of energy and environmental policy objectives. Notably, point 399 of the 2022 Guidelines clarifies that such levies are not considered '*environmental levies*' within the meaning, and for the purposes, of section 4.7.1, given that they do not target any negative externality. Finally, general system charges for electricity, or levies on the consumption of other forms of energy (e.g., natural gas) are not covered by this section.

The rationale for allowing this type of is, however, similar in many respects to reduction in environmental taxes: while electricity levies are needed to fund the Union's decarbonisation objectives, energy-intensive industries may be disproportionately impacted to the point of causing severe drawbacks to society because, if energy-intensive industries were fully exposed to such levies, there will be: (a) an increase in the cost of electrification in crucial sectors, and/or (b) delocalisation towards third countries.

In order to minimise the distortions on competition and trade potentially arising from the reduction of electricity levies, the 2022 Guidelines require Member States to meet the following requirements.

– ***Eligibility***

Annex I of the 2022 Guidelines lists the sectors that meet eligibility criteria, which are divided into two categories: (1) sectors at significant risk and (2) sectors at risk. The distinction is a new feature of the 2022 Guidelines compared to the 2014 Guidelines and reflects the incidence of electricity costs on enterprise turnover.

Moreover, eligibility criteria are listed for each category, leaving it to Member States to include other sectors, provided that they respect the trade intensity and electro-intensity criteria calculated according to point 405, letters (a) and (b) of the 2022 Guidelines.

Finally, a non-discrimination clause is set out at point 407 of the 2022 Guidelines, pursuant to which any decision by a Member State to grant different levels of support to a subset of eligible beneficiaries falling within the same category of sectors ('at significant risk' or 'at risk'), must be made according to objective, non-discriminatory, and transparent criteria.

- ***Proportionality***

The 2022 Guidelines set out a method to calculate proportionality entailing two alternative systems, both foreseeing differences between sectors at significant risk and sectors at risk, plus a further provision, which, provided that certain conditions are respected, extends the beneficial criteria for sectors at significant risk to sectors at risk.

(i) Under the first system, described at point 408 of the 2022 Guidelines, two levels of aid are possible, depending on the sectors that form the object of the scheme, plus a threshold that applies to both:
   - For sectors at significant risk, the beneficiaries must pay at least 15% of the costs generated by the electricity levies that are part of the aid scheme, whereas for sectors at risk, the percentage is increased to 25%.
   - Further, the aid schemes must not result in a levy below EUR 0.5 per MWh, irrespective of the sector.

(ii) Under the second system, described at point 409 of the 2022 Guidelines, two levels of aid are possible, depending on the sectors that form the object of the scheme, plus a threshold that applies to both:
   - For sectors at significant risk, Member States can limit the additional costs resulting from the electricity levies to 0.5% of the gross value added of the undertakings concerned, whereas for sectors at risk, the percentage is increased to 1%.
   - Further, also under this system, the aid schemes must not result in a levy below EUR 0.5 per MWh, irrespective of the sector.

Finally, under point 410 of the 2022 Guidelines, the aid intensities described under both systems above and referred to enterprises in sectors at significant risk may be extended to sectors at risk, provided that: (i) beneficiaries will cover at least 50% of their electricity consumption from carbon-free sources, out of which either (ii) at least 10% will be covered by a forward instrument (such as a power purchase agreement), or (iii) at least 5% will be covered by on-site or near-site generation.

Form of State aid

The 2022 Guidelines prescribe that Member States can grant the aid: (a) in the form of a reduction in levies, (b) as a fixed annual compensation amount (refund), or (c) as a combination of the two. If the aid is granted, in total or in part, in the form of a reduction in levies, the 2022 Guidelines request that an *ex-post* monitoring mechanism be put in place to avoid overcompensation.

- ***Energy Audits and Management Systems***

Beneficiaries receiving aid in the form of reductions from electricity levies for energy-intensive users must comply with the obligation to conduct an energy audit (as per Article 8 of Directive 2012/27/EU) and commit to doing one or more of the following: (a) implement recommendations of the audit report, which result in a pay-back time not exceeding three years, (b) cover at least 30% of its electricity consumption from carbon-free sources, and (c) invest at least 50% of the aid amount in projects that lead to substantial reductions of its greenhouse gas emissions.

When comparing the rules under the 2022 Guidelines with the TCTF, the following aspects are relevant:

Beneficiaries

The following sectors eligible for aid are included in the TCTF but not in the 2022 Guidelines:

- Extraction of crude petroleum
- Manufacture of malt
- Manufacture of coke oven products
- Manufacture of bricks, tiles and construction products in baked clay
- Manufacture of ceramic household and ornamental articles
- Manufacture of lime and plaster
- Kaolin and other kaolinic clays
- Frozen potatoes, prepared or preserved (including potatoes cooked or partly cooked in oil and then frozen; excluding vinegar or acetic acid)
- Dried potatoes in the form of flour, meal, flakes, granules and pellets
- Concentrated tomato puree and paste
- Whole milk powder
- Skimmed milk powder
- Casein
- Lactose and lactose syrup
- Whey and modified whey in powder, granules or other solid forms, whether or not concentrated or containing added sweetening matter
- Bakers' yeast
- Vitrifiable enamels and glazes, engobes (slips) and similar preparations for ceramics, enamelling or glass
- Liquid lustres and similar preparations; glass frit and other glass in powder; granules or flakes.
- Open die forged ferrous parts for transmission shafts, camshafts, crankshafts and cranks, etc.

Commitments for decarbonisation

While in the 2022 Guidelines, there are commitments for energy-intensive users (to use carbon-free electricity and/or to have an energy audit and follow the recommendations therein), no such commitments are needed under the TCTF.

In sum, there are significant differences between the emergency rules and the normal rules. However, the emergency rules build on the normal rules, given that in the 2022 Guidelines, there are already provisions for the benefit of energy-intensive users. Therefore, the distance between emergency and normal rules in section 2.4 is less than that in section 2.1.

4.3 Section 2.5: The Aid for Accelerating Roll-out of Renewables Compared with the Normal State Aid Rules in the 2022 Guidelines

Points 77-134 of the 2022 Guidelines introduce a single category of aid to support investment and operating costs connected with a wide range of technologies, whose common aim is to reduce greenhouse gas emissions. Subsidies for the generation of electricity from renewable energy sources ('RES') would fall into this category of aid.

For the purposes of the comparison, one can single out the following aspects.

Tenders

As it is well known, a competitive bidding process is the normal *modus operandi* for allocating aid to renewables.[22] There are limited exceptions to this rule in the 2022 Guidelines:

- bidders are too few so the competitive process cannot function[23] or
- the aid is for small projects, defined as projects below or equal to 1 MW of installed capacity for electricity generation.[24]

In the TCTF, tenders are not necessary for awarding aid to solar photovoltaic, onshore and offshore wind, and hydropower installations when:

- the aid granted per undertaking per project does not exceed EUR 30 million; and
- the supported projects are small projects, i.e., projects with an installed capacity equal to or below 1MW.[25]

For solar photovoltaic, onshore and offshore wind above the thresholds, tenders are mandatory.[26]

For all other technologies, there is a choice between tenders or prices set through regulation.[27]

---

22. *See* point 103 ('Aid for reducing greenhouse gas emissions should in general be granted through a competitive bidding process as described in points 49 and 50, so that the objectives of the measure can be attained in a proportionate manner which minimises distortions of competition and trade').
23. *See* point 107, (a) ('Exceptions from the requirement to allocate aid and determine the aid level through a competitive bidding process can be justified where evidence, including that gathered in the public consultation, is provided that one of the following applies:

    (a) there is insufficient potential supply or number of potential bidders to ensure competition; in that case, the Member State must demonstrate that it is not possible to increase competition by reducing the budget or facilitating participation in the bidding process (for example by identifying additional land for development or adapting pre-qualification requirements) as appropriate').

24. *See* point 107(b). The other exceptions are based on the type of beneficiary (e.g., SME). The thresholds for energy consumption and heat generation are not relevant here.
25. *See* points 77(h) and 78(h).
26. *See* points 77(g) and 78(g).
27. *See* points 77(f) and 78(f).

The rules on tenders affect the ceilings on aid intensity:[28]

- 100% of the total investment costs when the aid is set in a competitive bidding process;
- 45% of the total investment costs when the aid is administratively set (with the possibility to increase by 20% for aid granted to small undertakings and by 10% for aid granted to medium-sized undertakings).

Deadlines

In the 2022 Guidelines, Member States must set deadlines by which aided projects must be completed, albeit this requirement is rather 'light' in the sense that there are no prescribed deadlines (there is also a flexibility clause for projects by SMEs or renewable energy communities).[29]

In the TCTF, there is a binding deadline for completion of the aided project: thirty-six months after the date of granting (with the exception of offshore wind technologies).[30] And Member states must have an effective system of penalties in case this deadline is not met.[31]

Contracts for difference

The 2022 Guidelines mention the possibility of using contracts for differences. This can be linked to an obligation on Member States to monitor and update the production costs on which the aid amount is based.[32]

In the TCTF, the use of two-way contracts for difference is mandatory, with the maximum permissible duration being set at twenty years after the aided installation starts operations.[33]

The amount of the aid may be set by competitive bidding process or through regulation. If the latter, the energy regulator must set the strike price at a level covering

28. *See* point 77(i).
29. *See* point 120 ('To avoid a budget being allocated to projects that are not realised, potentially blocking new market entry, Member States must demonstrate that reasonable measures will be taken to ensure that projects granted aid will actually be developed, for example setting clear deadlines for project delivery, checking project feasibility as part of pre- qualification for receiving aid, requiring collateral to be paid by participants, or monitoring project development and construction. However, Member States may grant more flexibility regarding pre-qualification requirements for projects developed and 100 % owned by SMEs or by renewable energy communities as a means to reduce barriers to their participation').
30. *See* points 77(d) and 78(d).
31. *See* points 77(d) and 78(d).
32. *See* points 120-121 ('Aid for decarbonisation can take a variety of forms including upfront grants and contracts for ongoing aid payments such as contracts for difference. Aid which covers costs mostly linked to operation rather than investment should only be used where the Member State demonstrates that this results in more environmentally- friendly operating decisions. Where aid is primarily required to cover short-term costs that may be variable such as biomass fuel costs or electricity input costs, and paid over periods exceeding 1 year, Member States should confirm that the production costs on which the aid amount is based will be monitored and the aid amount updated at least once per year').
33. *See* point 78(e).

expected net costs, including the estimated WACC, and taking into account all main revenues and any aid already received.[34]

Incentive effect

In the TCTF, there is a strong presumption that 'given the exceptional economic challenges that undertakings face due to the current crisis, it is generally the case that in the absence of the aid, beneficiaries would continue their activities without changes…'.[35]

Point 26 of the 2022 Guidelines recalls the usual principles on incentive effect and that the incentive effect is lost if the beneficiary already started the necessary works prior to applying for the aid. However, point 31 of the 2022 Guidelines introduces certain exemptions from the general rules outlined above. In particular, a beneficiary can still claim the incentive effect in the following exceptional circumstances:

- 'the aid is granted automatically in accordance with objective and non-discriminatory criteria and without further exercise of discretion by the Member State, and the measure has been adopted and is in force before work on the aided project or activity has started'.
- Another exceptional scenario is where the national authorities have published, before the start of works, a notice of their intention to establish the proposed aid measure, conditional upon the Commission's approval of the measure as required by Article 108(3) TFEU. In this case, there is still an obligation on the beneficiary to inform the granting authority prior to the start of works about the proposed aid measure having been a condition for the decision to invest.
- Finally, the incentive effect is still preserved 'where there is no "start of works" because there is no significant new investment'. This exception applies to operating aid granted to existing installations for environmentally friendly production. In these cases, the beneficiary must show what is in essence a counterfactual scenario where the installation operates in an alternative cheaper mode of operation that is less environmentally friendly.

In sum, the rules under the TCTF display a mix of relaxation and more stringent criteria compared to the normal rules:

- There is a relaxation from the normal rules insofar as there is more flexibility on tenders – there is more leeway for administratively set prices.
- The emergency rules are stricter than the normal rules insofar as (i) there are binding deadlines for completion of aided projects, and (ii) the use of two-way contracts for differences is mandatory.
- Thus, the emergency rules are firmly based on the normal rules, providing even for certain 'improvements' such as mandatory deadlines and the use of two-way contracts for differences.
- The distance between emergency and normal rules is therefore small.

34. *See* point 78(f).
35. *See* points 77(p) and 78(o).

4.4 Section 2.8: The Aid for Net Zero and the Matching Clause Compared to the Normal Measures

There are no corresponding provisions in the 2022 Guidelines. However, there are provisions in other "normal" State aid instruments which can provide a useful benchmark.

(a) Commission Communication on 'Criteria for the analysis of the compatibility with the internal market of State aid to promote the execution of important projects of common European interest' ('IPCEI Communication').[36]

The IPCEI Communication enables Member States to finance major innovative projects up to their first industrial deployment phase.[37]

To show the incentive effect, it is possible to present a counterfactual scenario where the beneficiaries have considered 'an alternative project that is wholly or partly carried out outside the Union'.[38] This rule is somewhat similar to scenario 2 under the Regional Aid Guidelines.[39]

Finally, in the balancing exercise, the IPCEI Communication enables the Commission and Member States to take into account/adduce, respectively,

---

36. Published in the OJ dated 30 December 2021 (https://eur-lex.europa.eu/legal-content/EN/TXT/PDF/?uri = CELEX:52021XC1230(02)&from = EN).
37. *See* points 22-24 and ('*22*. Research & Development & Innovation ("R&D&I") projects must be of a major innovative nature or constitute an important added value in terms of R&D&I in the light of the state of the art in the sector concerned. *23*. Projects comprising of first industrial deployment must allow for the development of a new product or service with high research and innovation content or the deployment of a fundamentally innovative production process. Regular upgrades without an innovative dimension of existing facilities and the development of newer versions of existing products do not qualify as first industrial deployment. *24* For the purpose of this Communication, first industrial deployment means the upscaling of pilot facilities, demonstration plants or of the first-in-kind equipment and facilities covering the steps subsequent to the pilot line including the testing phase and bringing batch production to scale, but not mass production or commercial activities (24). The end of first industrial deployment is determined taking into account, inter alia, the relevant R&D&I- related performance indicators pointing at the ability to start mass production. First industrial deployment activities can be financed with State aid as long as the first industrial deployment follows on from an R&D&I activity and itself contains an important R&D&I component which constitutes an integral and necessary element for the successful implementation of the project. The first industrial deployment does not need to be carried out by the same entity that carried out the R&D&I activity, as long as that entity acquires the rights to use the results from the previous R&D&I activity, and the R&D&I activity and the first industrial deployment are both described in the project').
38. *See* point 31 ('The Member States must provide the Commission with adequate information concerning the aided project as well as a comprehensive description of the counterfactual scenario, which corresponds to the situation where no aid is awarded by any Member State. The counterfactual scenario may consist in the absence of an alternative project, where evidence supports that this is the most likely counterfactual, or in an alternative project considered by the beneficiaries in their internal decision-making, and may relate to an alternative project that is wholly or partly carried out outside the Union. To demonstrate the credibility of the counterfactual scenario presented by the beneficiaries, the notifying Member States are invited to provide relevant internal documents of the beneficiaries, such as board presentations, analyses, reports and studies').
39. *See* Commission Communication (published in the OJ from 29 April 2021) on 'Regional State aid', point 59 ('The incentive effect can be proven in two ways:

'aid of an equivalent intensity for similar projects', received by competitors of the beneficiary located outside the EU.[40]

(b) Commission Communication on 'Framework for State aid for research and development and innovation' ('R&D&I Communication').[41]

The R&D&I Communication has a provision that is identical to the one in the (earlier) IPCEI Communication about the aid received by competitors located outside the EU.[42]

For the purposes of the comparison, the following aspects are relevant:

Scope

The aid is granted for the 'production' of certain equipment, which also includes mass production.[43]

---

(1) the aid gives an incentive to take a positive decision to invest in the area concerned because otherwise the investment would not be sufficiently profitable for the aid beneficiary anywhere in the EEA (scenario 1, investment decision);

(2) the aid gives an incentive to locate a planned investment in the area concerned rather than elsewhere because it offsets the net disadvantages and costs of investing in a location in the area concerned (scenario 2, location decision)').

40. *See* point 38 ('In order to address actual or potential direct or indirect distortions of international trade, the Commission may take account of the fact that, directly or indirectly, competitors located outside the Union have received, in the last three years, or are going to receive, aid of an equivalent intensity for similar projects. However, where distortions of international trade are likely to occur after more than three years, given the particular nature of the sector in question, the reference period may be extended accordingly. If at all possible, the Member State concerned will provide the Commission with sufficient information to enable it to assess the situation, in particular the need to take account of the competitive advantage enjoyed by a third country competitor. If the Commission does not have evidence concerning the awarded or proposed aid, it may also base its decision on circumstantial evidence. The Commission may also take appropriate action to address competition distortions arising from subsidies received outside the Union').

41. Published in the OJ dated 28 October 2022.

42. *See* point 98 ('In order to address actual or potential direct or indirect distortions of international trade, higher intensities than generally permissible under this framework may be authorised if, directly or indirectly, competitors located outside the Union have received in the last three years or are going to receive aid of an equivalent intensity for similar projects. However, where distortions of international trade are likely to occur after more than three years, given the particular nature of the sector in question, the reference period may be extended accordingly. Where possible, the Member State concerned must provide the Commission with sufficient information to enable it to assess the situation, in particular the need to take account of the competitive advantage enjoyed by a third country competitor. Where the Commission does not have evidence concerning the awarded or proposed aid, it may also base its decision on circumstantial evidence').

43. *See* point 85(a) ('[The aid is granted to incentivize] (i) the production of relevant equipment for the transition towards a net-zero economy, namely batteries, solar panels, wind turbines, heat-pumps, electrolysers, and equipment for carbon capture usage and storage (CCUS); or (ii) the production of key components designed and primarily used as direct input for the production of the equipment defined under (i); or (iii) the production or recovery of related critical raw materials necessary for the production of the equipment and key components defined in (i) and (ii) above').

Ceilings – matching aid

There are limitations on the maximum aid amount. However, there is a matching clause, i.e., a clause that allows raising the maximum aid amount when the beneficiary could receive aid for a similar project from a foreign country. These provisions are worth quoting in full:

Point 85 (g) TCTF

> 'The aid intensity may not exceed 15 % of the eligible costs and the overall aid amount may not exceed EUR 150 million per undertaking per Member State. However,
>
> (i) for investments in assisted areas designated in the applicable regional aid map for the Member State concerned in accordance with Article 107(3)(c) TFEU ('c' areas), the aid intensity may be increased to 20 % of the eligible costs and the overall aid amount may not exceed EUR 200 million per undertaking per Member State;
>
> (ii) for investments in assisted areas designated in the applicable regional aid map for the Member State concerned in accordance with Article 107(3)(a) TFEU ('a' areas) the aid intensity may be increased to 35 % of the eligible costs and the overall aid amount may not exceed EUR 350 million per undertaking per Member State'.

Point 86 TCTF

> 'Exceptionally, by derogation from point 85(b) and on the basis of individual notifications, for the production of the relevant goods for the transition towards a net-zero economy as defined in point 85(a) of this Communication, the Commission may approve on the basis of Article 107(3)(c) TFEU individual aid up to the amount of subsidy, which the beneficiary could demonstrably receive for an equivalent investment in a third country jurisdiction outside the EEA, provided the following conditions are met:
>
> a) The aid incentivises the beneficiary to locate the investment project or to trigger linked investment projects necessary for the production of the relevant goods defined in point 85(a) either:
>   i. fully in an assisted area as defined in the applicable regional aid map; or
>   ii. in at least three EEA Member States where a significant part of the capital investment takes place in at least two assisted areas. An important part of such significant investment should take place in an 'a' area as defined in the applicable regional aid map(s);
>
> b) The aid is granted by 31 December 2025;
>
> c) The beneficiary must commit to use for the production of goods defined in point 85(a) of this Communication the latest commercially available state-of-the-art production technology from an environmental emissions perspective;"
>
> d) The beneficiary must provide solid evidence of subsidies it would credibly receive in a non-EEA jurisdiction for a similar project and must demonstrate that without the aid the planned investment would not take place in the EEA. In addition, the beneficiary must provide evidence that the aid does not create counter-cohesion effects;
>
> e) The aid may not exceed the minimum amount needed to incentivise the aid beneficiary to locate the investment in the area concerned in the EEA (funding gap)'.

In sum, the emergency measures go beyond the normal measures as regards scope and maximum aid amount:

- Under the emergency measures, aid can be granted for production, without being limited to the first industrial deployment phase.
- Whereas in the IPCEI Communication, it was permissible to take into account aid received by competitors located outside the EU, the emergency measures enable a Member State to enter into a race with a third country grantor, up to the point of matching such foreign aid.

There are mitigating elements, though:

- the project must be located in assisted areas (at least in part); and
- the technology for the production must be state-of-the-art from an environmental emissions perspective.

Taken together, these elements indicate that the distance between emergency and normal rules is significant, but there is also a continuity between the two.

5 CONCLUSIONS

The table below provides a summary of the above considerations, with a tentative quantification of the distance between emergency and normal rules, with three marking the highest distance.

Type of Measure	*Level 1*	*Level 2*	*Level 3*
Section 2.1 – aid to alleviate higher energy costs			X
Section 2.4 – aid for energy-intensive users		X	
Section 2.5 – the aid for accelerating roll-out of renewables	X		
Section 2.8 – the aid for Net Zero		X	

First of all, the emergency rules are not a complete break away from the normal rules:

- Even the 'matching clause', admittedly a significant departure from normal rules, is an amplification of a possibility already existing in the normal IPCEI Communication.
- And the exceptions from tenders for small renewables projects are in many respects identical to those in the normal rules (the 1 MW threshold).

Second, the fact that the emergency rules in many respects build on the normal rules suggests a dynamic process, where the experience gained with the emergency rules may be usefully applied to the normal rules.

- For instance, introducing deadlines to complete an aided project and the widespread use of contracts for differences seem likely to remain also after 2025.

Third, this (tentative) comparison of the emergency and normal rules of State aid for energy yields a picture with blurred lines between the two in the sense that some of the emergency provisions fit equally well with Article 107(3)(c) TFEU (which is often quoted). Or, to put it differently, some of the emergency provisions could have been introduced also under normal State aid rules. This indicates that to paraphrase the quote from Monet, State aid is a part of EU law which is ready for every crisis.

Part VI Competition Enforcers' Perspectives on the Energy Dilemma

CHAPTER 15

Tackling the Crisis from Energy to Inflation Through the Competition Lens: An Austrian Perspective

Natalie Harsdorf-Borsch & Lukas Cavada

1 INTRODUCTION

In the past years and months, consumers have faced numerous challenges due to disruptions to their daily lives and interactions. Businesses have to deal with economic shocks and price increases. Multiple crises from the COVID-19 pandemic to the war in Ukraine have highlighted the vulnerabilities of our markets and supply chains, prompting questions about our attitudes towards competition and globalisation, and the application of competition law during crises.

The Austrian Federal Competition Authority (AFCA) has been very successful in the past years in fighting distortions of competition. This focus sharpened in the current economic and social crisis. The main objective was to keep markets open and fair for both businesses and consumers. By September of this year, AFCA had already brought a record of cases per year, twenty, before the Cartel Court.

We are pleased to present an overview of the various activities by AFCA to address the crises.

2 TACKLING THE CRISIS: ENERGY AND FOOD MARKETS

The Austrian Competition Act prescribes that the AFCA has a mandate, under section 2(1)(3), to conduct comprehensive investigations of an economic sector if there are indications that competition may be restricted or distorted. Since its establishment, the

AFCA has conducted numerous sector inquiries, for example, in recent years regarding e-charging infrastructure and healthcare.[1]

2.1 Sector Enquiry into the Austrian Fuel Market

Against the backdrop of soaring fuel prices due to the war in Ukraine on 24 February 2022, the AFCA launched a sector enquiry into the Austrian fuel market in March 2022 in response to a growing number of submissions and complaints from the market.[2]

The AFCA issued requests for information to five leading oil companies that run ten refineries in and around Austria while also controlling petrol stations in Austria. These refineries have been identified as the primary sources of fuel supply for petrol stations in Austria. The Austrian Mineral Oil Administration Stock Company (OMV), located near Vienna, is the sole refinery in Austria. In the requests for information, the AFCA demanded quarterly production volumes, capacities, and operating expenses from Q1 2019, among other information. Additionally, discussions were held with three major fuel wholesalers and petrol station operators who are unaffiliated with refineries.

Besides this, the AFCA collected publicly available data and obtained proprietary data from Argus Media, a recognised price reporting agency (PRA) on the worldwide energy and commodity markets. Argus Media furnishes price details and publishes price evaluations on a wide variety of energy goods and commodities, such as petrol and diesel, both of which were pertinent for the sector enquiry's analyses. In particular, PRA-published price assessments for petroleum products function as benchmark prices within supply contracts between refineries and a variety of clients, such as fuel wholesalers and fuel retailers.

The competitive assessment can be summarised as follows.

2.1.1 Competitive Assessment of Market Conditions

2.1.1.1 Fuel Retailing

In the fuel retailing market, the competitive assessment centres on markets with a geographic scope of thirty minutes travel time around the respective location of the fuel retailer. Within this area, there is substantial competition between fuel retailers. However, it is plainly evident that this intensity of rivalry diminishes with distance. Given the geographically small scope of these markets, there are several local fuel markets for small customers in Austria, where over 3,000 petrol stations with both petrol and diesel fuels available are active.

Between 2017 and 2021, nearly 50% of all petrol stations in Austria were managed and run by leading oil companies such as BP, ENI, JET, OMV, or Shell. As the

1. Full reports are available at www.bwb.gv.at/en/sector_inquiries.
2. Full report (currently in German only) available at www.bwb.gv.at/fileadmin/user_upload/Abschlussbericht_BU_Kraftstoffe_2022_final_barrierefrei.pdf.

overall number of petrol stations in Austria has maintained stability over the last five years, this proportion has remained almost constant. Independent petrol stations play a vital role in ensuring healthy competition. In particular, an objective analysis conducted in Austria demonstrates that fuel prices, on average, are systematically lower (approximately 3-5 pence per litre) in the Western part of Austria, particularly in Vorarlberg and Tyrol, than in the Eastern parts where there is a significantly higher proportion of independent fuel retailers.

Petrol stations in Austria are subject to a 2011 statutory order that restricts their pricing policy. They are permitted to raise fuel prices solely once per day at noon. Conversely, price reductions can be made at any time and as frequently as desired. Generally, fuel prices are the lowest during the day immediately before noon.

Major-owned and -operated petrol stations, independent fuel wholesalers, and larger fuel retailers negotiate medium-term supply contracts, or 'term contracts', with refineries or tank farms. These contracts are negotiated in the autumn for the following year. Spot purchases and long-term contracts are of little to no significance, although independent fuel wholesalers are progressively employing contracts with terms of several years.

Smaller fuel retailers typically do not procure directly from refineries or tank farms, but rather from independent or major-controlled wholesalers. They generally do not enter into term contracts. Nevertheless, the pricing approach taken by these fuel traders is influenced by reference prices, as seen in the aforementioned term contracts. As such, both independent wholesalers and smaller and larger fuel retailers are susceptible to fluctuations in said reference prices.

2.1.1.2 Oil Refining

In 2021, Europe housed roughly ninety-three refineries, out of which about seventy-five can be classified as 'mainstream' refineries that generate a diverse line of petroleum products (diesel, heating oil, kerosene, petrol, naphtha, propane, bitumen, etc.) through combined production. The remaining eighteen refineries concentrate on producing lubricants and bitumen, among others.

When focusing solely on petrol and diesel, approximately seventy-four refineries in Europe compete intensely with each other. Additionally, global elements are accounted for with diesel imports and petrol exports. This deduction is based on the geographic range of the market, which has been previously defined as EEA-wide by the European Commission (EC). On the product level, a market exists for refined products which can be categorised further into a market for ex-refinery sales (primary customers: wholesalers and large resellers) and a market for non-retail sales (primary customers: small independent resellers, independent retailers). In Austria, there is only one refinery located close to Vienna, operated by OMV. For the geographical area of Austria, five major oil companies (BP, ENI, JET, OMV, and Shell) operate ten refineries, which are significant sources of fuel supply.

The supply of refined petroleum to petrol stations and fuel wholesalers is primarily governed by medium-term supply agreements, as mentioned previously.

These agreements are renegotiated annually in the autumn and take effect the following year. They specify both delivery quantities and pricing formulas which comprise fixed and variable components. The variable price component is a petrol or diesel price assessment provided by a PRA, typically either Argus Media or S&P Global Platts. These price assessments fluctuate on weekdays due to reassessments by PRAs. Conversely, the fixed component in the pricing formula remains unchanged throughout the year and generally amounts to a few pence per litre. The sum of the variable and fixed components provides the cost that petrol stations and fuel wholesalers must pay for their fuel purchases.

In contrast to medium-term supply agreements, spot sales or long-term supply contracts have a minimal impact on refineries' revenues. However, pricing policies for spot sales or negotiations for long-term supply contracts are still influenced by price assessments provided by PRAs. Therefore, international PRAs, including Argus Media, Platts or OPIS, have a considerable impact on the business activities and profitability of European refineries. It should be noted that price assessments from PRAs are also utilised to determine the price of crude oil.

2.1.2 Competitive Assessment Regarding Development of Profitability

2.1.2.1 Fuel Retailing

The gross margins for petrol stations in Austria were computed as the variance between net sales prices (i.e., gross prices without VAT and energy taxes) and corresponding Argus price notations. The AFCA's method of gross margin calculation closely follows that of Wood MacKenzie, a renowned energy consultancy. However, the AFCA report excludes freight costs, which Wood MacKenzie includes in their equation.

The calculations indicate a significant rise in gross margins for petrol stations in March 2022. In the subsequent months, the gross margins marginally exceeded their pre-war level. Nevertheless, to determine whether the profitability of petrol stations has been impacted or whether the higher costs have offset the small increase in gross margins, other factors such as increased transportation costs must be considered.

Although there are certainly noteworthy price disparities among gasoline stations, particularly between motorway service areas and regular stations, the analysis reveals no significant variations in prices or gross margins within individual subgroups or across all fuel stations in Austria since 24 February 2022. While variations are visible in the short term, they dissipate after a few weeks. In other words, a long-term equilibrium relationship appears to exist between Argus price notations for diesel and petrol, and the prices of diesel and petrol (excluding VAT and energy taxes), respectively.

The absence of conspicuous changes in prices and gross margins in the vehicle fuel market for small customers suggests that a reduction in competition between petrol stations is unlikely to be the reason behind the increased fuel prices following Russia's invasion of Ukraine. After a month of significant uncertainty in March 2022, global price indicators and petrol station fuel prices (excluding VAT and energy tax) have mainly moved in tandem in the subsequent months. However, there has been higher volatility compared to before the war's outbreak.

2.1.2.2 Oil Refining

A widely used and simple indicator to estimate refinery profitability is the crack spread. Crack spreads calculate the discrepancy between the selling price of refined goods and the cost of crude oil, using either individual products or product bundles. A 3:2:1 crack spread calculation is a popular method employed to estimate the gross margins of British refineries. This calculation utilises three barrels of crude oil on the cost side and a product bundle comprising two barrels of petrol and one barrel of diesel on the revenue side. Technical abbreviations will be explained upon first usage. The resulting figure is then divided by the input quantity of three barrels of crude oil to determine gross margin per barrel.

In a refinery representative of Europe, the product yield has a diesel-to-petrol ratio of approximately 2:1. This ratio is reversed in US refineries, where petrol is produced twice as much as diesel. Due to this discrepancy, the AFCA has derived a European iteration of the 3:2:1 crack spread. We found that while there was no discernible trend in gross margins before the start of the war in Ukraine, there was a significant and sudden increase in margins afterwards. In certain cases, gross margins have even quadrupled. On average, gross margins have tripled since 24 February 2022. The data suggests a significant increase in the profitability of European refineries since the beginning of the war. The cause for this increase is a decoupling of international price assessments for diesel and petrol, which are used as reference prices in supply contracts, from crude oil prices.

2.1.2.3 Operating Expenses

The market enquiry reveals that oil companies' reported operating expenses indicate a significant increase in the refineries' actual profit margins (i.e., gross margins minus operating expenses) since the commencement of the war in Ukraine. This observation can be linked to the steep price hikes of natural gas and electricity since 2021.

In the first quarter of 2022, wholesale gas and electricity prices increased by approximately 600% and 160%, respectively, compared to the first quarter of 2021. Over the same period, refinery operating expenses, which include gas and electricity costs, increased by less than 1 penny per litre on average. This illustrates the secondary importance of gas and electricity costs compared to crude oil costs, which increased by about USD 0.25 per litre over this period.

In light of the shift in operating costs, the AFCA has determined that a significant rise in operating expenses during Q2 2022 is improbable. This is due to a mere 40% and 20% increase in gas and electricity prices, respectively, compared to the previous quarter. Therefore, it can be inferred that actual profit margins have doubled or even tripled, given the average tripling of gross margins since the outbreak of the war.

2.2 Task Force on Energy Markets in Austria

Both the AFCA and the energy regulator E-Control have experienced a significant surge in requests and grievances from concerned customers, predominantly caused by substantial price hikes within the energy industry. A major source of discontent has been the sizable variations in price between old and new client agreements, along with the varied supply patterns of numerous providers. Against this backdrop, the AFCA and E-Control collaboratively decided to establish a common task force in January 2023 to investigate the situation in the electricity and gas markets. The preliminary findings of this task force reveal significant results.[3]

The preliminary (work ongoing) competitive assessment can be summarised as follows:

> The accessibility and affordability of energy are fundamental to consumers. Efficient and effective competition, as has been the norm since energy market liberalisation in 2001 (electricity) and 2002 (gas), is the foundation of consumer trust in fair market prices and a diverse selection of options. What had worked effectively for over two decades was significantly disrupted last year. In the past year, there has been a substantial shakeup. Energy prices have already risen sharply towards the end of 2021, which was further intensified due to the war in Ukraine in 2022. The increasing market concentration is a significant concern and contributing factor to the ongoing crisis. This has sparked considerable uncertainty among consumers. Companies have withdrawn temporarily from the market or restricted operations to their supply area, leading to additional price increases, cancelled contracts, and renewed contracts with significantly higher rates.

2.2.1 Partial Increase in Market Concentration on the Electricity Market

In regards to the Herfindahl-Hirschman Index (HHI), an economic measure of market concentration, it was observed that from 2021 to 2022, a significant increase in market concentration occurred in provinces of Lower Austria, Burgenland, Salzburg, Tyrol and Vorarlberg. Vorarlberg exhibited the highest concentration with an HHI of 9,741, surpassing all other federal provinces. This demonstrates the dominant market position of the regional energy suppliers, with Vorarlberg as the leader. A high concentration of market power often hinders effective competition.

2.2.2 Switching Figures Decrease Significantly

Regarding switching suppliers, the domestic electricity and gas markets in 2022 have reached a virtual standstill in terms of competition. This is evident from the considerable decrease in switching rates, as well as the limited range of products available. Changing providers was hardly advantageous anywhere last year, leading to decreased

3. Full report (currently in German only) available at e-control.at/documents/1785851/1811582/BWB+Zwischenbericht+Taskforce+Strom-+und+Gasmärkten_FINAL.pdf/1fe1f6a3-ff40-5a0b-f1cc-4e9683caa0ad?t=1687851944530.

switching figures of 2.2% for electricity and 4% for gas in 2022. Just under 23% of household electricity switches and just under 17% of gas household switches could be attributed to market exits. As of 2021, the switching rates remained at 4.2% for electricity and 5.6% for gas. Consumers' only option during this time was to report to the complaints department of their respective energy providers, thereby drawing attention to their grievances. Switching to alternative suppliers was barely feasible. This could be attributed to adverse changes in the transparency, conditions, and customer service offered by energy companies in the electricity and gas markets last year. These changes frequently led to complaints directed towards both AFCA and, even more prominently, the energy regulator E-Control.

2.2.3 Hardly Any Competition, Hardly Any Offers

If there is a lack of functioning competition in the market, it inevitably impacts consumers. In 2022, this was evident through both the decline in product offers and the withdrawal of several suppliers from the new customer market. The absence of offers from these suppliers only exacerbated the situation. As a result, some companies chose to leave the market entirely. Companies responded to the changed market conditions in four distinct ways: (i) the large-scale termination of customer contracts; (ii) withdrawal of offers from the core region; (iii) cessation of Austria-wide offers for new customers; and (iv) orderly winding down of business operations in Austria.

2.2.4 Exceptional Differences Between New and Existing Customers

In 2022, significant price disparities arose between new and existing customers, with many perceiving an arbitrary and inequitable treatment. Numerous consumers expressed dissatisfaction with the unequal regional, customer group, and contract completion time distinctions made. If customers were compelled to seek a new supplier during the winter of 2022/2023, they frequently ended up in exceedingly high price categories. Analyses conducted within the task force demonstrated that prices for electricity and gas for existing customers were mostly increased to align with modifications in wholesale prices. Nevertheless, it is noteworthy that in contrast, electricity prices for new customers were frequently raised disproportionately. Furthermore, the prices charged to new customers by the incumbent companies surveyed are significantly higher than the corresponding wholesale prices. It is evident that these companies do not engage in direct price competition, or only to a limited extent, as new customer prices in the overall market are continuously decreasing. Suppliers can retain current customers and attract new ones by implementing a dual strategy, as they have few choices for a prolonged period. The study revealed that companies frequently referred to government support measures, including the federal government's electricity cost brake and several state subsidies, in their external communications. This raises the question as to whether the elevated prices for newly acquired customers were subsidising less expensive plans for pre-existing patrons. Nevertheless, the findings indicate that superior proposals ought to be formulated based on wholesale expenditures.

2.2.5 Customers Were Subjected to Discrimination

It was also revealed that certain suppliers engage in discriminatory practices against their customers. Discriminatory treatment was observed on the basis of regional factors and customer segments. Established companies retreated to their network regions where they hold a dominant market position. Meanwhile, prices were increased for customers located 'outside the network', at times even after those customers had cancelled their contracts. Customers within the 'own networks' continued to receive favourable prices. Furthermore, certain discount brands selectively terminated their customers. Consequently, market-dominant companies' unequal treatment needs to be critically evaluated from an antitrust perspective. The investigations conducted focused on household customers. Discriminatory behaviour towards commercial clients and small enterprises is also crucial from an antitrust standpoint, as it disrupts competition among the firms.

2.2.6 Electricity Subsidy Causes Price Increase?

As part of the task force, our analysis examined price fluctuations in relation to the electricity cost subsidy. We observed a correlation between the announcement or implementation of the subsidy and subsequent price hikes for certain suppliers. Notably, in comparison to gas prices, the reduction in wholesale electricity prices did not result in immediate adjustments to new customer prices, even for the most competitive options. Furthermore, the pricing for new customers at many established suppliers is not aligned with the market. It is noteworthy that the design of the electricity cost subsidy affects the pricing of suppliers. Therefore, this factor should be considered in the development of the system, within the confines of legal measures.

2.2.7 Outlook

Furthermore, the AFCA (working alongside E-Control) has issued compulsory information requests to the distribution firms of provincial energy suppliers and major municipal utilities as part of the sector enquiry under section 2(1)(3) Austrian Competition Act. These corporations make up around 80% of the Austrian electricity market. The outcomes are presently under examination. The task force's surveillance will at least be continued until mid-2024.

2.3 Sector Enquiry into the Austrian Food Industry

Since late 2021, particularly following the onset of the war in Ukraine, food costs have sharply increased in Austria, imposing a significant strain on households, particularly those with lower incomes. This has resulted in complaints. The disparity between the increase in prices for food and other items and services within the shopping basket was extremely noticeable. Against this background, in October 2022, the AFCA initiated a sector enquiry into the food industry.[4]

The preliminary competitive assessment can be summarised as follows.

2.3.1 Focus on the Last Two Stages of the Food Value Chain

The sector enquiry is primarily concerned with the final two stages of the food value chain, processing and retail. An overview of upstream stages, including agriculture and agricultural inputs, is provided in less detail.

The enquiry focuses on four core questions, specifically:

- (i) Where within the value chain, particularly in processing or retail, did food price increases primarily manifest themselves in 2022:
  - (a) Can any specific trade practices between suppliers and retailers be connected to these price shifts? And
  - (b) Have international food companies obtained any advantage?
- (ii) How have competitive factors changed in the grocery industry recently?
- (iii) How has the concentration within various product categories and the proportion of own-branded products sold by food retailers changed over time? And
- (iv) What impact does the growing significance of online sales have on competition in the food sector.

The core objective of this examination is to ascertain whether competitive factors or competitive shifts can be attributed to the price developments observed in food products since the start of 2022.

2.3.2 Development and Current Status

Following the sector enquiry's launch in October 2022, preliminary discussions were held with stakeholders and industry representatives to gain an initial overview of the structure of the markets (agricultural, processed agricultural products and food) and the food value chain. The AFCA has conducted interviews with a wide range of firms operating in the two main sectors of interest, namely food and processed agricultural products. The purpose of these interviews is to gather essential information, data, and opinions to enable a comprehensive competitive analysis.

The AFCA is presently assessing the responses to information requests and examining the obtained price data for thirty-four product categories. Taken together, these categories represent a collection of commonly consumed foodstuffs. The chosen product groups are analysed to evaluate the competitive situation amongst food retailers and to investigate the product characteristics linked with high price increases.

4. Full report will be available in the course of October 2023 at www.bwb.gv.at.

These characteristics may include production costs, shortage of raw materials, concentration measures, own-brand share, brand share of international food groups, and others.

Various potential correlations between the price developments of different product groups and competitive factors are presently under analysis. For instance, concentration measures, share of own-brand products, share of brands from international food groups, frequency of specific trading practices, and other variables are being examined.

The responses received from food retailers and suppliers regarding trade practices are currently being collated, interpreted, and analysed using descriptive statistics. The report provides an overview of the incidence of specific trade practices among suppliers, contrasted with food retailers' evaluation. The partial report was published after evaluating the responses to a voluntary information request sent to seven price comparison platforms. This publication presents the AFCA's recommendations to enhance the service function of price comparison platforms while promoting consumer freedom of choice.[5] Another section of the report focuses on the significance of online food trade for competition in the Austrian food industry.

2.3.3 Outlook

To determine the beneficiaries of price increases since the beginning of 2022, cost data analyses and price development comparisons are required. The AFCA will increase efforts to undertake this task as food retailers and the food industry have not yet responded to information requests. Further questioning and complementary inquiries to food retailers and the food industry could be likely or even feasible to enhance the analysis's level of detail, specifically for costs and profit margins. In this regard, universal advancements at the early stages of the food supply chain (such as agriculture, agricultural ingredients, energy sources, electricity, etc.) will be examined to establish their responsibility for the price escalation witnessed. If there is enough initial suspicion under the Fair Competition Act related to trading practices between food retailers and suppliers, it will initiate separate proceedings for AFCA investigations.

Additional information requests to the food industry were recently prepared. Manufacturers of fresh products (i.e., eight product groups) and private label manufacturers (i.e., twenty-six product groups) were the primary addressees. Furthermore, a thorough interrogation of major global food corporations is scheduled. Moreover, a consumer survey has been commissioned and will be conducted soon, with a focus on competitive factors including store density, perceived transparency of prices, online shopping as a substitute for physical retail outlets, and own-brand products. Following the evaluation of Information requests and data analysis, a report summarising the results of sector studies will be prepared. This report will offer recommendations for future action.

5. Full report (currently in German only) available at www.bwb.gv.at/fileadmin/user_upload/Fokuspapier_Preisvergleichsplattformen_Sept_2023_barrierefrei_14.09.2023.pdf.

3 ANNOUNCEMENT REGARDING STRENGTHENING OF COMPETITION LAW

The Council of Ministers announced in May 2023 its intention to strengthen competition law in Austria. In this context, the Government plans to strengthen competition law, for example, by extending the AFCA's powers when conducting sectoral inquiries and by tightening merger control. However, details are still very open and would have to pass through the parliamentary process. Also, it has been agreed to strengthen the resources of the agency.

4 CONCLUSIONS

Current times call for a particularly active competition authority. For obvious reasons, the public is calling on competition authorities to provide solutions to these challenges. At least in Austria, this has to do with not only the solid reputation of the Federal Competition Authority but also the general mandate of competition agencies to make sure the market economy functions well. It is certainly a time to not only strengthen the resources of competition authorities but also widen their toolbox so that they can live up to the task. Maintaining open and fair markets for businesses and consumers is arguably more important than ever.

CHAPTER 16

Energy Markets in Troubled Times: The Spanish Response

Cani Fernandez

1 ASSESSING THE EUROPEAN ENERGY CRISIS: REGULATORY MEASURES AND MARKET DYNAMICS IN THE SPANISH ENERGY SECTOR

Energy is a vital input for all economic activities and everyday life. Energy supply impacts the productivity of businesses and the well-being of households. It must therefore be considered a priority for both regulators and competition agencies.

Some activities in the energy market value chain tend to be natural monopolies because of the unaffordability of replicating the operating network that generates a decreasing average cost. In particular, this includes energy transmission and distribution.

It is very common to find vertical integration in commodity production, distribution and supply. Furthermore, some companies, sometimes formerly state-owned, can accrue a large market share leading to highly concentrated markets. These elements introduce high entry barriers for new actors and potential market abuse in an activity that is essential for economic performance, and which requires specific supervision.

All economic actors should be bound by the same set of rules and conditions, and due to the factors already mentioned, competition agencies have always paid extreme attention to the energy sector, which has traditionally been exposed to severe technical restrictions and complex regulation based on the existence of market failures and highly concentrated structures.

In recent years, the transition of energy systems to green production together with the exponential evolution of big data technology has led to important opportunities to not only decarbonise energy production but also introduce new sources of competition. Boosting this transition requires both changes in the regulatory framework and antitrust supervision to prevent possible action from incumbents against the dilution of their market power.

To this endeavour, scarcity risks, energy market volatility, and high prices linked to the war in Ukraine have incorporated new and pressing challenges forcing governments to deal with affordability, inflation, and industrial sector viability in the EU. All Member States have adopted immediate and rigorous interventions to alleviate the impact of high energy prices on consumers. Spain has implemented several measures to contain the energy crisis, which affected peripheral countries despite their low level of interconnection during the first and most severe stages of the crisis. Spanish households are particularly exposed to spot electricity prices due to the important role of gas in electricity price formation.

Therefore, together with the immediate impact of increased energy prices on inflation, the energy shock had considerable second-round effects on the inflation rate through input costs. Spain responded by implementing various measures in the petrol, gas and electricity markets, including the Iberian exception, tax reductions, and market intervention. Among these, the most relevant have been:

(i) Measures to protect the most vulnerable consumers and industries, such as aid to low-income consumers, SMEs, small farmers, and fishing communities. The government has progressively extended bonifications in terms of electricity price, reduced electricity grid tariffs, and implemented tax reductions or new subsidies. Some of these measures are:
- Electricity tax reduction.[1]
- Increased discounts for vulnerable consumers ranging from 25% to 80%.[2]
- 80% discount on electricity transmission and distribution network tolls for electro-intensive industries.[3]
- Direct aid to gas-intensive industries, such as paper and cardboard, glass, and ceramics.[4]
- Aid package with specific measures for the agricultural and fishing sector.[5]

1. Royal Decree-Law 12/2021, of 24 June, adopting urgent measures in the field of energy taxation and energy generation, and on the management of the regulation canon and the water use tariff, 25.06.2021, and Royal Decree-Law 23/2021, of 26 October, adopting urgent measures to protect energy consumers and bring transparency into the wholesale and retail electricity and natural gas markets, 27.10.2021.
2. Royal Decree-Law 18/2022, of 18 October, approving measures to reinforce the protection of energy consumers and to contribute to the reduction of natural gas consumption in application of the 'Plan + seguridad para tu energía (+SE)', as well as measures regarding the remuneration of public sector personnel and the protection of temporary agricultural workers affected by the drought, 19.10.2022.
3. Royal Decree-Law 6/2022, of 29 March, adopting urgent measures as part of the National Plan in response to the economic and social consequences of the war in Ukraine, 30.3.2022.
4. Article 3 of the Royal Decree-Law 6/2022, of 29 March, adopting urgent measures as part of the National Plan in response to the economic and social consequences of the war in Ukraine, 30.3.2022.
5. Royal Decree-Law 6/2022, of 29 March, adopting urgent measures as part of the National Plan in response to the economic and social consequences of the war in Ukraine, 30.3.2022.

- Direct aid for transport companies, particularly impacted by fuel price raises (taxis and chauffeured cars, buses, autonomous carriers).[6]
- Public transport bonification for urban and intraurban train tickets.[7]

(ii) Cap on household gas prices and on central heating gas tariffs in buildings, resulting in price savings for consumers of more than 50%. The State has subsidised gas retailers with a specific EUR 3,000 m budget line.

(iii) Motor fuel bonifications: from April 2022 to December 2022, petrol stations implemented a EUR 20 c/l discount on all fuel sales prices that were subsequently reimbursed by the State. The oil incumbents with refining infrastructures in Spain had to add, at their own expense, an extra EUR 5 c/l discount on sales of their brand at petrol stations.

(iv) Windfall profits detraction:[8] in September 2021, in order to mitigate the impact of energy prices in the electricity retail market, the government approved a reduction in non-emitting inframarginal plant revenues, proportional to Iberian gas market (MIBGAS) quotations. This tool has faced limitations as most energy was subject to an exemption as it was already sold either wholesale or retail (vertically integrated companies).

(v) Compulsory long-term contracts for inframarginal plants: in March 2022, the government introduced an alternative voluntary mechanism to detract windfall profits, inducing bilateral agreements between producers and consumers unlinked to electricity spot prices at a fixed price of 67 EUR/MWh. The measure seeks to reduce consumer prices by inducing integrated companies and inframarginal plants to commit to production at fixed and non-gas-linked prices. The measure does not aim to reduce spot and forward prices, which are still linked to gas prices.

(vi) The Iberian exception: the new rule requires gas power plants to determine their market bids based on a reference gas price, initially 40 EUR/MWh but which will progressively reach 65 EUR/MWh by the end of 2023. Other inframarginal and non-emitting technology plants continue bidding as usual. The merit order of technologies does not change.

Gas and coal generators are compensated for the difference between the intervention price of 40-65 EUR/MWh and the daily MIBGAS price. Consumers pay the cost of the gas price compensation for these gas generators and benefit from a lower market price.

Inframarginal technologies do not benefit from high gas prices: all technologies receive lower revenues, and only gas and coal-powered generators obtain similar revenue levels as before.

6. Article 4 of the Royal Decree-Law 14/2022, of 1 August, on economic sustainability measures in the field of transport, in terms of scholarships and study aid, 2.8.2022.
7. Royal Decree-Law 14/2022, of 1 August, on economic sustainability measures in the field of transport, in terms of scholarships and study aid, 2.8.2022.
8. Royal Decree-Law 17/2021, of 14 September, on urgent measures to mitigate the impact of rising natural gas prices on the retail gas and electricity markets, 16.9.2021.

Demand hedged or committed at a fixed price before the entry into force of the mechanism is temporarily exempted since it does not benefit from the exception.

The compensation mechanism is only triggered if gas prices are higher than the cap. As observed, since the end of March, gas prices fell to under 50 EUR/MWh, in other words, below the intervention price.

(vii) Regulatory measures to improve market design: several reforms to reduce warranty schemes for independent retailers or remove barriers for renewable generation promoters.

The implemented measures appear to have reduced energy prices (both directly and as an input cost) in the short term in Spain. Specifically, the Iberian exception, which relaxed the increase of gas prices impacting the electricity sector, has successfully contained Spanish spot and forward electricity prices compared to other Northern marketplaces.

However, the energy crisis has not affected all competitors equally. Independent retailers struggled in these volatile conditions, finding it challenging to maintain competitiveness due to increased financial costs for long-term coverage and prime risk downgrade. In contrast, vertically integrated companies saw their market shares rise as they enjoyed natural protection from market instability. They have experienced consistent growth since the beginning of the crisis.

Amidst soaring prices, the renewable sector has been progressing rapidly, marked by new deployments of plants and self-consumption as consumers sought ways to reduce their bills. Nonetheless, challenges such as distribution grid capacity and conflicts of interest with integrated operators might hinder further advancements, and therefore we have been extremely vigilant both from the regulatory and competition supervision.

2 TOWARDS A RESILIENT AND SUSTAINABLE ENERGY SYSTEM: STRUCTURAL REFORMS AND REGULATORY PRIORITIES IN THE EU

In October of 2021, the EU Commission adopted a document known as the 'Toolbox', regarding short-term measures to mitigate the impact of a crisis. A more significant market reform has been discussed since then at the EU level. In March 2023, the European Commission proposed this reform to the Parliament. Currently under negotiation by Member States and the European Parliament, the planned adoption of this reform coincides with Spain's Presidency of the European Council in the second half of 2023. This proposal encompasses two key approaches: a long-term perspective aiming for a net-zero economy and affordable prices and a targeted intervention addressing current market deficiencies.

A fundamental position of this reform is that it must be structural and ensure the long-term resilience of the energy system. The focus must extend beyond short-term price concerns and aim to provide signals to long-term investments, particularly in renewable energy, storage, grid investments or cogeneration, as we transition to a net zero emissions scenario. The reform intends to enhance flexibility incentives, promote new markets, and optimise responses from both the supply side, including investments in networks and storage, and the demand side.

To achieve stability in price formation, the reform considers that the price volatility inherent to short-term markets based on marginal pricing should be complemented by risk hedging through long-term contracts: Power Purchase Agreements (PPAs) and Contracts for Differences (CFDs). While these provide a degree of certainty and introduce additional positive aspects as reducing the incentive to exercise market power in day-ahead markets, they are not exempted from some concerns, particularly:

- If the weight of long-term contracts is too high, short-term market signals may be lost.
- Even though CfD inevitably implies that the electricity system (or Member State) acts as counterparty on behalf of consumers, we should prioritise 'market behaviour' as the most efficient mechanism for allocating resources, economic growth, and job creation.

The proposed surgical intervention addresses several critical areas; specifically it seeks to improve:

- The consumers' rights in the event of retailer bankruptcy: Member States are obliged to designate last-resort retailers, at least for household consumers. We already have this concept in Spain.
- Regarding effective third-party capacity access and grid connection: Transmission System Operators (TSOs) and Distribution System Operators (DSOs) must publish their capacity access on nodes, as well as the status of access requests. In Spain, we implemented this transparency requirement two years ago to aid investor decision-making.
- Facilitating supplier access to collaterals to participate in long-term markets (forwards or PPAs) to properly manage risks from short-term price volatility. However, the National Regulatory Authority (NRA) must ensure that retailers adopt an appropriate hedging strategy to honour their fixed-term contracts.

The European reform prioritises enhanced liquidity in forward markets. A centralised approach at a pan-European level could be considered, but it is crucial to analyse different factors before implementing such an approach. Some essential factors to be analysed are the existing market structures in individual European countries, regulatory frameworks, economic stability, competition among market participants, and the potential impact on consumers and businesses. Additionally, it is vital to assess the readiness of regions and stakeholders to adapt to a centralised system.

Additionally, the reform focuses as well on the necessity for the NRAs of each Member State to lead and oversee specific aspects of liquidity promotion since they have a better understanding of their respective countries. To illustrate this, a couple of examples include:

- In Spain, we have a differential factor that is increasingly contributing to competition in the market: a large number of small retailers. These small retailers are able to develop innovative products that cater to the specific needs of consumers.
- Making gate closure time closer to real-time (from H-60 to H-30) by 2028 as the reform proposes, may impact countries with reserve replacement needs and low interconnection levels.

To reach this new scenario and implement the necessary new regulation, the efforts of governments and national regulatory agencies will be required. Under this proposal, NRAs are entrusted with these additional responsibilities:

- The NRAs will approve the methodology proposed by system operators for establishing the conditions and sizing of a specific 'peak shaving product' to reduce demand, as well as the method for measuring consumption reduction.
- NRAs should introduce performance targets to give incentives to TSOs and DSOs to increase the efficiency of networks (including energy efficiency, use of flexibility services, and development of smart grids and smart meters).
- NRAs must use the methodology proposed by the European Network of Transmission System Operators for Electricity (ENTSOE) and EU-DSO to prepare a biennial national study of daily and seasonal flexibility needs with a five-year horizon, starting in January 2025.
- NRAs must remove obstacles to connecting flexible resources.
- NRAs must ensure that retailers adopt an appropriate hedging strategy to limit the risk of changes in the wholesale market.
- NRAs must enable network operators (TSOs-DSOs) to consider the potential of flexibility as an alternative to network development in their planning.

These roles will be added to the new roles that regulatory agencies shouldered during the energy crisis. In Spain, only in 2022, the Spanish energy regulator became responsible for twenty-four new functions, including monitoring service station subsidies, subsidy compliance checking from Recovery Plans to smart grid projects, and assessing the impact of energy taxes. It's important to highlight (and insist) that, for NRAs to be able to carry out these new additional responsibilities along with the roles already assumed during the energy crisis, it is necessary to allocate adequate financial and human resources to enable them to fulfil these new functions.

3 THE DUTY OF REGULATORY AGENCIES: BALANCING CRISIS REGULATION AND LONG-TERM COMPETITION

In general terms, regulatory interventions to tackle the energy crisis should be transitory. Addressing the energy crisis through crisis regulation should be progressively transformed into structural measures aimed at ensuring competition and reinforcing the market economy. Measures for crisis regulation such as price controls, restrictions, subsidies, or other interventions to stabilise supply and demand in the short term, are not a definitive solution: they provide relief in the short term but bring unintended consequences such as market distortions and may deter long-term investments. Therefore, regulators and governments must shift their focus toward implementing long-term solutions that address the root causes of the energy crisis.

This must involve measures that promote competition in the energy sector, encourage the adoption of renewable energy sources, and strategic investment in infrastructure, and flexibility assets to support these initiatives. Embracing a market-based approach that promotes competition and innovation is more likely to provide sustainable solutions to the energy crisis in the long run. By ensuring a level playing field for market participants and removing barriers to entry, policymakers will stimulate innovation and competition, fostering the development of efficient and sustainable energy systems.

In Spain, the crisis regulation has been progressively removed, allowing for structural reforms to be implemented. For instance, fuel bonification was abolished in December 2022 and discounts were limited to the first half of 2023 only for specific sectors (professional transport, agriculture and fisheries). However, the challenge to reduce fuel dependence still needs to be tackled as it increases our economic risks; it is crucial to explore solutions such as using renewable energy sources, such as biofuels, and considering the integration of electric vehicles, accompanied by new charging models and regulatory developments, facilitated by the Spanish National Markets and Competition Commission's (CNMC) efforts to remove entry barriers to attract investors.

Currently, measures such as the cap on gas tariffs for households and for centrally heated buildings, or reduced VAT on gas consumption are less necessary as gas prices have stabilised, hovering under 50 EUR/MWh, 55% less than a year ago. However, the market situation could change rapidly, and the pertinent tools are still imperative. In the electricity sector, the Iberian mechanism might still be needed to prevent instability caused by gas price spikes, even though the current level of gas prices is not triggering the mechanism. As a precaution, the Iberian mechanism has been extended until December 2023.

At the same time, a broader and more effective regulatory approach is being adopted, with measures such as:

- Identification and analysis of the difficulties in deploying renewables: lack of regulatory clarity and territorial planning, the duplication of procedures, delays in response and the scarcity of resources in local authorities hinder their development.
- Better and more transparent access and capacity procedures to encourage new renewable generation.
- Better economic conditions for smart grid investments: a shorter payback period.
- Better consumer information, supervision of energy companies' behaviour, and enforcement of best practices (the CNMC has implemented an obligation to include a QR code in all electricity bills that gives domestic consumers direct access to the price comparison tool published on the CNMC website so that

they can check which is the best offer for their consumption pattern. This measure promotes competition among different retailers).

In addition, new regulations governing renewable gases like biomethane and hydrogen are being designed. The CNMC is currently preparing a public consultation on access and connection procedures, indicating a forward-looking approach. Strategic storage obligations and energy efficiency programmes for homes and buildings are also part of this strategy, reflecting a commitment to addressing the crisis in a sustainable manner.

Considering the long-term landscape, a flexible and proactive regulatory strategy is required. Regulatory frameworks must evolve in harmony with shifting market dynamics and emerging technologies.

NRAs, providing an independent view, are vital in this context. Their responsibility extends beyond immediate policy concerns, demanding a contribution of technical and regulatory expertise and a long-term vision which transcends political cycles. These agencies are tasked with the goal of creating an environment that supports competition, innovation, and sustainability. Ultimately, their efforts aim to ensure consumers have access to energy services that are not only affordable but also reliable, a commitment which requires a proactive approach that adapts to an ever-changing energy landscape and anticipates the needs of the industry and of the consumers in the long run.

www.ingramcontent.com/pod-product-compliance
Lightning Source LLC
Chambersburg PA
CBHW071243230926
51849CB00001B/206
9789403522388